AQA German

GCSE

Roy Dexter
David Riddell
Sue Smart
Marcus Waltl

Nelson Thornes

Published in 2009 by:
Nelson Thornes Ltd
Delta Place
27 Bath Road
CHELTENHAM
GL53 7TH
United Kingdom

10 11 12 13 / 10 9 8 7 6 5 4

A catalogue record for this book is available from the British Library

978 1 4085 0428 4

Cover photograph by Alamy/Hayden Richard Verry
Illustrations by Kathy Baxendale, Mark Draisey, Robin Edmonds, Stephen Elford, Tony Forbes, Dylan Gibson, Celia Hart, Abel Ippolito, Martin Sanders
Page make-up by eMC Design Ltd, www.emcdesign.org.uk

Printed and bound in China by 1010 Printing International Ltd

Contents

Context 1 – Lifestyle

Context 2 – Leisure

Context 3 – Home and environment

Context 4 – Work and Education

Nelson Thornes has worked in partnership with AQA to ensure this book and the accompanying online resources offer you the best support for your GCSE course.

All resources have been approved by senior AQA examiners so you can feel assured that they closely match the specification for this subject and provide you with everything you need to prepare successfully for your exams.

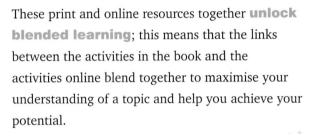

These print and online resources together **unlock blended learning**; this means that the links between the activities in the book and the activities online blend together to maximise your understanding of a topic and help you achieve your potential.

These online resources are available on  which can be accessed via the internet at **www.kerboodle.com/live**, anytime, anywhere. If your school or college subscribes to kerboodle! you will be provided with your own personal login details. Once logged in, access your course and locate the required activity.

For more information and help on how to use kerboodle! visit **www.kerboodle.com**

How to use this book

Lernziele

Look for the list of **Lernziele** based on the requirements of this course so you can ensure you are covering everything you need to know for the exam.

AQA Examiner's tip

Don't forget to read the **Examiner's Tips** which accompany the Controlled Assessment sample tasks, to help you prepare for the Speaking and Writing assessments. Listening and Reading **Examination-style questions** are available online so you can practise and prepare for the exam papers.

Visit **www.nelsonthornes.com/aqagcse** for more information.

AQA GCSE German

■ How to use this book

This book is arranged in a sequence approved by AQA which matches precisely the structure of the GCSE specification:

- The book is split into four sections, one for each Context of the specification.
- Each Context is split into two Topics.
- The Topics are divided into sub-topics which fit the Purposes of the specification.

At the beginning of each Context you will find the sub-topics, grammar and communication strategies listed, so you can see precisely how the content you are learning matches the GCSE specifications and be sure you are covering everything you need to know for your exams.

The features in this book include:

📖 **Reading icon** – you can listen to the reading texts in your book on **kerboodle!**, so you can hear the language spoken by native speakers as you read it. Interactive reading activities are also available.

🎧 **Listening icon** – audio material for listening and/or reading activities is online. Interactive listening activities are available on **kerboodle!**.

📹 **Video icon** – videos can be found online to support listening activities, with further interactive activities also available on **kerboodle!**.

🗩 **Speaking icon** – an activity designed to practise speaking skills. Worksheets for further practice are also available on **kerboodle!**.

✎ **Writing icon** – an activity designed to practise writing skills. Worksheets for further practice are available on **kerboodle!**.

Strategie – outlines different strategies you can employ to help you communicate effectively. The strategy box includes the icon of the activity it supports: Listening, Reading; Speaking or Writing.

🌐 **Strategy icon** – When this icon appears next to an activity, you should use the communication strategy introduced in the strategy box on that page to complete the task.

Tipp – provides handy hints which you can use to help you with your language learning.

Grammatik – provides a summary of the main grammar point. Further grammar points are also provided here. Go to the pages listed to find activities to practise them.

G Grammar icon – an activity designed to help you practise the grammar point introduced on the page. You will also find interactive grammar practice on **kerboodle!**.

V Vocabulary icon – a vocabulary learning activity. The essential vocabulary used within each Topic is listed on Vocabulary pages. Here you can learn key words for each Topic. You can also go to **kerboodle!** to hear how they sound. Some words are in light grey. This is to indicate that you do not need to learn them for your Listening and Reading exams, but you may still want to use them in your Speaking and Writing Controlled Assessments.

> **Language structure** – boxes show you how to construct key sentences designed to help you carry out the Speaking and Writing tasks.

Controlled Assessment – Controlled Assessment tasks are designed to help you learn language which is relevant to the GCSE Topics and Purposes.

These tasks are not designed to test you and you cannot use them as your own Controlled Assessment tasks and submit them to AQA. Although the tasks you complete and submit to AQA may look similar to the tasks in this book, your teacher will not be able to give you as much help with them as we have given with the tasks in this book.

Go to **kerboodle!** to see sample answers. Look at them carefully and read the AQA Examiner's Tips to see how you can improve your answers.

AQA Examiner's tip

These provide hints from AQA examiners to help you with your study and prepare for your exams.

Teste dich! – a summary quiz at the end of each Context tests key language and grammar learnt in that Context. This is also available as a multiple-choice quiz, with feedback, on **kerboodle!**.

Wusstest du schon? – an anecdotal insight into facts/figures relating to the Context.

Numbers 1–20, ages and days of the week

Ich habe zwei Schwestern und keine Brüder. Ich bin fünfzehn Jahre alt, aber Marlies ist achtzehn und Claudia ist neun.

Jan

Ich habe zwei Brüder und eine Schwester. Karl ist elf Jahre alt und Michael ist sechzehn. Gabi ist erst sechs Monate alt.

Monika

Meine Geschwister sind älter als ich. Ich bin vierzehn Jahre alt und Hans ist siebzehn. Brigitte ist zwei Jahre älter als Hans.

Susanne

1a 📖🎧 Read the texts above and answer the following questions in English:

a How old is Jan's younger sister?

b Who has two brothers?

c How old is Susanne's brother?

d Who is the youngest person mentioned?

e How old is Monika's older brother?

f Who doesn't have any brothers?

g How old is Brigitte?

1b 💬 Work in pairs. One person makes a statement based on the texts above and the other identifies who it is. Then swap roles.

Beispiel: Ich bin achtzehn Jahre alt. Du bist Marlies.

Vokabeln

Wie alt bist du? How old are you?

Ich bin ... Jahre alt. I am ... years old.

0	*null*	11	*elf*
1	*eins*	12	*zwölf*
2	*zwei*	13	*dreizehn*
3	*drei*	14	*vierzehn*
4	*vier*	15	*fünfzehn*
5	*fünf*	16	*sechzehn*
6	*sechs*	17	*siebzehn*
7	*sieben*	18	*achtzehn*
8	*acht*	19	*neunzehn*
9	*neun*	20	*zwanzig*
10	*zehn*		

2a 📖🎧 Read Lena's plans for what she will do when she is on holiday. Then put the sentences into the order she will do them (her holiday starts on a Monday).

a Am Mittwoch kaufe ich Souvenirs.

b Am Sonntag spiele ich Tennis.

c Am Dienstag spiele ich Fußball.

d Am Samstag mache ich eine Bootsfahrt.

e Am Montag gehe ich schwimmen.

f Am Freitag gehe ich kegeln.

g Am Donnerstag mache ich eine Stadtrundfahrt.

Vokabeln

Montag	Monday
Dienstag	Tuesday
Mittwoch	Wednesday
Donnerstag	Thursday
Freitag	Friday
Samstag / Sonnabend	Saturday
Sonntag	Sunday

2b 📖🎧 Now write down in English what Lena is going to do each day. If you are unsure of some of the activities, look them up in the glossary.

2c ✏️💬 Using Lena's sentences as a model, write down what you do each day. Then work with a partner. One person asks the other what he or she does on a particular day. Then swap roles.

Beispiel: Was machst du am Mittwoch? Am Mittwoch gehe ich schwimmen.

Days of the week

If you want to say which day you do something, use *am* followed by the day:

Am Montag gehe ich schwimmen. – On Monday I am going swimming.

If you do something regularly on a particular day, miss out *am* and add *–s* to the day, but don't give it a capital letter (unless starting a sentence):

Wir gehen samstags zum Fußballspiel. – We go to the football match on Saturdays.

Grammatik

Weather and seasons

1a 📖🎧 Read the weather forecast below and compare it to the map. Correct the mistakes in the forecast.

> Heute schneit es in Berlin meistens. Im Norden in Hamburg regnet es mit Temperaturen bei 0 Grad Celsius. In Köln im Westen von Deutschland ist es sehr sonnig und in Dresden an der Elbe ist es ziemlich kalt. Und in Nürnberg ist es den ganzen Tag windig.

1b ✏️ Complete the following sentences, checking against the map to get the correct weather reading.

a In München _____ .
b In Stuttgart _____ .
c In Hannover _____ .
d In Frankfurt am Main _____ .
e In Bremen _____ .

2a 📖🎧 Which season is it? Match up the sentences with the pictures.

a Es ist Herbst.
b Es ist Frühling.
c Es ist Winter.
d Es ist Sommer.

Vokabeln

Wie ist das Wetter?	What's the weather like?
Es regnet.	It's raining.
Es schneit.	It's snowing.
Es friert.	It's freezing.
Es donnert und blitzt.	There's thunder and lightning.
Es ist sonnig.	It's sunny.
Es ist windig.	It's windy.
Es ist heiß.	It's hot.
Es ist kalt.	It's cold.
Es ist neblig.	It's foggy.
Es ist wolkig.	It's cloudy.

2b 💬 What is the weather like during the different seasons? One person asks questions and the other answers. Then swap roles. Try to add some qualifiers (*sehr, ziemlich* etc.) if you can.

Beispiel:

> Wie ist das Wetter im Frühling?

> Im Frühling ist es ziemlich windig.

Inversion

Grammatik · *Seite 186*

The verb is the second idea (not word) in a sentence. So if you put something other than the subject at the start, the verbs still comes next:

*Es **regnet** in Berlin.*
*In Berlin **regnet** es.*

To practise using inversion more, see page 21.

Telling the time, months and birthdays

1a 📖🎧 Put the sentences below into the correct order, then note down each time in figures.

Beispiel: **a** 7:30, …

a Ich frühstücke um halb acht.

b Zwischen sechs Uhr und sieben Uhr am Abend mache ich meine Hausaufgaben.

c Um Viertel nach zwei esse ich zu Hause zu Mittag.

d Um ein Uhr verlasse ich die Schule und gehe nach Hause.

e Zwischen halb elf und zehn vor elf quatsche ich mit Freunden in der Pause.

1b ✏️ Write down the correct times in words for each of these clocks using the German 12-hour clock.

Beispiel: **a** Es ist zehn nach zwei.

2a 📖🎧 Match up the dates on the calendars with the birthdays.

Beispiel: **a** 3

a Ich habe am einundzwanzigsten Mai Geburtstag.

b Ich habe am siebzehnten November Geburtstag.

c Sie hat am dritten Januar Geburtstag.

d Sie hat am ersten Dezember Geburtstag.

e Er hat am achten Oktober Geburtstag.

1 December
2 8 October
3 21 May
4 17 November
5 3 January

2b 💬 Interview at least eight people in your class, asking them when their birthdays are. Each person has to answer using a full sentence.

Beispiel:

> Wann hast du Geburtstag?

> Ich habe am siebten Juli Geburtstag.

Vokabeln

Wie spät ist es? /Wie viel Uhr ist es?	What time is it?
Es ist …	It is …
Uhr	o'clock
Viertel nach	quarter past
Viertel vor	quarter to
halb	half **to**
halb neun	half past eight
Mittag	midday
Mitternacht	midnight
um	at
zwischen … und …	between … and …

24-hour clock

Grammatik

The 24-hour clock is often used in German. When you use the 24-hour clock you need to add the minutes as a number, for example 15:10 is *fünfzehn Uhr zehn*.

Vokabeln

Januar	January
Februar	February
März	March
April	April
Mai	May
Juni	June
Juli	July
August	August
September	September
Oktober	October
November	November
Dezember	December

Birthdays

Grammatik

To give your birthday, you say *Ich habe am* [number] [month] *Geburtstag*. The numbers you use (*ersten, zweiten* etc.) are called ordinal numbers.

Seite 187–88

kerboodle!

Classroom equipment and colours

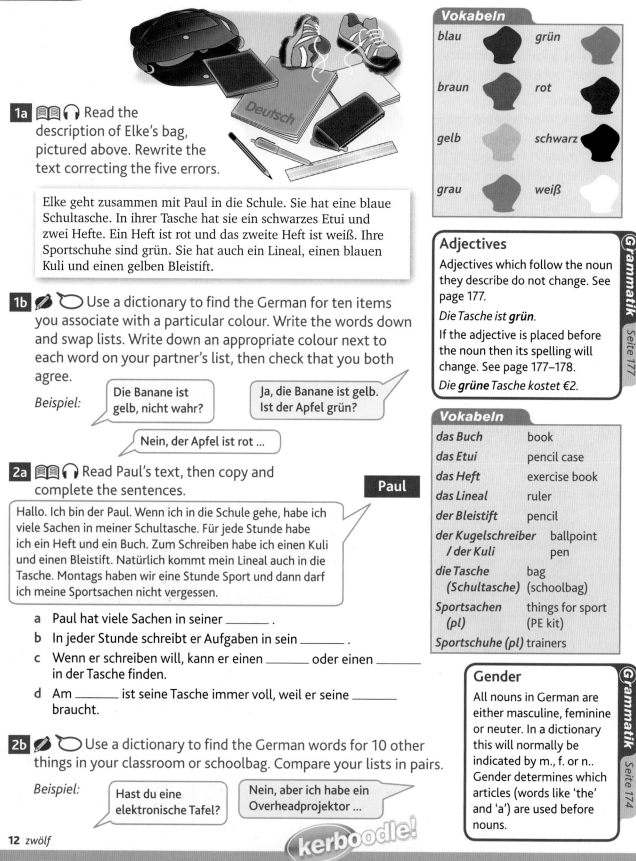

1a 📖🎧 Read the description of Elke's bag, pictured above. Rewrite the text correcting the five errors.

> Elke geht zusammen mit Paul in die Schule. Sie hat eine blaue Schultasche. In ihrer Tasche hat sie ein schwarzes Etui und zwei Hefte. Ein Heft ist rot und das zweite Heft ist weiß. Ihre Sportschuhe sind grün. Sie hat auch ein Lineal, einen blauen Kuli und einen gelben Bleistift.

1b ✏️💭 Use a dictionary to find the German for ten items you associate with a particular colour. Write the words down and swap lists. Write down an appropriate colour next to each word on your partner's list, then check that you both agree.

Beispiel:

> Die Banane ist gelb, nicht wahr?

> Ja, die Banane ist gelb. Ist der Apfel grün?

> Nein, der Apfel ist rot ...

Adjectives

Adjectives which follow the noun they describe do not change. See page 177.

*Die Tasche ist **grün**.*

If the adjective is placed before the noun then its spelling will change. See page 177–178.

*Die **grüne** Tasche kostet €2.*

Grammatik Seite 177

2a 📖🎧 Read Paul's text, then copy and complete the sentences.

Paul

> Hallo. Ich bin der Paul. Wenn ich in die Schule gehe, habe ich viele Sachen in meiner Schultasche. Für jede Stunde habe ich ein Heft und ein Buch. Zum Schreiben habe ich einen Kuli und einen Bleistift. Natürlich kommt mein Lineal auch in die Tasche. Montags haben wir eine Stunde Sport und dann darf ich meine Sportsachen nicht vergessen.

a   Paul hat viele Sachen in seiner _____ .

b   In jeder Stunde schreibt er Aufgaben in sein _____ .

c   Wenn er schreiben will, kann er einen _____ oder einen _____ in der Tasche finden.

d   Am _____ ist seine Tasche immer voll, weil er seine _____ braucht.

Vokabeln

das Buch	book
das Etui	pencil case
das Heft	exercise book
das Lineal	ruler
der Bleistift	pencil
der Kugelschreiber / der Kuli	ballpoint pen
die Tasche (Schultasche)	bag (schoolbag)
Sportsachen (pl)	things for sport (PE kit)
Sportschuhe (pl)	trainers

2b ✏️💭 Use a dictionary to find the German words for 10 other things in your classroom or schoolbag. Compare your lists in pairs.

Beispiel:

> Hast du eine elektronische Tafel?

> Nein, aber ich habe ein Overheadprojektor ...

Gender

All nouns in German are either masculine, feminine or neuter. In a dictionary this will normally be indicated by m., f. or n.. Gender determines which articles (words like 'the' and 'a') are used before nouns.

Grammatik Seite 174

kerboodle!

Numbers and dates

1a 📖 🎧 Read the description of a city in Germany. For each of the following statements write T (True) or F (False).

a There are 32 underground stations.

b The city has 270,000 inhabitants.

c There are 41 youth clubs.

d There are 22 parks available.

e The city has 300 buses.

f On the roads are 59,000 cars.

g There are 3 major stations.

h There are 56 schools.

> In meiner Stadt gibt es zweihundertachtzigtausend Einwohner. Wir haben fünfundneunzigtausend Autos und dreihundert Busse auf den Straßen. Es gibt auch vier große Bahnhöfe und zweiunddreißig U-Bahnstationen. Für die Kinder gibt es sechsundfünfzig Schulen, aber wir haben auch einunddreißig Jugendclubs und zweiundwanzig Parks.

1b ✏️ Work out the answer to these sums in German and write the answer in words.

Beispiel: **a** siebenundzwanzig

a acht + neunzehn =

b fünfzig – zwanzig =

c fünfundneunzig – dreiundvierzig =

d einundzwanzig x vier =

2a 📖 🎧 Three famous people are saying when they were born. Match up the year of birth with the name of the person.

a Ich heiße Michael Ballack und bin Fußballspieler. Ich bin am sechsundzwanzigsten September neunzehnhundertsechsundsiebzig in Görlitz geboren.

b Mein Name ist Barack Obama und ich bin Präsident der USA. Ich bin am vierten August neunzehnhunderteinundsechzig in Hawaii geboren.

c Ich heiße Heidi Klum und bin Fotomodell. Am ersten Juni neunzehnhundertdreiundsiebzig bin ich in Bergisch Gladbach geboren.

| 1961 | 1976 | 1973 |

2b 💬 Work in pairs. One person names a famous person below and the other person gives his or her date of birth.

Beispiel:

> Du bist Angela Merkel. Wann bist du geboren?

> Ich bin am siebzehnten Juli neunzehnhundertvierundfünfzig geboren.

Vokabeln

21	*einundzwanzig*	60	*sechzig*
22	*zweiundzwanzig*	70	*siebzig*
23	*dreiundzwanzig*	80	*achtzig*
29	*neunundzwanzig*	90	*neunzig*
30	*dreißig*	100	*(ein)hundert*
31	*einunddreißig*	200	*zweihundert*
40	*vierzig*	201	*zweihunderteins*
50	*fünfzig*	311	*dreihundertelf*

836	*achthundertsechsunddreißig*
1,000	*(ein)tausend*
2,000	*zweitausend*
2,009	*zweitausendneun*
3,684	*dreitausendsechshundertvierundachtzig*

Dates

When talking about a particular year, include 'hundred' and 'thousand':

1995 = *neunzehnhundertfünfundneunzig* (nineteen hundred and ninety-five)

2001 = *zweitausendeins* (two thousand and one)

Note that there are two ways of saying when you were born:

> *Ich bin **1995** geboren.*

or *Ich bin **im Jahre 1995** geboren.*

Grammatik

Wayne Rooney, 24/10/1985 | Angela Merkel, 17/07/1954

Daniel Brühl, 16/06/1978 | Britney Spears, 02/12/1981

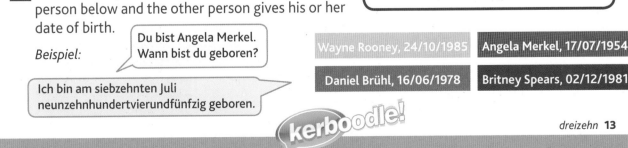

kerboodle!

Parts of the body, useful words

Ich heiße Richard. Das bin ich im Bild. Ich habe blaue Augen und einen Kinnbart. Neben mir steht meine Freundin Marion. Sie hat lange Fingernägel und trägt ein Armband. Ihr Aussehen ist ihr sehr wichtig: in ihrer Handtasche hat sie immer einen Lippenstift. Mein Freund Georg ist dort links. Er hat lange Haare und eine große Nase. In der Schule spielen Georg und ich oft Fußball zusammen. Marion macht nicht mit, aber sie ist immer noch sportlich – gestern hat sie sogar einen Schulterstand gemacht. Fantastisch!

1a 📖🎧 Read the text and answer the following questions in English:

a Which of the two boys is Georg (a or c)?
b What four things does Richard mention about his and Marion's appearance?
c What does Marion have in her bag?
d How many compound nouns which include a part of the body can you find in the text?

1b ✎ Match up the following words to make compound nouns which include a part of the body.

Hand Fuß Ohr	Harmonika Ring
Schulter Mund	Blatt Bad Schuh

2a 📖🎧 Read the following text then fill in the gaps in the sentences, using the words from the box.

Hallo, ich bin Lothar. Ich mag meine Schulroutine nicht. Ich finde alles so langweilig. Ich spiele gern Handball, aber wir müssen leider Hockey spielen. Wir lernen alle Französisch oder Spanisch aber ich würde lieber Japanisch lernen. Jeden Tag stehe ich um 6 Uhr auf, und ich bin also immer müde. Das ist doch blöd nicht wahr? Das Klassenzimmer gefällt mir auch nicht. Es stinkt immer. Meiner Meinung nach ist die Schule schrecklich. Was finde ich gut? Nichts!!

a Lothar steht _____ um 6 Uhr auf.
b Lothar muss Hockey spielen _____ Handball ist besser.
c Lothar findet _____ gut in der Schule.
d Lothar fährt nach Japan _____ will _____ Japanisch lernen.

immer   aber   nichts   also   und

2b ✎ Now write five sentences, each including one of the words from the vocab box on the right.

Vokabeln

die Lippen	lips
die Hand	hand
die Schulter	shoulder
der Fuß	foot
der Arm	arm
der Finger	finger
das Kinn	chin
die Nase	nose
die Augen	eyes
die Haare	hair
der Mund	mouth

Compound nouns

Many nouns in German are made up of two nouns put together:

Körper (body) + *Sprache* (language) = *Körpersprache* (body language)

The gender of these nouns is the same as the gender of the second noun. To find out more about compound nouns see page 42.

Grammatik Seite 42

Vokabeln

aber	but
alles	everything
also	therefore
auch	also, too
immer	always
nichts	nothing
noch	still
oder	or
schon	already

kerboodle!

1 Lifestyle

Health

Food and drink, ailments and solutions

1a 📖 🎧 Read Jürgen's description of his food preferences, then order a three-course meal with drinks for him.

> Ich esse gern Kartoffeln, aber Hähnchen schmeckt mir nicht. Tomaten und Mayonnaise sind schrecklich. Ich esse gern Eis und Schokolade, aber Erdbeeren esse ich am liebsten. Ich trinke nicht gern Kaffee oder Limonade.

Jürgen

1b 💬 Work in pairs. Take it in turns to make an order, based on the preferences given below (then order something you would really like!).

Beispiel: a Ich möchte Tomatensuppe, …

a You like soup, you love chips, you like cake but not fruit and you want a hot drink.

b You enjoy salad, you don't eat sausage or pasta and you want a cold, non-alcoholic drink.

2a 📖 🎧 Read the following conversation in a doctor's surgery then answer the questions in English.

Trude

> Guten Tag, Trude. Was ist los?

> Guten Tag, Frau Doktor. Ich habe Kopfschmerzen.

Ärztin

> Also, nehmen Sie diese Tabletten dreimal pro Tag nach dem Essen und bleiben Sie vier bis fünf Tage im Bett.

> Danke schön.

> Bitte schön. Auf Wiedersehen.

a What exactly is wrong with Trude?

b How often does she have to take the tablets?

c When does she have to take them?

d What else is she told to do?

2b 💬 Work in pairs, using the doctor and Trude's dialogue as a model. One partner says what is wrong based on the images and the other gives advice, choosing from the statements given. Then swap roles.

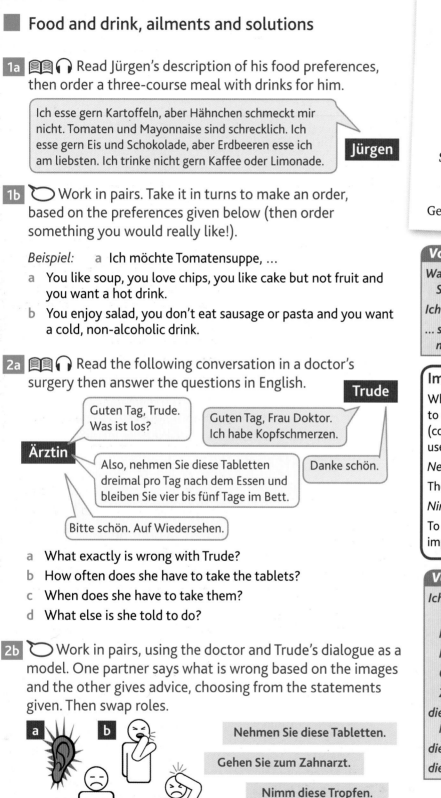

| a | b |
| c | d |

Nehmen Sie diese Tabletten.

Gehen Sie zum Zahnarzt.

Nimm diese Tropfen.

Nehmen Sie dieses Medikament und bleiben Sie im Bett.

Speisekarte

Tomatensuppe
Fleischsalat
Eier mit Mayonnaise
*****
Hähnchen mit Kartoffeln
Nudeln mit Tomatensoße
Wurst mit Pommes
*****
Vanilleeis mit Nüssen
Schokoladenkuchen mit Sahne
Erdbeertorte
*****
Getränke: Wein, Limonade, Kaffee

Vokabeln

Was möchten Sie?	What would you like?
Ich möchte …	I'd like …
… schmeckt mir (nicht).	I (don't) like the taste of …

Imperative forms

When the doctor tells Trude what to do, she uses the imperative (command) form of the verb. She uses the polite *Sie* form:

Nehmen Sie. Bleiben Sie.

There is also an informal *du* form:

Nimm. Bleib.

To find out more about imperatives, see page 185.

Grammatik   Seite 185

Vokabeln

Ich habe …	I have / I've got …
Halsschmerzen	a sore throat
Kopfschmerzen	a headache
Ohrenschmerzen	earache
Zahnschmerzen	toothache
dieses Medikament	this medicine
diese Tabletten	these tablets
diese Tropfen	these drops

Relationships and choices

Family members and pets

Robert

1a 📖🎧 Read the text then for each of the following statements, write T (true) or F (false).

Ich heiße Robert. Ich stelle meine Familie vor. Ich habe einen Bruder und eine Schwester. Mein Bruder heißt Viktor und meine Schwester heißt Ursula. Wir wohnen in Stuttgart mit meiner Mutter Manuela und meinem Vater Helmut. Mein Onkel heißt Uwe. Er wohnt in Bonn mit seiner Frau, meiner Tante Anja, und ihren Kindern, meiner Cousine Franziska und meinem Cousin Karlheinz. Der Vater von meiner Mutter und meinem Onkel heißt Jürgen. Er wohnt in der Nähe von uns mit meiner Großmutter, Ute.

Vokabeln	
der Bruder	brother
der Cousin / die Cousine	cousin
die Eltern	parents
die Geschwister	brothers and sisters
der Großvater	grandfather
die Großmutter	grandmother
die Mutter	mother
der Onkel	uncle
die Schwester	sister
die Tante	aunt
der Vater	father

a Robert's mother is called Manuela.

b His female cousin is called Karlheinz.

c His aunt is married to Helmut.

d His grandparents have two children.

e His father is called Helmut.

f His grandparents have four grandchildren.

1b ✏️📖 Using Robert's text as a model, write several sentences on your own family. Then swap with a partner and draw each other's family trees.

2a 📖🎧 Read the two texts below then answer the questions.

Hallo. Mein Name ist Karl und ich wohne in Bonn in Deutschland. Ich habe ein Kaninchen, Mindy, und es hat einen Stall im Garten. Ich habe auch vier Katzen. Die sind so süß! Ich gehe gern reiten, aber leider habe ich kein Pferd. Ich habe auch eine Maus und sie liebt meine Katzen!

Grüezi. Ich heiße Bärbel. Ich komme aus Luzern in der Schweiz. Ich habe drei Haustiere und finde sie toll. Ich möchte einen Hund, aber keine Katzen, weil ich zwei Goldfische habe, Schlipp und Schlapp. Ich habe auch ein Meerschweinchen. Es heißt Max und ist sehr lieb.

Indefinite and negative articles

Grammatik Seite 174

You'll notice that different words are used in the emails to say 'a / an' and 'no / not a':

Ich habe **ein** Kaninchen.

Ich habe **einen** Hund.

Leider habe ich **kein** Pferd.

Ich möchte **keine** Katzen.

To learn more about these words, see pages 28 and 29.

Vokabeln	
Ich habe ...	I have / I've got ...
... einen Goldfisch	... a goldfish
... einen Hund	... a dog
... eine Katze	... a cat
... eine Maus	... a mouse
... ein Meerschweinchen	... a guinea-pig
... ein Pferd	... a horse
... ein Kaninchen	... a rabbit

a Who has a guinea pig?

b Whose pet lives outside?

c Who doesn't have a horse?

d Who would like a dog?

e Who has six pets?

- Hast du ein Haustier?
- Wie heißt es? / Wie heißen sie?
- Wie alt ist es? / Wie alt sind sie?
- Wie ist es? / Wie sind sie? (süß, schön, niedlich, groß, ...)

2b 💬 Work in pairs. One person asks the other the following questions about pets. Then swap roles. (If you don't have any pets, why not talk about a pet you would like?)

kerboodle!

1.1

Gesund essen, gesund leben!

Lernziele

Talking about different diets

Using the present tense

Keeping conversations going

◀ ◯ [   ] 🔍 Suche

Startseite | Index | Hilfe | Kontakt | Textversion

Gesund leben online Forum
> Diskussion > Diät
Isst deine Familie gesund?

Klaus
Registriert seit: 08.04.2008
Beiträge: 8

Ich glaube, meine Familie ernährt sich meistens gesund. Jeden Tag essen wir fünf Portionen Obst und Gemüse, weil sie voller Vitamine sind, und wir trinken zwei Liter Wasser. Ich persönlich esse gern Fastfood, aber vielleicht nur einmal in der Woche, weil es so fetthaltig ist. Am liebsten essen wir Fisch – Forelle und Lachs schmecken besonders gut und sind gesund, wenn man sie grillt.

Meine Schwester Monika ist 17 Jahre alt und trainiert für die Olympischen Spiele. Sie läuft sehr gern. Sie isst wenig Fett und viele Kohlenhydrate, zum Beispiel Nudeln und Reis. Natürlich trinkt sie viele Mineralwasser, aber keine Cola. Nach jeder Mahlzeit isst sie einen Apfel oder eine Banane.

Meine Mutter Sabine isst kein Fleisch, keinen Fisch und keine Eier, denn sie ist Vegetarierin. Biokost findet sie auch wichtig für die Gesundheit. Ihr Lieblingsessen ist ein Salat mit Bohnen, Käse, Tomaten und Gurken. Sie ist ein richtiger Fruchtsaft-Fan. Ananas, Himbeeren und Pfirsiche findet sie lecker. Ich auch!

Jochen, mein Bruder, ist allergisch gegen Jogurt, Milch und Käse. Das findet er nicht so schlimm, weil er viele andere Sachen essen kann, zum Beispiel Schinken und Hähnchen. Er trinkt gern Cola oder Limonade.

Leider isst mein Onkel Hans sehr ungesund: Pommes, Pizza, Bratwurst, Kuchen und Sahne. Außerdem sitzt er abends mit Bier und Chips vor dem Fernseher. Er ist wirklich nicht fit!

---

1 📖🎧 Who is talking in each sentence?

Beispiel: **a** *Jochen*

a Ich esse keine Milchprodukte.

b Meine Ernährung ist nicht gesund.

c Ich laufe gern.

d Ich esse nach jeder Mahlzeit Obst.

e Fastfood esse ich nur manchmal.

f Mein Lieblingsessen ist Gemüse.

g Ich finde Grillen gesund.

h Cola trinke ich nicht gern.

2a Ⓖ Add the correct endings to the stem to complete the table for the regular verb *spielen*. Look at the endings Klaus uses in his text or refer to page 180 if you get stuck.

ich spiel_____	
du spielst	
er/sie/es spiel_____	
wir spiel_____	
ihr spielt	
sie spielen	
Sie spielen	

2b Ⓖ Now do the same for the irregular verbs *essen* and *laufen*.

Ⓖ Grammatik *Seite 180*

Using the present tense

The present tense is used to talk about what you are doing now. To form the present tense for regular verbs, take the *-en* from the infinitive to find the stem:

Infinitive   Stem
spielen → *spiel*

Then add the correct endings for each person (*ich, du, er/sie/es, wir, ihr, sie, Sie*).

With irregular verbs the stem usually changes in the *du* and the *er/sie/es* form e.g.

ich esse but *du **isst**, er/sie/es **isst***

ich laufe but *du **läufst**, er/sie/es **läuft***

Learn also how to say 'I eat a / an … .'

See page 28 ➡

3 🎧 Listen to some young people talking about their diet. What do they eat? Is it healthy or not? Do they enjoy it? Copy and complete the table.

🎧 You can work out in advance what you need to listen for. It doesn't matter if you don't know every food mentioned; you will probably know at least one and that will provide a big clue to whether or not the person is a healthy eater.

Tipp

	What is eaten?	Healthy	Unhealthy	🙂	🙁
a Maria	Ham, sausage …		✔	✔	
b Christoph					
c Silke					
d Jürgen					
e Daniela					
f Heiko					

4a 🗨️ 👤 Work with a partner to conduct interviews on healthy eating. One partner asks the questions and the other answers. Then swap roles.

Was isst du (zum Frühstück / in der Pause / zu Mittag / am Abend)?

(Zum Frühstück) esse ich _____

Und was trinkst du?

Ich trinke _____

Und wie findest du deine Ernährung?

Ich finde meine Ernährung (gesund / lecker _____)

🗨️ **Keeping conversations going**

In speaking tasks, don't worry if you don't know the exact word for what you want to say. You can make up an answer using the language you do know.

Also, rather than try to think what the German words are for 'shepherd's pie' (there may be no equivalent!), just give some ingredients: *Fleisch mit Kartoffeln* … etc.

Strategie

4b 🗨️ Now describe what your partner eats and drinks.

Zum Frühstück	esse ich	Müsli / Toast / Schinken / Pizza …
In der Pause	isst er / sie	einen Apfel / eine Banane / ein Butterbrot …
Zu Mittag	essen wir	viel / nichts.
Um drei Uhr	trinke ich	Fruchtsaft / Tee / Kaffee / Cola …
Abends	trinkt er / sie	
	trinken wir	
Das	finde ich	gesund / ungesund / lecker …
	findet er / sie	
	finden wir	

1 📖🎧🌐 Answer these multiple-choice questions by choosing an appropriate answer. Work out how many points you have scored to see how healthy you are.

Das Gesundheitsquiz!

1 Ich esse Fastfood **a** nie **b** manchmal **c** jeden Tag.

2 Ich esse 5 Portionen Obst und Gemüse **a** täglich **b** fast jeden Tag **c** nie.

3 Ich treibe Sport **a** jeden Tag **b** ziemlich oft **c** selten.

4 Pro Nacht schlafe ich **a** 7–8 Stunden **b** 5–6 Stunden **c** weniger als 5 Stunden.

5 Mein Leben ist **a** nicht stressig **b** etwas stressig **c** sehr stressig.

6 Ich rauche **a** nie **b** 5–10 Zigaretten pro Tag **c** mehr als 10 Zigaretten täglich.

7 Ich trinke Alkohol **a** nie **b** manchmal am Wochenende **c** jeden Abend.

8 Ich entspanne mich **a** den ganzen Abend lang **b** ein paar Stunden **c** nur selten.

Antworten mit **a** = 3 Punkte; **b** = 2 Punkte; **c** = 1 Punkt. **<u>Aber</u>** wenn du rauchst oder Alkohol trinkst, bekommst du **– 3 Punkte** pro Antwort.

Wenn du 22–24 Punkte hast, bist du sehr gesund. So musst du weiter leben!
Wenn du 15–21 Punkte hast, bist du relativ gesund, aber du kannst mehr machen, um gesünder zu werden!
Wenn du 7–14 Punkte hast, bist du ziemlich ungesund. Du musst mehr für deine Gesundheit machen!
Wenn du 2–6 Punkte hast, bist du sehr ungesund. Du brauchst Hilfe!

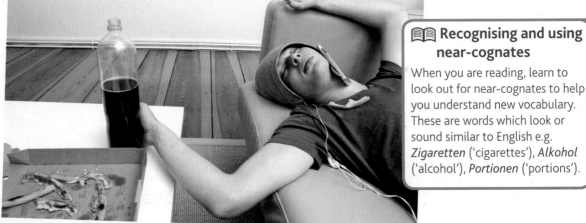

2 Ⓖ Re-write the following sentences starting each with the underlined word or phrase:

Beispiel: Am Wochenende spiele ich Tennis.

a Ich spiele <u>am Wochenende</u> Tennis.

b Wir essen Fastfood <u>einmal pro Woche</u>.

c Mein Bruder sieht <u>jeden Tag</u> vier Stunden fern.

d Meine Freundin schwimmt <u>dreimal pro Woche</u> im Hallenbad.

e Stress ist <u>manchmal</u> ein Problem für mich.

f Meine Eltern haben <u>leider</u> nicht genug körperliche Bewegung.

g Mein Onkel und ich gehen <u>am Samstag</u> windsurfen.

3 🎧 Listen to these young people talking about their lifestyles. Choose the appropriate picture for each.

Beispiel: **a** *Katharina = 2*

Ⓖ **Grammatik** *Seite 186*

Using inversion

In a normal sentence, the subject (the person or thing doing the action) comes before the verb. The verb is the second idea in the sentence:

Subject	Verb		
Ich	*treibe*	*manchmal*	*Sport.*
Mein Freund	*raucht*	*10 Zigaretten*	*pro Tag.*

If a sentence does not start with the subject, the verb and subject have to be turned around so that the verb stays as the second idea. This is called inversion.

	Verb	Subject	
Manchmal	*treibe*	*ich*	*Sport.*
Pro Tag	*raucht*	*mein Freund*	*10 Zigaretten.*

Learn also how to use adverbs of frequency. *See page 28* ➡

Tipp

Ⓖ Remember that the verb is not necessarily the second word in the sentence, but the **second idea** e.g.

First idea	Second idea	
Am Samstag	*spielt*	*mein Bruder Squash.*
Nach der Schule	*lese*	*ich eine Zeitschrift.*

 1

 2

3 (cigarette crossed out)

4 (ice skate)

5 (hamburger)

 6

 7

 8

---

4 🗨️ ✏️ Interview your partner to find out how he or she keeps healthy, noting down the responses. Use the questions on the clipboard.

Um fit zu bleiben,	mache ich	viel / überhaupt nichts.
	esse ich	gesund / Obst / Biokost …
	trinke ich	Saft / keinen Alkohol …
Manchmal / Oft / Normalerweise	spiele ich	Fußball / Tennis …
	gehe ich	reiten / schwimmen …
Das mache ich	im	Hallenbad / Stadion …
	in der	Schule / Stadt.
Um mich zu entspannen,	lese / schlafe	ich.
	höre	ich Musik.

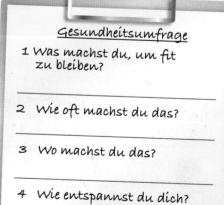

Gesundheitsumfrage

1 Was machst du, um fit zu bleiben?
_____

2 Wie oft machst du das?
_____

3 Wo machst du das?
_____

4 Wie entspannst du dich?
_____

---

ker**boodle!**

Rauchen ist doch ungesund!

1 Ⓥ Match the following German and English words:

Beispiel: **a** *2*

a Raucherhusten
b verschwenden
c süchtig
d Außenseiter
e Öffentlichkeit

1 public
2 smoker's cough
3 addicted
4 to waste
5 outsider

Kirsten, 15 Jahre alt

Stefan, 17 Jahre alt

Jörg, 14 Jahre alt

Hannah, 16 Jahre alt

Ich rauche überhaupt nicht. Es stinkt und es ist auch sehr gefährlich für die Gesundheit, weil es Lungenkrebs und andere Krankheiten verursacht. Ich habe einmal eine Zigarette probiert, aber sie hat furchtbar geschmeckt. Ich kann einfach nicht verstehen, warum so viele Leute rauchen.

Ich rauche schon seit acht Jahren. Meine Eltern finden das schrecklich, aber alle meine Freunde rauchen auch und ich will kein Außenseiter sein. Ich fühle mich wirklich cool mit einer Zigarette in der Hand. Manchmal habe ich einen Raucherhusten, aber ich habe keine Angst vor Krankheiten. Ich bin süchtig und ich kann nicht aufhören zu rauchen.

Meiner Meinung nach ist Rauchen total blöd. Meine Großmutter ist vor drei Jahren gestorben, weil sie geraucht hat. Ich finde es toll, dass man in der Öffentlichkeit nicht rauchen darf. Rauchen ist auch so teuer. Ich will mein Geld nicht verschwenden. Ich spare mein Geld lieber für Kleidung oder die Ferien.

Ich rauche zehn Zigaretten pro Tag. Meine Freundinnen sagen, es macht schlank. Es schmeckt gut und entspannt. Außerdem fühle ich mich erwachsen, wenn ich eine Zigarette rauche. Es ist ungesund und ich soll das Rauchen jetzt aufgeben, aber ich kann aufhören, wenn ich älter bin!

2 📖 🎧 ⓔ Match the following sentence beginnings and endings so that they make sense. Then decide who might make each statement – Kirsten, Stefan, Jörg or Hannah? (It could be more than one person!)

Beispiel: **a** *5 Meiner Meinung nach soll man nie rauchen. Kirsten, Jörg*

a Meiner Meinung nach
b Ich fühle mich wirklich cool,
c Ich habe nur einmal
d Ich kann nicht aufhören,
e Ich will kein Außenseiter sein,

1 also rauche ich mit meinen Freunden.
2 weil ich süchtig bin.
3 eine Zigarette probiert.
4 wenn ich rauche.
5 soll man nie rauchen.

📖 **Using context to predict meanings**

Ⓢ Strategie

Using the context (here it is smoking) can help you predict the meaning of new words, e.g.

Ich kann nicht aufhören ('I cannot <u>stop</u>'), *Lungenkrebs* ('lung cancer'). Notice that *Lungenkrebs* is a compound noun (two nouns joined together – *Lungen* + *Krebs*).

3 **G** Translate the following sentences into English:

Beispiel: **a** *I ought to give up smoking now.*

a Ich soll das Rauchen jetzt aufgeben.

b Wir können nicht aufhören.

c Mein Freund will keine Zigarette probieren, weil das ungesund ist.

d Willst du einen Raucherhusten haben?

e Er kann nicht aufhören, weil er süchtig ist.

f Ihr sollt im Garten und nicht im Haus rauchen.

4 🎧 Read the statements below and check that you understand them. Then listen to the radio interview about smoking in Germany and decide whether the statements are true (T) or false (F).

a In Deutschland rauchen 25 Prozent aller Erwachsenen.

b Es rauchen mehr Jungen als Mädchen.

c Rauchen verursacht Gesundheitsprobleme, und schädigt insbesondere das Gehirn und die Leber.

d Wenige Leute wollen aufhören zu rauchen.

e Es gibt Nikotinpflaster und Sprays in Deutschland.

f In Bussen ist Rauchen manchmal erlaubt.

g Rauchen ist in allen Restaurants verboten.

5 🗨🖊 Prepare a presentation in German for or against smoking. Try to give reasons.

@rammatik *Seite 181*

Using the modal verbs *wollen*, *können*, *sollen*

Modal verbs are verbs like 'want to', 'can' and 'should'. There are six in all. Learn each one as you meet it.

***wollen* –** to want to	***können* –** to be able to / can	***sollen* –** to be supposed to / should
ich will	*ich kann*	*ich soll*
du willst	*du kannst*	*du sollst*
er/sie/es will	*er/sie/es kann*	*er/sie/es soll*
wir wollen	*wir können*	*wir sollen*
ihr wollt	*ihr könnt*	*ihr sollt*
sie wollen	*sie können*	*sie sollen*
Sie wollen	*Sie können*	*Sie sollen*

Modal verbs are often used with another verb which must be in the **infinitive** form at the **end of the sentence or clause.**

*Ich **will** mein Geld nicht **verschwenden**.*

Also revise how to form the negative with *nicht* and *kein.*

See page 29 ➡

Tipp

You may often hear German speakers using *Ich sollte* rather than *Ich soll*, especially when talking about things they really ought to do (but might not):

Ich sollte gesund essen. – I (really) should eat healthily.

This is called using the subjunctive. You may learn more about this later.

Tipp

Try to use *weil* to make your sentences longer, more interesting and more impressive!

Ich rauche (nicht)		weil	es _____ schmeckt.
Meiner Meinung nach ist Rauchen	toll, ekelhaft,		es entspannt. ich mich _____ fühle. es stinkt.
Rauchen kann	Herzprobleme Atembeschwerden		verursachen.

Man soll nicht rauchen, weil es _____ ist.

---

kerboodle!

1.4 Alkohol und Drogen brauchen wir nicht!

Lernziele

Talking about alcohol and drugs

Using the modal verbs *dürfen*, *müssen* and *mögen*

Understanding word order better

■ Alkohol, Drogen und die Schweizer Jugend

Prozent der Jugendlichen in der Schweiz, die . . .

einmal in der Woche Alkohol trinken	25% der 15–jährigen Jungen
	18% der 15–jährigen Mädchen
schon zweimal betrunken waren	28% der 15–jährigen Jungen
	19% der 15–jährigen Mädchen
schon Erfahrung mit Cannabis haben	34% der 15–jährigen Jungen
	27% der 15–jährigen Mädchen

1 📖 🎧 Two teenagers are discussing the above survey about alcohol and cannabis use among young people in Switzerland.

Franz: Das kann ich mir vorstellen. Meine Freunde und ich treffen uns abends hinter dem Bahnhof und wollen schnell betrunken werden. Cannabis rauchen wir auch.

Marion: Mensch, bist du dumm! Kannst du nichts anderes mit deinem Leben anfangen?

Franz: Warum denn? Darf ich keinen Spaß haben? Schule und Eltern machen mir so viel Stress, weil ich immer viel arbeiten muss – Hausaufgaben, im Haushalt helfen und so weiter: ich darf nie machen, was ich will. Ich habe überhaupt keine Freiheit!

Marion: Das stimmt doch nicht. Du weißt, dass Alkohol dich total kaputt machen kann, besonders deine Leber, außerdem kannst du süchtig werden. Und Cannabis ist genauso schädlich wie Zigaretten. Du kriegst bestimmt Motivationsprobleme. Hast du keine Angst?

Franz: Mir ist das egal. Ich bin kein Alkoholiker und ich habe keinen Lungenkrebs. Meine Freunde und ich müssen irgendwie unsere Sorgen vergessen!

Marion: Das ist schade, weil du bestimmt Probleme bekommst, wenn du weiter so trinkst und rauchst.

Franz: Darfst du denn kein Bier trinken?

Marion: Doch, aber ich mag Alkohol und Drogen überhaupt nicht. Für mich ist Abstinenz wichtig, weil ich Sportlerin bin. Ich muss meine Gesundheit schützen, wenn ich erfolgreich sein will.

Answer the following questions in German. Try to use full sentences.

Beispiel: a *19% der 15–jährigen Mädchen waren schon zweimal betrunken.*

a Wie viele 15–jährige Mädchen waren schon zweimal betrunken?

b Wie viele junge Leute in der Schweiz haben heute Erfahrung mit Cannabis?

c Wo treffen sich Franz und seine Freunde abends?

d Was machen sie dort?

e Warum hat Franz so viel Stress?

f Was kann passieren, wenn er weiter soviel trinkt?

g Warum ist Marion gegen Alkohol und Drogen?

2 **G** Copy the sentences and fill in the gaps with the correct form of *müssen* or *dürfen*.

Beispiel: **a** *Mein Cousin ist 10 Jahre alt und er darf keinen Alkohol trinken.*

a Mein Cousin ist 10 Jahre alt und er _____ keinen Alkohol trinken.

b In der Schule _____ wir eine Uniform tragen.

c Ich _____ abends nicht zu spät ausbleiben.

d _____ du diesen Film sehen? Bist du alt genug?

e Jeden Samstagmorgen _____ ich mein Zimmer aufräumen.

f Meine Eltern _____ am Samstag nach Kiel fahren, weil mein Opa krank ist.

3 🎥 Watch the interview with the rock star, Blitz, and fill in the gaps in the sentences below.

Beispiel: **a** *Der Rockstar Blitz hat Probleme mit Alkohol gehabt.*

a Der Rockstar Blitz hat Probleme mit _____ gehabt.

b Jetzt geht's ihm _____.

c Für ihn waren Drogen _____.

d Die Party war in einem _____.

e Ein Bandmitglied hat eine _____ genommen.

f Blitz hat eine _____ in einer Klinik gemacht.

g Jetzt _____ er überhaupt keine Drogen mehr nehmen.

h Das neue Lied von der Band können wir nächsten _____ hören.

Using the modal verbs *dürfen, müssen, mögen*

There are three more modal verbs to learn:

dürfen – to be allowed to	*müssen* – to have to	*mögen* – to like
ich darf	*ich muss*	*ich mag*
du darfst	*du musst*	*du magst*
er/sie/es darf	*er/sie/es muss*	*er/sie/es mag*
wir dürfen	*wir müssen*	*wir mögen*
ihr dürft	*ihr müsst*	*ihr mögt*
sie dürfen	*sie müssen*	*sie mögen*
Sie dürfen	*Sie müssen*	*Sie mögen*

As with the other modal verbs, remember that the other verb being used must be in the **infinitive** form at the **end of the sentence or clause.**

*Ich **darf** keinen Alkohol **trinken**, weil ich zu jung bin.*

Also revise how to use *man*.   *See page 29* ➡

Alkohol	normal	Hotel

Entziehungskur	Monat

darf	nie	besser

Überdosis	Woche

4 💬 Work in pairs to conduct interviews similar to those in the video. One of you is the interviewer while the other is either a hard-living celebrity or a clean-living sportsperson. Then swap roles.

Tipp
If you want to say 'must not' in German, use *dürfen nicht* rather than *müssen nicht*.

5 ✏️ 🌐 Write up your interview for a magazine, describing your interviewee's attitude to drugs and alcohol using the third person.

Ich darf / will	keinen Alkohol trinken, keine Drogen nehmen,	weil	ich gesund bleiben will. es gefährlich / ungesund ist. es Spaß macht.
Alkohol trinken Drogen nehmen	finde ich blöd finde ich toll		
Alkohol kann	der Leber schaden. in großen Mengen zum Tod führen.		
Drogen können	Motivationsprobleme verschiedene Krankheiten	verursachen.	
	in sehr kleinen Mengen zum Tod führen.		

Strategie

✏️ Understanding word order

Remember that when you are using *weil* with modal verbs, there will be two verbs at the end of the sentence or clause. The modal verb must go last:

*Ich rauche Cannabis nicht, weil er Motivationsprobleme **verursachen kann**.*

Health

Um länger zu leben, muss man richtig leben!

Hier schreiben Schüler und Schülerinnen der Klasse 10b über Gesundheit und geben Tipps für ein gesundes Leben.

Raucher sind doof, oder? Sie müssen Geld ausgeben, um krank und unfit zu werden.

Zigarettenrauch schadet den Lungen, dem Herz und den Adern. Dann stirbt der Raucher früher als der Nichtraucher. Das ist aber Unsinn! Du brauchst nicht nikotinabhängig zu sein. Rauchen ist nicht mehr cool – für ein gutes Image ist eine Zigarette gar nicht nötig.

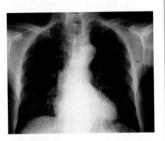

Andreas

Der Körper braucht keinen Alkohol. Er verursacht Probleme für die Leber und das Gehirn. Zuerst wird man betrunken, wenn man zu viel trinkt. Dann kann man das Bewußtsein verlieren und sogar sterben. Wenn man regelmäßig trinkt, kann man süchtig werden. Heute ist der Alkoholismus ein steigendes Problem.

Helga

Drogenhändler am Schuleingang? Spritzen auf dem Kinderspielplatz? Wie schrecklich!

Wenn du leben willst, sollst du kein Rauschgift nehmen. Das erste Mal kann das letzte Mal sein. Wenn du ein(e) Drogensüchtige(r) bist, musst du zur Drogenberatungsstelle gehen. Dort kannst du eine Therapie machen und die Sucht loswerden.

Wilhelm

Es ist wichtig, dass du genug isst, sonst kannst du magersüchtig werden. Besonders Mädchen gehen das Risiko ein, magersüchtig zu werden. Sie wollen schlank sein, aber zu schlank zu sein ist nicht normal.

Dirk

Zu viel Salz kann hohen Blutdruck verursachen. Sechs Gramm pro Tag ist genug. Deshalb sollst du lieber mit Paprika oder Knoblauch würzen. Die geben dem Essen einen sehr guten Geschmack.

Ulrika

Um fit zu bleiben, muss man sich jeden Tag bewegen. Es ist egal, ob man spazieren oder joggen geht, Tischtennis oder Fußball spielt, aber Bewegung ist notwendig für einen gesunden Körper.

Dieter

1a 📖 🎧 Read the students' tips, then read the following sentences. For each sentence write T (true) or F (false), in accordance with what the students advise.

- a You should exercise occasionally.
- b You don't need to smoke to look cool.
- c Anorexia affects boys and girls equally.
- d The problem with alcohol abuse is decreasing.
- e You should eat more than 6g of salt per day.
- f Table-tennis is as good as football for providing exercise.

1b 📖 🎧 Read the tips again and answer the following questions in English.

- a Who talks about not eating too little?
- b Who is likely to be interested in cooking?
- c Who writes about a problem that is getting worse?
- d Who writes about people spending money on making their health worse?
- e Who talks about something that is necessary in order to stay healthy?
- f Who warns that doing this activity just once can be dangerous?

2a 🎧 Listen to Karla getting advice from her mother about living healthily. Put the pictures in the correct order.

2b 🎧 Listen to Kurt talking about taking drugs then answer the following questions in English.

Part 1
- a How old was Kurt when he started smoking cannabis?
- b What did his parents make him do?
- c What happened most days?

Part 2
- d How old was he when he met Sonja?
- e What did Kurt want to do?
- f What happened after six months?

Part 3
- g How do Kurt and Sonja make money?
- h What do they think is awful?
- i What is Kurt afraid of?

AQA *Examiner's tip*

When reading, look in the text for **key words** from the question which will enable you to focus on the right section. For example, the key word in the first statement in Activity 1a is **exercise** (*Um fit zu bleiben, muss man sich jeden Tag bewegen*).

Vokabeln

die Ader	vein
das Bewußtsein verlieren	to lose consciousness
steigend	growing, increasing
der Drogenhändler	drug dealer
die Spritze	syringe
die Drogenberatungsstelle	drugs advice centre
das Risiko eingehen, etw. zu tun	to run the risk of doing sth.
der Blutdruck	blood pressure

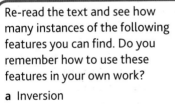

Grammatik Seite 181 & 186

Re-read the text and see how many instances of the following features you can find. Do you remember how to use these features in your own work?

a Inversion
*Zuerst **wird man** betrunken, wenn man zu viel trinkt.*

See page 21 ➡

b Present tense modal verbs
*Sie **müssen** Geld **ausgeben**.*

See page 25 ➡

AQA *Examiner's tip*

Don't panic when faced with longer listening passages. Use skills you've already practised, such as checking the questions for clues and listening out for key words. Remember, you will get to hear each recording twice, so don't get distracted if you've missed something the first time around.

kerboodle!

G Health

1 📖 Underline all the indefinite articles in the accusative case. Take care because not every article is in the accusative!

Beispiel: a Ich trinke gern <u>eine</u> Cola, aber ein Orangensaft schmeckt besser.

a Ich trinke gern eine Cola, aber ein Orangensaft schmeckt besser.

b In der Pause isst sie ein Käsebrot oder einen Apfel.

c Zu Mittag isst sie einen Hamburger mit Pommes und trinkt ein Glas Limonade.

d Mein Lieblingsessen ist ein halbes Hähnchen mit Kartoffelsalat.

e Zum Abendessen esse ich normalerweise eine Portion Fleisch mit Gemüse.

f Der Junge hat eine Zigarette in der Hand, aber er sieht nicht cool aus.

Using the indefinite article and the accusative case

In German, the word you use for 'a' or 'an' depends on the gender of the noun (masculine, feminine or neuter) and the case. You use the nominative case for the subject of a sentence:

Ein Apfel *ist sehr gesund.*

For the direct object of the sentence, you need the accusative:

Ich esse **einen Apfel** *in der Pause.*

These are the different forms you need to remember:

	masc.	fem.	neut.
nominative (nom.)	ein	eine	ein
accusative (acc.)	einen	eine	ein

As you can see, the only articles which are different depending on whether they are nominative or accusative are masculine.

2a 📖 Translate the following sentences into English.

1 Ich gehe ab und zu mit meinen Freunden ins Kino.

2 Meine Familie und ich gehen oft kegeln, weil es Spaß macht.

3 Fleisch esse ich nie, weil ich Vegetarier bin.

2b ✏ Now translate these sentences into German. Be careful with the word order!

1 I rarely eat cheese or butter.

2 We play table-tennis now and again.

3 I sometimes go swimming at the weekend.

2c 🗨 Work with a partner: one partner asks the questions on the clipboard and another answers, using full sentences and a different adverb each time. Then swap roles. (Remember to use inversion if you start the sentence with an adverb.)

- Wie oft treibst du Sport?
- Wie oft isst du Pommes frites?
- Wie oft trinkst du Mineralwasser?
- Wie oft gehst du zum Arzt?
- Wie oft gehst du kegeln?
- Wie oft hörst du Musik?

Using adverbs of frequency

Adverbs are words which qualify the action of the verb, e.g. slowly, loudly, neatly etc. Adverbs of frequency describe how often you do something e.g. sometimes, often etc. Here are some common ones in German:

immer – always

oft – often

ab und zu – now and again

selten – rarely

nie – never

In German the adverb comes after the verb (never between the verb and subject, as sometimes happens in English):

Er geht **manchmal** *ins Sportzentrum.* – He sometimes goes to the sports centre.

3a ✏ Write a suitable negative response to each of the following questions. You need to work out whether to use *nicht* or *kein* each time.

Beispiel: **a** Nein, ich esse nicht gern Spinat.

A ← Isst du gern Spinat?

B

Hast du eine Banane?

C ← Rauchst du?

Trinkst du Alkohol? **D**

E ← Hast du Angst vor Krankheiten?

F

Bist du Raucher / Raucherin?

Grammatik Seite 174

Forming negative phrases using '*nicht*' and '*kein*'

To say that you do not do something, you should use *nicht*:

> *Ich will nicht rauchen.* – I don't want to smoke.

Be careful, though – if you need to say 'not a/an' or 'not any', you should never say *nicht ein*. You have to use the negative article (*kein*) instead.

> *Ich habe keine Zigaretten geraucht.* –
> I haven't smoked any cigarettes.

Remember that *kein* takes the same endings as *ein* (but there is also a plural form):

	masc.	fem.	neut.	pl.
(nom.)	kein	keine	kein	keine
(acc.)	keinen	keine	kein	keine

3b 🗨 Say in German what your friend has / hasn't got in her shopping basket, based on the pictures below.

Beispiel: **a** Sie hat keine Wurst, ...

4a ✏ Re-write the following sentences replacing *du* with *man*. You will need to make sure you change the verb ending too!

Beispiel: **1** Man soll keine Drogen nehmen.

1 Du sollst keine Drogen nehmen.
2 Du musst jeden Tag spazieren gehen.
3 Darfst du hier rauchen?
4 In der Schule musst du eine Uniform tragen.
5 Pro Tag sollst du fünf Portionen Obst und Gemüse essen.

Grammatik Seite 179

Using *man*

Man means 'you', 'one', 'people', 'we or 'they', used when you aren't referring to anybody in particular. It is followed by the same form of the verb as *er/sie/es*:

> *Man darf im Restaurant nicht rauchen.* – You aren't allowed to smoke in the restaurant.

4b ✏ Now translate these sentences into German using *man*.

1 You should often eat fruit.
2 People aren't allowed to smoke in restaurants.
3 We must do more physical exercise.
4 They aren't allowed to wear trainers in school.
5 You can't sleep here because it is too loud.

Health

Gesund essen, gesund leben! ➡ *Seite 18–19*

das	Abendessen	dinner
die	Allergie	allergy
die	Ananas	pineapple
der	Apfel	apple
die	Banane	banana
das	Bier	beer
die	Biokost	organic food
der	Blumenkohl	cauliflower
die	Bohne	bean
die	Bratwurst	(fried) sausage
das	Butterbrot	sandwich
die	Chips (pl)	crisps
die	Diät	diet
das	Ei	egg
die	Ernährung	diet
	essen	to eat
	fettig / fetthaltig	greasy / fatty
der	Fisch	fish
das	Fleisch	meat
die	Forelle	trout
der	Fruchtsaft	fruit juice
das	Frühstück	breakfast
das	Gemüse	vegetables
	gesund	healthy / healthily
	grillen	to grill
die	Gurke	cucumber
die	Haferflocken (pl)	rolled oats
das	Hähnchen	chicken
die	Himbeere	raspberry
der	Jogurt	yoghurt
der	Kaffee	coffee
die	Kartoffel	potato
der	Käse	cheese
die	Kohlenhydrate (pl)	carbohydrates
	köstlich	delicious
der	Kuchen	cake
der	Lachs	salmon
	lecker	delicious
	magersüchtig	anorexic
die	Mahlzeit	meal
die	Milch	milk
die	Milchprodukte (pl)	dairy produce

das	Mineralwasser	mineral water
das	Mittagessen	lunch
das	Müsli	muesli
die	Nahrung	food
die	Nudeln (pl)	pasta, noodles
das	Obst	fruit
die	Pause	breaktime
der	Pfirsich	peach
die	Pommes (frites) (pl)	chips
der	Reis	rice
die	Sahne	cream
der	Salat	salad
	satt	full
der	Schinken	ham
	schlank	slim
	schmecken (es schmeckt)	to taste (it tastes good)
der	Schokoriegel	chocolate bar
das	Spiegelei	fried egg
der	Spinat	spinach
der	Tee	tea
die	Tomate	tomato
	trainieren	to train
	trinken	to drink
	nicht fit	unfit
	ungesund	unhealthy / unhealthily
	vegetarisch (adj)	vegetarian
die	Vitamine (pl)	vitamins
das	Wasser	water

Ich bin in Form! ➡ *Seite 20–21*

die	Bewegung	movement / exercise
	dick	fat
	entspannen (sich)	to relax
	fernsehen	to watch TV
	fit bleiben	to keep fit
das	Fitnesszentrum	fitness centre
	Fußball spielen	to play football
die	Gesundheit	health
das	Hallenbad	indoor swimming pool
der	Körper	body
	körperlich	physical
	lesen	to read

die	Portion	portion
	reiten gehen	to go riding
	schlafen	to sleep
	Schlittschuh laufen	to go ice skating
	schwimmen	to swim
	Spaß haben	to have fun
	spazieren gehen	to go for walks
	Sport treiben	to take part in sports
das	Stadion	stadium
der	Stress	stress
	stressig	stressful
	Tennis spielen	to play tennis
die	Zeitschrift	magazine

Rauchen ist doch ungesund! Seite 22–23

	Angst haben	to be afraid
der	Atem	breath
	atmen	to breathe
	aufgeben	to give up
	aufhören	to stop
der	Außenseiter	outsider
	fühlen (sich)	to feel
	gefährlich	dangerous
das	Herz	heart
die	Krankheit	illness
der	Krebs	cancer
die	Lunge	lung
der	Lungenkrebs	lung cancer
die	Öffentlichkeit	public
	(in der Öffentlichkeit)	(in public)
	probieren	to try
	rauchen	to smoke
der	Raucherhusten	smoker's cough
	riechen	to smell
das	Risiko	risk
	sterben	to die
	stinken	to stink
die	Sucht	addiction
	süchtig	addicted
der	Tabak	tobacco
	verschwenden	to waste
	verursachen	to cause
die	Zigarette	cigarette

Alkohol und Drogen brauchen wir nicht!

Seite 24–25

	abhängig	dependent
die	Abstinenz	abstinence
die	Ader	vein
der	Alkohol	alcohol
der	Alkoholiker	alcoholic (noun)
	alkoholisch	alcoholic (adj.)
der	Alkoholismus	alcoholism
	betrunken	drunk
der	Cannabis	cannabis
die	Droge	drug
die	Drogenberatungsstelle	drugs advice centre
der	Drogenhändler	drug dealer
der/ die	Drogensüchtige	drug addict
die	Entziehungskur	withdrawal treatment
die	Erfahrung	experience
	erfolgreich	successful
das	Gehirn	brain
	kaputt machen	to ruin, to wear out
die	Klinik	clinic
die	Leber	liver
das	Rauschgift	drug, narcotic
	schaden	to damage
	schädlich	damaging
	schützen	to protect
die	Sorge	worry
	tot	dead
	töten	to kill
	treffen	to meet
die	Überdosis	overdose
	verboten	forbidden

Extra! Modalverben

	dürfen	may, to be allowed to
	können	can, to be able to
	mögen	to like
	müssen	must, to have to
	sollen	should, ought to
	wollen	to want to

1.5 Familie und Freunde – zu Hause

■ Wie ist es in deiner Familie?

Interviewer: Hallo, Thomas, wo wohnst du, bitte?

Thomas: Hallo. Ich wohne in Salzburg in Österreich.

Interviewer: Kannst du bitte deine Familie beschreiben?

Thomas, 15 Jahre

Thomas: Ja, gerne. In meiner Familie gibt es 5 Personen: meinen Vater Klaus, meine Stiefmutter Monika, meinen Bruder Karl, meine Stiefschwester Sylvia und mich. Vor drei Jahren haben sich meine Eltern scheiden lassen.

Interviewer: Und wie habt ihr das gefunden?

Thomas: Damals waren mein Bruder und ich sehr traurig. Ein Jahr später hat mein Vater wieder geheiratet, aber meine Stiefmutter ist sehr nett. Jedes zweite Wochenende verbringe ich bei meiner Mutter in Hamburg.

Interviewer: Erzähl mir von deinen Geschwistern, bitte!

Thomas: Karl ist mein Zwillingsbruder und man sagt, dass wir sehr ähnlich sind. Er ist manchmal frech. Sylvia ist zwei Jahre jünger als ich. Meistens ist sie sehr freundlich, aber ab und zu ist sie ein bisschen eifersüchtig.

Interviewer: Grüß dich, Ayse. Wo wohnst du, bitte?

Ayse: Grüß dich. Ich wohne in Bremen in Norddeutschland. Ich bin hier geboren, aber meine Eltern Jusuf und Fadime stammen aus der Türkei. Sie sind vor zwanzig Jahren hierher gekommen.

Ayse, 16 Jahre

Interviewer: Und hast du Geschwister?

Ayse: Nein. Leider bin ich Einzelkind und ich fühle mich manchmal einsam. Letztes Jahr ist mein Großvater in der Türkei gestorben. Deswegen wohnt meine Oma Leyla bei uns.

Interviewer: Wie findest du das?

Ayse: Eigentlich ganz gut. Oma hat eine eigene Wohnung im Haus. Sie kann selbstständig leben, wenn sie es will, aber normalerweise essen wir alle zusammen. Ich finde sie sehr lieb und immer großzügig.

---

1 📖 🎧 🔊 In the text find the German for these phrases:

Beispiel: a Normalerweise essen wir alle zusammen.

a Usually we all eat together.

b My parents separated three years ago.

c I spend every second weekend in Hamburg with my mother.

d I feel lonely sometimes.

e People say that we are very similar.

f Now and again she is a little jealous.

g I think she is very kind and always generous.

h At the time my brother and I were very sad.

> 📖 **Identifying patterns between German and English** ⟳ Strategie
>
> Using common patterns between German and English can help you understand words. For instance, *d* in German can become 'th' in English (*Bruder* → 'bro**th**er'), and *v* can become 'f' (*Vater* → '**f**ather').

2 Ⓖ Read the interview with Jutta and fill in the gaps with the correct form of *haben* or *sein*.

Beispiel: **a** ist

3 🎧 Paul, Julia and Michael are talking about their families. First make notes on each person. Then answer the questions below with the name of the relevant person.

Beispiel: **a** Michael

a   Whose parents are divorced?

b   Whose mother has died?

c   Who has three brothers?

d   Who has a half-brother?

e   Who doesn't live in Germany?

f   Who has a grandparent at home?

g   Who doesn't mention his / her age?

h   Whose family all share in the housework?

4 🗨 Work in pairs. Using the interviews above as examples, interview your partner about his or her family, before swapping roles. Here are some questions to get you started:

Interviewer: Guten Tag, Jutta. Woher kommst du?

Jutta: Grüezi. Ich komme aus Bern in der Schweiz.

Interviewer: Und wie (a) _____ deine Familie, bitte?

Jutta: Wir (b) _____ drei Personen: meine Mutter, mein jüngerer Bruder Anton und ich. Ich (c) _____ keine Schwestern. Leider (d) _____ meine Mutter alleinstehend.

Jutta, 15 Jahre

Interviewer: Und wie findet ihr das?

Jutta: Meine Mutti (e) _____ ein schweres Leben, weil mein Vati seit letztem Jahr mit seiner Freundin im Ausland wohnt. Anton (f) _____ erst acht Jahre alt und (g) _____ im Rollstuhl. Er braucht viel Hilfe. Nachts geht Mutti in einer Fabrik arbeiten und ich passe auf Anton auf. Leider (h) _____ ich wenige Freundinnen. Daher kann ich selber nicht oft ausgehen.

Wie viele Personen gibt es in deiner Familie?

Hast du Geschwister?

Wie alt ist er / sie? (Wie alt sind sie?)

Wohnen deine Eltern beide zu Hause?

Wohnt dein Großvater oder deine Großmutter bei dir?

Wie findest du das?

In meiner Familie gibt es	meinen Vater / Bruder / Stiefbruder / Halbbruder / Opa / Onkel.	
	meine Mutter / Schwester / Stiefschwester / Halbschwester / Oma / Tante.	
Ich habe	(k)einen (jüngeren / älteren) Bruder.	
	(k)eine (jüngere / ältere) Schwester.	
	zwei Brüder / Schwestern.	
Mein Vater	ist	gestorben / geschieden.
Meine Mutter	lebt	getrennt.
Meine Eltern	sind	
Meine Großeltern		
Mein Bruder / Meine Schwester ist ledig / verheiratet / verlobt.		

Ⓖrammatik *Seite 181*

Using the present tense of *haben* and *sein*

The German verbs for 'to have' and 'to be' are irregular so you need to learn them by heart.

haben – 'to have'   ***sein*** – 'to be'

ich habe	*ich bin*
du hast	*du bist*
er/sie/es hat	*er/sie/es ist*
wir haben	*wir sind*
ihr habt	*ihr seid*
sie haben	*sie sind*
Sie haben	*Sie sind*

Learn also how to use *ihr*.

See page 46 ➡

Tipp

The verbs *haben* and *sein* are particularly important because they can each be used when forming the perfect tense.

kerboodle!

1.6 Familie und Freunde – Beziehungen

Lernziele

Describing different relationship scenarios

Using possessive adjectives

Using your knowledge of grammatical categories

◼ Probleme zu Hause

Startseite | Index | Hilfe | Kontakt | Textversion

🔍 Suche

Jasmin (14)

Meine Familie wohnt in Köln in einem Zweifamilienhaus. Ich verstehe mich sehr gut mit meinem Vater und meiner Stiefmutter. Ich habe eine Stiefschwester. Sie heißt Sara und ist auch vierzehn, aber ich kann sie nicht leiden, weil sie immer meine Sachen nimmt. Sie ist so eifersüchtig und eingebildet. Außerdem bringt sie ihre Freundinnen mit nach Hause und sie schwatzen die ganze Zeit. Wir streiten uns oft.

Lutz (15)

Ich wohne mit meiner Mutter und meiner jüngeren Schwester in einem Wohnblock. Leider hat meine Mutter Gesundheitsprobleme, also kann sie nicht arbeiten. Sie ist sehr sympathisch und wir verstehen uns gut. Nach der Schule muss ich viel in der Wohnung helfen oder babysitten. Mein Leben ist nicht gerade einfach, aber ich bin zufrieden.

Natascha (16)

Meine beste Freundin heißt Laura und sie ist sehr nett. Sie ist ein Jahr älter als ich. Abends treffen wir unsere Freunde im Park und manchmal trinkt Laura Alkohol, aber ich mag das nicht. Normalerweise kommen wir spät nach Hause und mein Vater ist böse. Meine Eltern mögen Laura nicht und glauben, dass sie einen schlechten Einfluss auf mich hat. Ich finde das so gemein!

---

1 📖 🎧 🔊 Decide if these statements are true (T) or false (F).

Beispiel: a   F

a   Jasmin hat Probleme mit ihren Eltern.

b   Ihre Stiefschwester ist nicht sehr nett.

c   Lutz versteht sich gut mit seiner Mutter.

d   Er findet sein Leben manchmal hart.

e   Nataschas Freundin ist siebzehn Jahre alt.

f   Sie hat ein schlechtes Verhältnis zu ihr.

g   Nataschas Eltern haben keine Probleme mit Laura.

📖 **Using your knowledge of grammatical categories**

If you can recognise whether a word is a noun, a verb or an adjective, this will help you to have an educated guess at what it means.

In German, all nouns have capital letters.

Learn to recognise verbs with their different endings.

Adjectives can go immediately before a noun or often after *ist* and *sind*.

	Verb	Adjective	Noun
Deswegen	*habe ich*	*ein sehr gutes*	*Verhältnis zu ihnen.*

Strategie

2 **G** Copy out the sentences and fill in the missing possessive adjective.

Beispiel: a Mein bester Freund heißt Felix.

a _____ bester Freund heißt Felix. (mein / meine / meinen)

b _____ Familie wohnt in Köln. (mein / meine / meinen)

c Ich treffe _____ Bruder in der Stadtmitte. (sein / seine / seinen)

d Am Wochenende gehen _____ Freunde einkaufen. (ihr / ihre / ihren)

e Karl und ich besuchen am Samstag _____ Onkel. (unser / unsere / unseren)

f Beate muss _____ Hausaufgaben machen. (ihr / ihre / ihren)

g Hat _____ Vater ein deutsches Auto? (dein / deine / deinen)

3 🎧 Read the statements below then listen to Matthìas and Karla describing relationships important to them. Who says what? Write down the name of the person concerned.

Beispiel: a Matthias

a Meine Familie ist ziemlich groß.

b Ich kenne sie seit drei Jahren.

c Einmal im Monat besuchen wir unseren Vater.

d Er hat jetzt eine neue Familie.

e Leider arbeitet mein Stiefvater nicht.

f Jeden Samstag gehen wir in die Stadtmitte.

g Ich verstehe mich ziemlich gut mit meinem Bruder.

h Wir haben dieselben Interessen.

Using possessive adjectives

These are words which tell you who something belongs to, e.g. 'my', 'your' etc. The basic words are:

mein – my

dein – your (familiar singular)

sein – his, its (masc. or neut. nouns)

ihr – her, its (fem. nouns)

unser – our

euer – your (familiar plural)

ihr – their

Ihr – your (polite, sing./pl.)

They often add endings and this depends on the gender and case of the noun which follows:

	Masculine	Feminine	Neuter	Plural
Nominative	*mein*	*meine*	*mein*	*meine*
Accusative	*meinen*	*meine*	*mein*	*meine*

For a reminder about cases and gender, see pages 28, 39.

Learn also how to use adjectives after nouns and how to use qualifiers.   *See page 46* ➡

Grammatik — *Seite 175*

Tipp

Don't forget that the possessive adjective must **agree** with the person or thing it refers to.

Er kann seinen Bruder nicht leiden.

Ihre Mutter ist sympathisch.

---

4 ✏ Using the language support box, write an article about a fictional family (e.g. from a book or TV soap) and its problems. You should mention:

■ what the family is called and which soap or book they are in

■ who the main character is and what relatives and / or friends he or she has

■ what sort of characters they are and how they get on with each other.

Beispiel: Die Familie heißt Mitchell und sie ist in „EastEnders". In der Familie gibt es …

Die Familie heißt … und ist in …				
In der Familie gibt es … Personen.				
Der beste Freund / Die beste Freundin von … heißt …				
Sie verstehen sich (nicht) gut,		weil er / sie	nett / freundlich /	ist.
Sie streiten sich,			zu streng / eingebildet / unordentlich	
Er	kann	sie	nicht leiden	
Sie		ihn		

Zukunftspläne –
Heiraten, ja oder nein?

■ Willst du heiraten oder ledig bleiben?

Wolfgang (15)

Ich möchte auf die Uni gehen und später Geschäftsmann werden. Meine Karriere ist sehr wichtig für mich. Ich möchte auch vielleicht im Ausland arbeiten und natürlich viel Geld verdienen. Ich muss ein schnelles Auto und eine Luxuswohnung haben. Mit 35 Jahren kann ich dann heiraten und Kinder haben. Das ist früh genug.

Andrea (16)

Heiraten und Kinder haben – das ist nichts für mich. Meine Mutter wollte mich nicht als Baby und ich bin adoptiert. Ich kenne meinen Vater nicht. Deswegen will ich viel Spaß in meinem Leben. Das heißt, mit meinen Freundinnen ausgehen, viel Alkohol trinken und Jungen treffen. Ich möchte auf jeden Fall Single bleiben!

Gisela (16)

Mein Freund und ich heiraten nächstes Jahr. Ich kann es kaum erwarten. Ich habe schon den Verlobungsring und ich möchte eine traditionelle Hochzeit. Dann will ich zwei oder drei Kinder. Für mich ist Familie das Wichtigste. Meiner Meinung nach sollen der Mann und die Frau verheiratet sein und nicht einfach nur zusammenleben. Ein Kind muss Stabilität haben.

Dominic (14)

Meine Eltern streiten sich so viel und sind immer unglücklich – ich heirate nie! Ich möchte mit einer Freundin zusammenleben und alles teilen – den Haushalt, das Geld und die Verantwortung. Heutzutage kann ein Kind auch bei unverheirateten Eltern glücklich sein.

Wolfgang   Gisela   Andrea   Dominic

1 📖🎧 Find the following sentences in the German text above:

Beispiel: a Ich möchte auf jeden Fall Single bleiben.
a I'd definitely like to stay single.
b My career is very important to me.
c Family is the most important thing for me.
d My parents argue so much and are always unhappy.
e I'd like to live together with a girlfriend.
f I must have a fast car and a luxury apartment.
g I'd like a traditional wedding.
h That's why I want lots of fun in my life.

2 Ⓖ Unscramble the statements about the future so that they make sense. Start with the underlined word. Take care with the word order.

Beispiel: a Hoffentlich habe ich einen guten Beruf.
a ich einen <u>hoffentlich</u> Beruf habe guten.
b Jahren <u>ich</u> in heirate 10.
c Mathe ich Englisch September studiere <u>im</u> und.

d treffen Abend Freunde <u>heute</u> wir unsere.

e besucht Freundin <u>im</u> sie ihre Sommer.

f <u>heute</u> und sie Biologie Sport Nachmittag haben.

g <u>nächsten</u> ich eine meine Radtour machen und Schwestern Samstag.

3 🎧 Listen to five young people talking about whether they want to get married and have children. Decide whether the sentences are true (T) or false (F).

Beispiel: a   T

a Petra will heiraten.

b Sie hat Kinder nicht gern.

c Lars will nicht heiraten.

d Er will im Ausland arbeiten.

e Sophie will eine traditionelle Hochzeit haben.

f Sie möchte zwei Kinder haben.

g Achim will nicht heiraten.

h Er will jeden Abend mit seiner Frau ausgehen.

i Elke will ledig bleiben.

j Ihre Eltern leben nicht mehr zusammen.

4 🗨 ✏ 🌐 Class survey. Using the questions below, find out people's views on marriage. Use the table to help you give your own responses. When you have completed the survey, you can write up people's different viewpoints (but remember to use the third person!).

- Willst du heiraten oder Single bleiben?
- Und warum?
- Wann willst du denn heiraten?
- Möchtest du Kinder haben?
- Warum (nicht)?

Using the present tense to talk about the future

You don't always have to use 'will' or 'shall' when talking about the future. Provided you have a **future indicator**, you can just use the present tense. For example, 'I am getting married in **20 years time**' refers to what you are going to do in the future. It is the same in German:

Ich heirate in 20 Jahren.

Nächstes Jahr gehe ich auf die Uni. ('I am going to university next year.')

Learn also about adverbial phrases of time.   *See page 46* ➡

Grammatik *Seite 184*

🗨 Asking for help when unsure

You need to be able to ask for help in German, if you aren't sure how to say something, e.g. *Wie sagt man … auf Deutsch?*

Strategie

Wie sagt man: "Will you marry me?" auf Deutsch?

Ich heirate,		weil	ich eine(n) Partner(in) will.
Ich will nicht ledig bleiben,		da	ich eine Familie möchte.
Ich bleibe Single,		denn	meine Karriere ist wichtiger.
Ich heirate noch nicht,			ich will reisen.
Ich heirate	in zehn Jahren,	weil	ich Spaß haben will.
	irgendwann,	da	ich im Moment keine Verantwortung will.
	erst mit 25 Jahren,		
Ich möchte (keine) Kinder haben,		denn	ich mag sie (nicht).

Tipp

Remember the pronunciation of *ei* in *heiraten* and *weil*. If you tend to get mixed up between *ei* and *ie*, just pronounce the last letter each time and you'll get it right!

Gleichheit für Männer und Frauen?

Das ist keine Stelle für dich, oder?

1 Grüezi. Ich heiße Rainer und komme aus Basel in der Schweiz. Seit zwei Jahren ist meine Schwester Lisa Feuerwehrfrau. Sie findet die Arbeit sehr interessant, aber das kann manchmal gefährlich sein. Am Anfang hatte mein Vater Angst. Er sagte: „Eine Frau kann diese Arbeit nicht machen, weil sie nicht stark genug ist!" Lisa hat aber alle Prüfungen bestanden. Ihre Kollegen akzeptieren sie total und mein Vater ist jetzt sehr stolz auf sie.

2 Guten Tag. Ich bin die Nicole und wohne in Linz in Österreich. Mein Vater arbeitet als Sekretär bei einer großen Baufirma. Er hilft seinem Chef, er schreibt Briefe, organisiert Geschäftsreisen und noch vieles mehr. Er macht, was eine Seketärin macht. Ein Mann kann die Arbeit genauso gut wie eine Frau machen!

3 Hallo. Mein Name ist Mehmet. Ich komme aus Regensburg in Süddeutschland. Mein Vater arbeitet den ganzen Tag zu Hause, weil er Hausmann ist. Einige Leute finden das komisch, aber warum soll er das nicht machen? Meine Mutter hat einen gut bezahlten Beruf als Ärztin. Mein Vater arbeitet im Haushalt, er bringt meine kleinen Schwestern zur Schule und er geht einkaufen. Das ist ideal.

4 Tag. Ich bin Yvonne und wohne in Innsbruck in Österreich. Mein Bruder ist Ballett-Tänzer in Wien. Meine Freunde lachen, wenn sie das hören, aber ich finde es toll. Er ist sehr stark und trainiert viel, um fit zu bleiben. Außerdem verdient er ziemlich viel Geld und er kann in andere Länder reisen.

> **Tipp**
> In English, we don't always distinguish between male and female jobs, e.g. 'doctor' can be male or female. In German, there are usually versions for both e.g. *Arzt / Ärztin*.

1a 📖 🎧 Read the text above and match the photos to the correct paragraphs.

a

b

c

d

1b 📖 🎧 🌐 Read the text again and find the German for these phrases:

a a well paid job
b sometimes dangerous
c organises business trips
d all day
e in the beginning
f Some people think it's funny.

📖 **Matching German and English phrases**

Take care – a phrase in English may be translated using more or fewer words in German:

just as well – *genauso gut*

all week – *die ganze Woche*

Remember this when you want to say or write something new in German. You may not be able to substitute one word directly for another!

Strategie

2 ⓖ Add the correct definite article for each of these nouns:

a _____ Limonade   f _____ Auge

b _____ Körper   g _____ Lineal

c _____ Gesundheit   h _____ Teppich

d _____ Gehirn   i _____ Lehrer

e _____ Meinung   j _____ Freundin

3 🎧 Listen to the radio report about gender discrimination in Germany and the UK. Complete the gaps in the sentences, using the words on the rght.

Beispiel: a illegal

a Die Diskriminierung zwischen Männern und Frauen ist _____.

b Mehr Männer als Frauen sind _____.

c Frauen verlassen die Schule mit _____ Qualifikationen.

d Frauen verdienen etwa 30% _____ als Männer.

e Frauen _____ oft zu Hause bleiben.

f _____ Männer als Frauen arbeiten als Manager.

g Diese Diskriminierung muss sofort _____.

> ### Understanding nouns and gender
>
> Deciding whether a noun is masculine, feminine or neuter can be tricky, but here are some ways to help. (There are some exceptions, though.)
>
> **Masculine**
>
> Usually words ending in *-ich, -ig, -us, -or*
>
> Many words ending in *-er*
>
> **Feminine**
>
> Words ending in *-ei, -heit, -ie, -in, -keit, -schaft, -tät, -tion, -ung, -ur*
>
> Most words ending in *-e* (but *der Käse, der Name, das Auge, das Interesse, das Ende*)
>
> **Neuter**
>
> Most words starting with *Ge-* (but *die Geschichte, die Gesundheit*)
>
> Many words ending in *-al, -ar, -ier, -o*
>
> Learn also how to use the correct word for 'it'.
>
> *See page 47* ➡

Ⓖrammatik   Seite 174

mehr	enden	wichtig
arbeitslos	zu Hause	illegal
weniger	besseren	müssen

4 🗨️ 💭 Study the Austrian poster about unequal pay and discuss it in pairs. Use the questions and table below to help you.

a Was ist „Equal Pay Day?"

b Warum verdienen Frauen weniger als Männer?

c Ist das gerecht?

d Warum (nicht)?

e Gibt es dieses Problem nur in Österreich?

Use the table below to write up your answers, including your own opinions.

Frauen verdienen weniger als Männer,	da	sie zu Hause bleiben müssen.
	weil	sie mehr Teilzeitjobs haben.
Männer verdienen mehr als Frauen		sie die besseren Stellen haben.
		sie nicht auf die Kinder aufpassen müssen.

| Ein Mann | ist manchmal | stärker / fleißiger / kreativer … | als eine Frau / ein Mann. |
| Eine Frau | | | |

Meiner Meinung nach ist die Situation blöd / ungerecht / unwichtig, da / weil …

Hat Ahmet keine Chance?

Interviewer: Guten Tag, Ahmet. Woher kommst du?

Ahmet: Ich komme aus Berlin in Deutschland. Ich bin hier geboren, aber meine Eltern kommen aus der Türkei. Wir wohnen in einer Wohnung im sozialen Wohnungsbau.

Interviewer: Wie findest du das?

Ahmet: Dort ist es nicht so schön, denn es gibt Probleme mit Vandalismus und Gewaltkriminalität.

Interviewer: Was für eine Schule besuchst du?

Ahmet: Ich besuche eine Hauptschule am Stadtrand.

Ahmet

Interviewer: Und bist du in der Schule glücklich?

Ahmet: Eigentlich nicht. Die meisten Schüler hier sind Türken, also sind fast alle meine Freunde Türken. Im Klassenzimmer müssen wir Deutsch reden, aber auf dem Schulhof sprechen wir nie Deutsch, nur Türkisch. Am Anfang habe ich Deutsch schwierig gefunden, aber jetzt geht's besser.

Interviewer: Und wie ist es zu Hause?

Ahmet: Meine Eltern können wenig Deutsch sprechen und zu Hause spricht niemand Deutsch. Jeden Tag sehen wir nur Sendungen aus der Türkei im Satellitenfernsehen. Das finde ich schade.

Interviewer: Hast du denn keine deutschen Freunde?

Ahmet: Doch, ich kenne ein paar Leute in der Schule, aber wir sind keine richtigen Freunde. Ich bleibe normalerweise in der Gegend und war noch nie in der Stadtmitte.

Interviewer: Und wie sind deine Noten in der Schule?

Ahmet: Nicht besonders gut – ich bin sehr schwach in Mathe. Ich möchte auf die Uni gehen, aber ich habe keine Chance!

1 📖 🎧 Read the interview with Ahmet and answer these multiple-choice questions:

a Wo ist Ahmet geboren?

   1 in Deutschland   **2** in der Türkei   **3** in der Schweiz.

b Wo wohnen Ahmets Eltern?

   1 in der Türkei   **2** in Berlin   **3** in Bern

c Was für Probleme gibt es, wo er wohnt?

   1 Probleme mit Türken   **2** Probleme mit der Wohnung   **3** Probleme mit Kriminalität.

d Wo ist Ahmets Schule?

   1 am Stadtrand   **2** in der Stadtmitte   **3** in der Nähe der Stadt.

e Wo spricht Ahmet Deutsch?

   1 mit seinen Eltern   **2** im Klassenzimmer   **3** auf dem Schulhof.

f Was macht er mit seinen deutschen Freunden?

   1 Sie gehen in die Stadtmitte.   **2** Sie sehen fern.   **3** Nichts – er trifft sie nur in der Schule.

2a ⓖ Join the two sentences together to form one new sentence by using the conjunction given in brackets.

a   Ich kenne ein paar Leute in der Schule.
    Wir sind keine richtigen Freunde. (aber)

b   Dort ist es nicht so schön.
    Es gibt Probleme mit Rassismus. (denn)

c   Wir besuchen eine Schule am Stadtrand.
    Sie ist nicht sehr groß. (und)

d   Meine Eltern bleiben meistens zu Hause.
    Sie haben Probleme mit der Sprache. (denn)

2b ⓖ Choose your own coordinating conjunctions for these sentences:

a   Ich möchte auf die Uni gehen.
    Ich bin nicht intelligent genug.

b   Meine Eltern kommen aus der Türkei.
    Sie leben seit 20 Jahren hier.

Using coordinating conjunctions

Coordinating conjunctions are words which join sentences together. The most common ones are *und* ('and'), *aber* ('but') and *denn* ('for', 'because'). They are easy to use because **they do not affect the word order**.

Ich habe wenig Geld. + Ich kann die Leute nicht verstehen.

Ich habe wenig Geld und ich kann die Leute nicht verstehen.

If you use *aber* and *denn* as conjunctions, put a comma before them.

Ich mag die Leute, aber es gibt Probleme mit dem Essen.

Learn also how to use adverbs of place.

See page 47 ➡

Grammatik   Seite 186

Tipp

Be careful if you use an adverb or adverbial phrase after *und* – you will still need to use inversion, e.g. ... *und jeden Tag sehen wir nur Sendungen aus der Türkei.*

---

3 🎧 Listen to this radio report about a project in Germany called "Schule ohne Rassismus – Schule mit Courage". Then match the sentence beginnings and endings.

SCHULE OHNE RASSISMUS
SCHULE MIT COURAGE

Beispiel: a 5

a   Es ist ein Projekt
b   Sie wollen eine Gesellschaft
c   Hautfarbe und Religion
d   Das Projekt hat
e   70% der Schüler und Lehrer müssen zeigen,
f   Die Schüler organisieren
g   Letzte Woche
h   Es gibt jetzt

1   ohne Gewalttätigkeit.
2   dass sie total gegen Diskriminierung sind.
3   Filme, Diskussionen und Konzerte.
4   weniger Angst.
5   von Schülern und Schülerinnen für Schüler und Schülerinnen.
6   hatten sie sogar ein Sportfest.
7   sind für sie nicht wichtig.
8   im Jahr 1988 in Belgien begonnen.

4 ✏ 🗨 Imagine that you have just moved to a new country. Write an email to friends and / or family in your home country describing the issues you now face living abroad. Use the table below to help you.

Ich komme aus	Großbritannien / Irland / Litauen / Polen / Rumänien.		
Ich lebe	seit	gestern / einer Woche / drei Monaten	hier.
Ich habe	wenig Geld / keine Freunde.		
Ich verstehe	die Leute / die Sprache	nicht.	
Es gibt Probleme mit	dem Wetter / dem Essen / der Eingliederung / der Gewalttätigkeit / anderen Leuten.		

✏ 🗨 Writing and speaking creatively

Don't be frightened if you have to make things up – be creative!

▪ Collect as many ideas as possible for your topic.

▪ Adapt structures from reading and listening material.

▪ If what you want to say is too complicated, simplify it or make up something else.

Strategie

Lernziele

Talking about poverty

Using subordinating conjunctions

Identifying compound nouns

Zwei junge Leute, zwei verschiedene Lebensstile

Claudia

Hallo, ich heiße Claudia und bin 19 Jahre alt. Mein Vater ist der Inhaber einer internationalen Firma, die Markenkleidung produziert. Wir haben ein wunderschönes Haus in der Schweiz an einem See. Hier befindet sich unsere Jacht. Zu meinem letzten Geburtstag habe ich einen roten Lamborghini bekommen – meine Freundinnen sind total neidisch! Normalerweise stehe ich gegen zehn Uhr auf, ziehe mich an und schminke mich. Dann rufe ich ein paar Freundinnen an. Manchmal treffen wir uns zu Mittag und dann gehen wir einkaufen. Nach so einem Tag bin ich sehr müde, aber ich muss mich für die Party bei meiner besten Freundin zurechtmachen. Das ist ganz schön anstrengend!

Bodo

Ich heiße Bodo und bin siebzehn Jahre alt. Meine Eltern haben mich vor drei Jahren rausgeschmissen, weil sie drogensüchtig sind. Jetzt bin ich obdachlos und mein „Schlafzimmer" ist der Eingang von einem Supermarkt. Abends finde ich oft alte Butterbrote in der Mülltonne, da ihr Mindesthaltbarkeitsdatum überschritten ist. Nachts kann ich aber nicht gut schlafen, weil ich Angst habe. Um Geld zu bekommen, sitze ich tagsüber mit meinem Hund vor dem Bahnhof. Wenn ich Glück habe, geben mir die Leute etwas. Ich habe wenige Freunde, weil so viele Obdachlose Alkoholiker sind. Ich finde mein Leben so langweilig, aber was kann ich tun? Ich bin schmutzig und meine Kleider riechen. Ich habe keine Aussicht auf einen Job, aber ich weiß, dass ich Hilfe brauche.

1 📖 🎧 🌐 Read the article above and decide if the following sentences are true (T) or false (F).

Beispiel: a   F

a   Claudia besitzt eine internationale Kleidungsfirma.

b   Sie hat ein rotes Auto.

c   Meistens steht sie früh auf.

d   Sie geht morgens einkaufen.

e   Bodo ist drogensüchtig.

f   Nachts schläft er in einem Heim.

g   Er hat nicht viele Freunde.

h   Mit seinem Leben ist er nicht zufrieden.

> 📖 **Identifying compound nouns**
>
> German sometimes uses long words, but these don't have to be daunting. Learn how to break them up to understand the meaning,
>
> e.g. *Mindesthaltbarkeitsdatum* = *Mindest* + *haltbarkeits* + *datum*
>
> = minimum keep-ability date, in other words, 'sell-by date'.
>
> **Strategie**

2a **G** Join the sentences together to form one new sentence by using the subordinating conjunction given in brackets.

Beispiel: a Nachts kann ich nicht gut schlafen, weil ich Angst habe.

a Nachts kann ich nicht gut schlafen. Ich habe Angst. (weil)

b Meine Freunde und ich gehen ins Kino. Wir haben genug Geld. (wenn)

c Ich kaufe ein neues Handy. Es ist sehr teuer. (obwohl)

d Meine Schwester geht sehr gern schwimmen. Sie ist gestresst. (wenn)

e Ich darf nicht ausgehen. Ich habe zu viele Hausaufgaben. (da)

f Sie arbeitet oft ehrenamtlich. Sie hat sehr viel zu tun. (obwohl)

> **Grammatik** Seite 187
>
> ## Using subordinating conjunctions
>
> Conjunctions join clauses together. Subordinating conjunctions make the main verb go to the end of the clause. The most common ones are *weil* ('because'), *wenn* ('if' / 'when'), *obwohl* ('although'), *dass* ('that') and *da* ('since' / 'because').
>
> *Ich will Karriere machen.* + *Meine Eltern sind sehr reich.*
>
>   **main clause**   **subordinate clause**
>
> *Ich will Karriere machen, obwohl meine Eltern sehr reich sind.*
>
> Learn also how to use *um … zu.*
>
> *See page 47* ➡

2b **G** Once your teacher has checked your answers, re-write the sentences starting with the subordinate clause.

Beispiel: a Weil ich Angst habe, …

> **Tipp**
>
> You can also start the sentence with the subordinate clause, but you must then use inversion in the main clause:
>
> **subordinate clause:**
>
> *Obwohl meine Eltern sehr reich sind,*
>
> **main clause:**
>
> *will ich Karriere machen.*

3a 🎧 Listen to these three young people being interviewed about their voluntary work for the homeless. Match these words and phrases to the English translations.

a	private Spenden	e	Es ist wichtig		1	every two weeks	5	sell cakes
b	so viele Bedürftige	f	für die meisten Leute		2	voluntarily	6	luxury
c	ehrenamtlich	g	alle zwei Wochen		3	for most people	7	It's important
d	verkaufen Kuchen	h	Luxus		4	private donations	8	so many needy people

3b 🎧 Now write down what voluntary work each person does. Give any extra details that you pick up.

4a ✏ Imagine that you are either very rich or very poor. Write about your lifestyle – *Ein Tag in meinem Leben*. Mention:

- your daily routine
- what you wear
- where you live
- any problems you face

Um … stehe ich auf.			
Ich trage	Markenkleidung, zum Beispiel …		
	eine schmutzige Jacke / alte Schuhe.		
Ich treffe	meine Freunde.		
Ich gehe	einkaufen / in die Stadtmitte.		
Ich sitze	auf der Straße / im Park / vor dem Bahnhof.		
Ich wohne	in einer Luxuswohnung.		
	unter der Brücke.		
	hinter dem Bahnhof.		
Ich habe	ein sehr stressiges Leben,	weil	ich so viel zu tun habe.
	kein Geld / keinen Job,	da	ich keine Arbeit finden kann.

4b 🗩 Use what you have written to give a presentation.

Relationships and choices

Zwei Brüder, zwei verschiedene Meinungen!

Zwei Brüder, Andrei und Petru, sprechen über ihren Lebensstil.

Guten Tag. Mein Name ist Andrei und ich wohne in Bremerhaven in Norddeutschland. Meine Familie und ich haben einen sehr angenehmen Lebensstil. Mein Vater ist Firmenchef und meine Mutter hat eine Boutique im Stadtzentrum. Ich liebe meine Eltern sehr, aber mein Bruder, Petru, geht mir auf den Wecker. Obwohl er erst siebzehn Jahre alt ist, hat er ein Auto und er ist so angeberisch. Er geht drei- oder viermal pro Woche auf Partys, er trinkt zu viel und er arbeitet nicht! Er bekommt das Geld dafür von unseren Eltern. Ich finde das furchtbar. Ich glaube, man soll anderen Leuten helfen und Geld nicht verschwenden. Deswegen arbeite ich jedes Wochenende mit den Obdachlosen neben dem Busbahnhof. Mein Bruder findet das blöd, aber ich finde ihn blöd. Wir haben Glück, dass wir viel Geld haben und uns ein schönes Leben machen können. Das sollen wir nicht vergessen.

Startseite | Index | Hilfe | Kontakt | Textversion

Hallo. Ich heiße Petru. Vor zehn Jahren ist unsere Familie von Rumänien nach Deutschland gekommen. Damals waren wir ziemlich arm, aber jetzt finde ich mein Leben hier toll, weil ich immer genug Geld habe. Ich brauche nicht zu arbeiten, denn meine Eltern sind sehr reich und großzügig. Sie haben fleißig gearbeitet, um einen besseren Lebensstil zu haben. Warum sollen wir das Leben nicht genießen? Mein Freundeskreis ist sehr wichtig für mich und ich habe viele Freundinnen. Später will ich eine reiche Frau heiraten und sie kann dann für mich sorgen. Ich habe einen jüngeren Bruder, Andrei, aber er ist sehr langweilig. Er sitzt abends zu Hause und macht seine Hausaufgaben. Samstags und sonntags arbeitet er sogar mit Obdachlosen. Ich kann einfach nicht verstehen, warum er das macht. Er braucht mehr Spaß am Leben!

1a 📖 🎧 Read the blog entries and answer the questions below, giving the name of the correct person each time.

a Who has lots of girlfriends?
b Who is the youngest?
c Who works hard for school?
d Who doesn't work?
e Who believes in not wasting money?
f Who believes in helping others?

Vokabeln	
auf den Wecker gehen	to get on someone's nerves
angeberisch	boastful
verschwenden	to waste
großzügig	generous
für jdn sorgen	to look after sb.
sogar	even

1b 📖 🎧 Read the blogs again and answer the following questions in English.

a What do Petru and Andrei's parents do for a living?

b Where exactly does Andrei work at the weekend?

c Why doesn't Petru need to work?

d What are Petru's marriage plans?

e What is Petru's opinion of his brother?

f What is Andrei's view of his family's lifestyle?

2a 🎧 Listen to these people talking about their families or life problems, before selecting the correct picture for each question.

a What does Tanja definitely not want to do?

 1  2   3

b Where does Horst live?

 1  2  3

c What does Erika's sister do for a living?

 1  2  3

d What does Ilse's grandmother need?

 1  2  3

2b 🎧 Listen to Anna talking about her family and answer the questions below.

Part 1

a How long ago were Anna's parents divorced?

b Where does her father live?

Part 2

c How does Anna get on with her stepfather?

d How does Anna feel about her mother?

Part 3

e How old is Anna?

f How does her stepfather react to Günther's behaviour?

Grammatik Seite 186–87

Look at how Andrei and Petru use the following features in their blogs:

a Coordinating conjunctions

*Ich liebe meine Eltern sehr, **aber** mein Bruder **geht** ...*

See page 41 ➡

b Subordinating conjunctions

*... **weil** ich immer genug Geld habe.*

***Obwohl** er erst siebzehn Jahre alt ist, ...*

See page 43 ➡

See how many instances of these you can identify in the blogs and in the recordings for activities 2a and 2b, and remember to use coordinating and subordinating conjunctions correctly in your own work.

AQA *Examiner's tip*

In a listening task there is often a question referring to numbers, so make sure you know them thoroughly. Keep practising them regularly.

Vokabeln

sich scheiden lassen	to get divorced
Das Wichtigste ist, ...	The most important thing is, ...

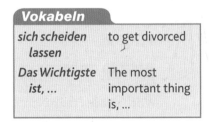

(G) Relationships and choices

1a ✏ Complete the following questions using the correct word for 'you' (*du, Sie* or *ihr*) and the appropriate form of the verb given in brackets.

a _____ ___ heute schwimmen, Peter und Ute? (gehen)

b Was _____ ___ , Kinder? (machen)

c _____ ___ einen Bruder, Lisa? (haben)

d Frau Bachmann, _____ ___ aus Österreich oder aus der Schweiz? (kommen)

e Marion und Klaus, _____ ___ eine Stiefschwester? (haben)

f _____ ___ in Nürnberg, Charlotte? (wohnen)

1b 💬 Work in groups of three or four. One person must ask the others a question using *ihr.* The others give answers, then swap roles.

Beispiel: **Wo wohnt ihr?** **Wir wohnen in ...**

2 📖 Read the following sentences and note down all the adjectives and quantifiers / intensifiers. Write 'A' or 'Q' above each one.

Beispiel:
        A   Q   A
a eifersüchtig, besonders, freundlich

a Meine Schwester ist eifersüchtig und nicht besonders freundlich.

b Unser Haus ist ziemlich groß und modern.

c Ich habe eine CD gekauft. Sie ist ganz toll.

d Das Baby ist laut, aber auch sehr süß.

e Das Auto ist schnell, aber es ist so teuer.

f Ihre Haare sind blond, lang und ziemlich lockig.

3 📖 Note down the adverbial time phrase in the following sentences. Then translate the sentences into English.

a In fünf Jahren heirate ich.

b Mein Vater fährt nächste Woche nach Frankreich.

c Im Winter gehe ich gern Ski fahren.

d Diesen Monat hat sie Prüfungen.

Using *ihr*

Ihr is the plural form of *du*, so you use it when talking to more than one person you know. So, for example, you might ask:

Wo wohnst du?

when talking to a friend, but

Wo wohnt ihr?

when talking to more than one friend. The verb is usually formed by adding *t* to the stem, e.g. *geh+t = geht, komm+t = kommt.* However, if the stem already ends in *t* or *d*, you must add *et*, e.g. *arbeit + et = arbeitet.*

Grammatik *Seite 179*

Adjectives after nouns

Adjectives are words which describe nouns. When they come after the noun, they work the same as in English and do not have to be changed in any way:

Mein Bruder ist groß.

Meine Schwester ist klein.

Quantifiers / intensifiers

Quantifiers or intensifiers are a type of adverb (words which qualify verbs or adjectives – these often end in 'ly' in English). Quantifiers indicate the extent of something:

*Mein Bruder ist **sehr** groß.*

*Meine Schwester ist **ziemlich** klein.*

Grammatik *Seite 177*

Adverbial phrases of time

These are phrases such as:

in zwei Jahren	in two years / in two years' time
nächstes Jahr	next year
diese Woche	this week
eines Tages	one day
in den Ferien	in the holidays
im Sommer	in the summer

Often these phrases can help you to talk about the future while using the present tense:

In den Ferien fahre ich nach Schottland.

(Note the use of inversion if the sentence starts with one of them.)

Grammatik *Seite 178*

---

4 ✏️ Complete the following sentences using the correct word for *it*:

Beispiel: a Ich esse einen Hamburger. Er ist ungesund, aber schmeckt sehr gut.

a Ich esse einen Hamburger. ____ ist ungesund, aber schmeckt sehr gut.

b Meine Familie wohnt in einer Wohnung. ____ ist klein, aber schön.

c Mein Bruder hat ein Handy gekauft. ____ ist einfach klasse!

d Meine Oma hat einen Rollstuhl, aber ____ ist nicht sehr bequem.

e Das Mädchen hat eine Katze. ____ ist braun und schwarz.

f Ich mag die Arbeit. _____ ist wirklich interessant.

> **Grammatik** *Seite 179*
>
> ## Using the word 'it'
> The German word for 'it' is not always *es*! It depends on the gender of the noun 'it' refers to. For the nominative case, you use *er* (masc.), *sie* (fem.) and *es* (neut.). So *das Buch* is *es*, but *die Banane* is *sie*. Don't be put off by the fact that *er* and *sie* also mean *he* and *she* – it should be clear from the context what the particular meaning is.

5a 📖 Match the following adverbs of place with the correct English translations.

Beispiel: a 3

a oben	1 everywhere
b draußen	2 there
c nirgendwo	3 above / upstairs
d hier	4 somewhere
e unten	5 outside
f irgendwo	6 here
g dort	7 nowhere
h überall	8 below / downstairs

> **Grammatik** *Seite 178*
>
> ## Adverbs of place
> These are words which tell us where something generally is e.g. *hier* = here, *dort* = there.
>
> *Wo ist dein Lineal?*
>
> *Dort ist es. / Es ist dort.*

5b 💬 Work in pairs. One person names a classroom item that both people can locate and the other says where it is, using an adverb of place. Then swap roles.

Beispiel:

> Wo ist der Kuli?

> Er ist dort. Wo ist der Schulhof? …

> **Grammatik** *Seite 185*
>
> ## Using *um … zu …*
> *Um … zu …* means 'in order to' and is always used with the infinitive at the end of the clause. Make sure that you separate the *um … zu …* clause from the rest of the sentence with a comma.
>
> *Um gesund zu bleiben, treibe ich viel Sport.*
>
> *Ich esse kein Fett, um schlank zu bleiben.*

6 📖✏️ Match the pictures below to the sentences. Then rewrite each pair of sentences as one sentence, using *um … zu …*.

Beispiel: a 5 Ich spende Geld, um den Obdachlosen zu helfen.

a Ich spende Geld. Ich helfe den Obdachlosen.

b Sie muss sehr fit sein. Sie wird Feuerwehrfrau.

c Am Samstag gehen wir ins Stadtzentrum. Wir kaufen ein Geschenk für Mutti.

d Ich gehe dreimal pro Woche einkaufen. Ich helfe meiner Mutter.

e Die Jugendlichen stehlen Handys. Sie bekommen Geld für Drogen.

Relationships and choices

Familie und Freunde – Zu Hause ➡ *Seite 32–33*

	ähnlich	similar
der/die	Alleinerziehende	single parent
	alleinstehend	single, living alone
der	Bruder	brother
	eifersüchtig	jealous
das	Einzelkind	only child
	Eltern (pl)	parents
die	Familie	family
	geboren	born
	Geschwister (pl)	siblings, brothers and sisters
	gestorben	dead
	Großeltern (pl)	grandparents
die	Großmutter	grandmother
der	Großvater	grandfather
	großzügig	generous
	Halb-	half-
	lieb	kind, nice, lovely
die	Mutter	mother
die	Oma	granny, gran
der	Onkel	uncle
der	Opa	granddad, grandpa
die	Person	person
die	Schwester	sister
	Schwieger-	-in-law
	selbstständig	independent
	Stief-	step-
die	Tante	aunt
der	Vater	father
das	Zuhause	home
	Zwillings-	twin (adj.)

Familie und Freunde – Beziehungen ➡ *Seite 34–35*

	angeberisch	boastful, pretentious
	ärgern	to annoy, to irritate
	auf den Wecker gehen	to get on somebody's nerves
	auf die Nerven gehen	to get on somebody's nerves
	blöd	stupid
	böse	angry
	egoistisch	selfish
der	Einfluss	influence
	eingebildet	conceited
	frech	cheeky, impudent
die	Freundschaft	friendship
	geduldig	patient
	gemein	mean
	gut / schlecht gelaunt	good- / bad-tempered
	sauer	cross
	schwatzen	to gossip, to chatter
	streiten (sich)	to argue
	streng	strict
	süß	sweet
	treffen (sich)	to meet
	unordentlich	untidy
	unternehmungslustig	likes doing lots of things (adj)
die	Verantwortung	responsibility
das	Verhältnis	relationship
	verstehen (sich mit)	to get on with
	weinen	to cry
	zufrieden	content, happy

Zukunftspläne – Heiraten, ja oder nein?
➡ *Seite 36–37*

	adoptiert	adopted
die	*Braut*	bride
der	*Bräutigam*	bridegroom
die	*Frau*	woman, wife
der	*Freund*	friend, boyfriend
die	*Freundin*	friend, girlfriend
	geschieden	divorced
	getrennt	separated
	heiraten	to marry, to get married
die	*Hochzeit*	wedding
	ledig	single
der	*Mann*	man, husband
	scheiden (lassen) (sich)	to get divorced
der	*Sohn*	son
die	*Tochter*	daughter
	trennen (sich)	to separate
	treu	faithful
	verheiratet	married
	verlobt	engaged
der/die	*Verlobte*	fiancé(e)
	zusammenleben	to cohabit

Gleichheit für Männer und Frauen?
➡ *Seite 38–39*

	arbeitslos	unemployed
	aufpassen (auf jemanden)	**to look after**
	ausgeglichen	balanced, equal
	benachteiligen	to disadvantage
	bevorzugen	to prefer, to favour
die	*Diskriminierung*	discrimination
das	*Geschlecht*	sex (male or female)
die	*Gleichheit*	equality
	herrschend	prevalent, current
	illegal	illegal
die	*Karriere*	career
der	*Lohn*	wages
	miteinander	with one another
	pessimistisch	pessimistic
die	*Stelle*	job, position
	stolz	proud
	ungerecht	unjust

Ethnische Probleme ➡ *Seite 40–41*

der	*Ausländer*	foreigner
die	*Eingliederung*	integration
der	*Einwanderer*	immigrant
	ethnische Probleme (pl)	racial issues
	freuen (sich)	to please, to be pleased
die	*Gesellschaft*	society
die	*Gewalt*	violence
die	*Gewalttätigkeit*	violence, acts of violence
die	*Hautfarbe*	colour of skin
	multikulturell	multicultural
der	*Rassismus*	racism
	rassistisch	racist
der	*soziale Wohnungsbau*	social housing
die	*Staatsangehörigkeit*	nationality
die	*vorgefasste Meinung*	preconceived opinion
das	*Vorurteil*	prejudice

Armut ➡ *Seite 42–43*

	arm	poor
die	*Armut*	poverty
	aussetzen	to abandon
	bedürftig	in need
der/ die	*Bedürftige*	person in need
	deprimiert	depressed
	ehrenamtlich	voluntary, voluntarily
das	*Heim*	hostel
die	*Hilfe*	help, assistance
das	*Mindesthaltbarkeitsdatum*	best-before date
die	*Mülltonne*	dustbin
die	*Not*	need
	obdachlos	homeless
	reich	rich
	riechen	to smell
die	*Spende*	donation
	spenden	to donate
	stehlen	to steal
das	*Verbrechen*	crime
die	*Wohltätigkeit*	charity

1 Meine Familie: heute und in der Zukunft

You are talking to a German friend about your family and your future plans.

Your teacher will play the role of the friend. He or she could ask you the following:

1 who is in your family?
2 what are they like?
3 who do you get on with?
4 who don't you get on with?
5 what problems do you have at home?
6 what are your future family and relationship plans?
7 !

Remember you will have to respond to something that you have not yet prepared.

It is natural to want to give a lot of information as quickly as you can, particularly when you start and might be nervous, so don't rush. Try to keep a reasonable pace throughout the conversation. After you have been speaking for a while, you will feel more relaxed! Careful planning in advance, as suggested below, should help you a great deal.

AQA Examiner's tips

1 **Who is in your family?**
- Say who lives with you
- Give their names and ages
- Say what your parents' situation is
- Say how you feel about that

Now start your notes. Write five or six words for each of the seven sections:

1 *Familie, geben, sein, Eltern, geschieden*
2 ......

Include one or more verbs in each list of words. Check that it is in the infinitive form and that you know how to change it.

If you come from a very large household, you needn't give information on every family member.

AQA Examiner's tips

2 **What are they like?**
- Say what your parents or brothers/sisters are like
- Give examples of their behaviour.
- Mention something you did together recently
- Say what you thought about it. Give a reason.

Try to use fewer than six words in some sections of your plan, as you might need more in others.

Don't waste words in your plan by writing something which is easy to remember. Pick words to prompt your memory. Each one should trigger a sentence (or more).

Use the perfect tense to say what you did recently, e.g. *Letzten Freitag sind wir zusammen kegeln gegangen*.

G See page 182 ➡

AQA Examiner's tips

3 **Who do you get on with?**
- Say who you have a good relationship with
- Explain why
- Say something about his/her personality
- Say what you think of this relationship

Remember that *ein gutes Verhältnis zu* is followed by the dative case.

G See page 176 ➡

When giving a reason, use *weil* or *da*, but don't forget that they will make the verb go to the end of the sentence or clause.

G See page 186 ➡

Using the cue words only, practise saying aloud the information for each section before you move on to the next one. Next do this for two sections, then three and so on.

AQA Examiner's tips

4 Who don't you get on with?
- Say who you have a bad relationship with
- Explain why
- Say something about his/her personality
- Say what you think of this relationship

AQA Examiner's tips

This bullet point is similar to the one before, but avoid using the same language. For example, instead of using *Verhältnis* again, you could say *Mein ... und ich verstehen uns nicht*.

Look for opportunities to show you can use different tenses. Don't wait to be asked!

Although visuals are allowed, do not use symbols in your plan.

5 What problems do you have at home?
- Say how you find your home life generally
- Say what problems you have because of someone at home
- Mention a problem you had recently
- Say what you thought about that. Give a reason.

AQA Examiner's tips

You might be lucky enough not to have any problems, so just make up the answers!

When talking about problems, this is a good opportunity to use *ich muss* or *ich darf nicht*, but try to relate the problem to a person, e.g. *Meine Mutter sagt, ich muss ... .* For a recent problem, you might say *Mein Vater hat gesagt, ich musste ... .*, using the perfect and imperfect tenses.

Perfect tense: **G** See page 182 ➡

Imperfect tense of modals: **G** See page 183 ➡

6 What are your future family and relationship plans?
- Say whether you intend staying at home for a few years or getting your own place
- Say whether you want to get married or stay single
- Explain why
- Say whether you want children. Give a reason.

AQA Examiner's tips

This whole section refers to the future, so make sure you include some future indicators, e.g. *in drei Jahren* or use the future tense.

Present tense with future indicators:
G See page 184 ➡

Future tense: **G** See page 184 ➡

Never hesitate to extend any answer, e.g. on the first bullet point, you could add on staying at home because you want to save for a flat.

Make sure that you know in advance how to pronounce all the words you are going to use.

7 **!** At this point you will be asked a question which you don't know in advance. However, you can try to guess what it might be and prepare various options:
- Describe your relationship with your best friend
- Talk more about your extended family
- Say whether it is better to live together or get married
- Talk about someone else's problems at home

AQA Examiner's tips

For each possibility, make three different points, e.g. best friend: why, type of person, what you do together. Next choose what you think are the two most likely points to be asked. Then pick three words to write in your plan for each point.

Now you should have a complete set of 40 cue words, in seven groups with either five or six words in each.

You should now have completed your plan and prepared your answers. Give your plan to your teacher for feedback. Compare your answers to the online sample version – you might find some useful hints to make yours even better.

kerboodle!

1 Ich will gesund leben

You are entering a competition and have to write an article in German about what you do to stay healthy. You could include:

1 how healthy you are at the moment
2 your diet
3 whether you exercise at the moment
4 your view on smoking
5 your view on drinking alcohol/taking drugs
6 an example of someone with an unhealthy lifestyle
7 how you intend to stay healthy in future

1 How healthy you are at the moment
- Introduce yourself, giving your name, age and where you live
- Say whether you are fit/healthy
- Say what you look like and how you feel about that
- Say whether you are stressed and mention how much sleep you get

2 Your diet
- Say what you consider to be a healthy diet. Give a reason.
- Mention what types of food you like, e.g. fast food, vegetarian. Say why you like them and whether they are good for you.
- Describe what you eat on a typical day (breakfast, lunch, evening meal and snacks)
- Say whether your daily diet is healthy enough.

3 Whether you exercise at the moment
- Say what you do to keep fit
- Mention who you exercise with, where and how often
- Mention an activity you did recently
- Say what you think about exercise and its importance for a healthy lifestyle

AQA Examiner's tips

Start off by giving your name and age.
Use *ich heiße* for giving your name and use *heißt* when talking later about someone else.
Make sure all the verbs you are using with *ich* have the correct –e ending, except for *ich bin*.

AQA Examiner's tips

Now start your notes. Write five or six words.
1 *wohnen, gesund, groß, zu dick, Asthma*
2 …
Remember to include one verb in each list of words. Check that it is in the infinitive form and that you know how to change it.
Don't mention details about eating, exercise etc. at this stage. They are discussed in later sections.

AQA Examiner's tips

When giving a reason, use *weil* or *da*, but don't forget that they will make the verb go to the end of the clause or sentence.
G page 186 ➡
Vary your language by making sure that not every sentence starts with *ich*. Use inversion (putting the verb before the subject but keeping it the second idea), e.g. *Zum Frühstück esse ich Haferflocken.*
G page 186 ➡
Keep adding words to your plan, but try to pick ones which you think you might find difficult to remember.

AQA Examiner's tips

When referring to what you usually do, use the present tense, e.g. *Gewöhnlich spiele ich . . .*
G page 180 ➡
Use the perfect tense to refer to what you did recently, e.g. *Letzte Woche habe ich . . . gespielt.*
G page 182 ➡
To say what you think, you could use *ich finde . . .*
Try to use fewer than six words in some sections of your plan, as your limit is 40 and you might need more in others.

4 Your view on smoking
- Say whether you have tried smoking
- If you do smoke, say how long you have done it for and how much and how often you smoke
- Mention some of the disadvantages of smoking, including health ones
- Give your overall opinion of smoking

To say how long you have done something for, use *seit* with the present tense.

G page 185 ➡

As well as giving your own opinion, you could mention what your parents and friends think of smoking.

You could use the modal verb *können* to list the things caused by smoking: *es kann … verursachen*. Take care with your word order.

G page 181 ➡

To say what 'you' or 'people' should do, use *man*: *man sollte nicht rauchen* etc.

G page 179 ➡

5 Your view on drinking alcohol/taking drugs
- Say whether you have tried alcohol
- Say what you think of alcohol and the consequences of drinking
- Say whether you have tried drugs
- Say what you think of them and their effects

If you have not tried alcohol, you could say whether you intend to try it in the future.

G page 184 ➡

To give an opinion, you could start a sentence with *Meiner Meinung nach*, but don't forget the inversion afterwards.

To discuss consequences, you could use *wenn … dann*, e.g. *Wenn man Drogen nimmt, dann wird man . . .*

G page 190 ➡

6 An example of someone with an unhealthy lifestyle
- Give the name and age of a friend or relative (real or imaginary)
- Explain why he or she is unhealthy
- Mention something unhealthy which he or she did recently
- Say what you think about his or her lifestyle

As you are writing about someone else here, be careful that you use the correct verb endings.

G page 180 ➡

You could also describe the lifestyle of someone who is much healthier than you.

You can use *zum Glück* ('fortunately') and *leider* ('unfortunately') to make your opinions sound more interesting.

7 How you intend to stay healthy in future
- Say what you plan to do about your diet
- Say how you will go about getting enough exercise and sleep
- Mention one thing which you shouldn't do
- Give reasons why you should start or continue to live healthily

Although you are referring to the future, you don't necessarily need the future tense. Just use the present tense with a future indicator e.g. *Morgen gehe ich joggen …*

G page 184 ➡

You could use the phrase *um gesund zu bleiben …* but remember the inversion afterwards.

G page 185 ➡

Now you should have a complete set of 40 cue words, in seven groups of either five or six words.

When you have written your article, compare it and your cue card with the online sample version – you might find some useful hints to make yours even better.

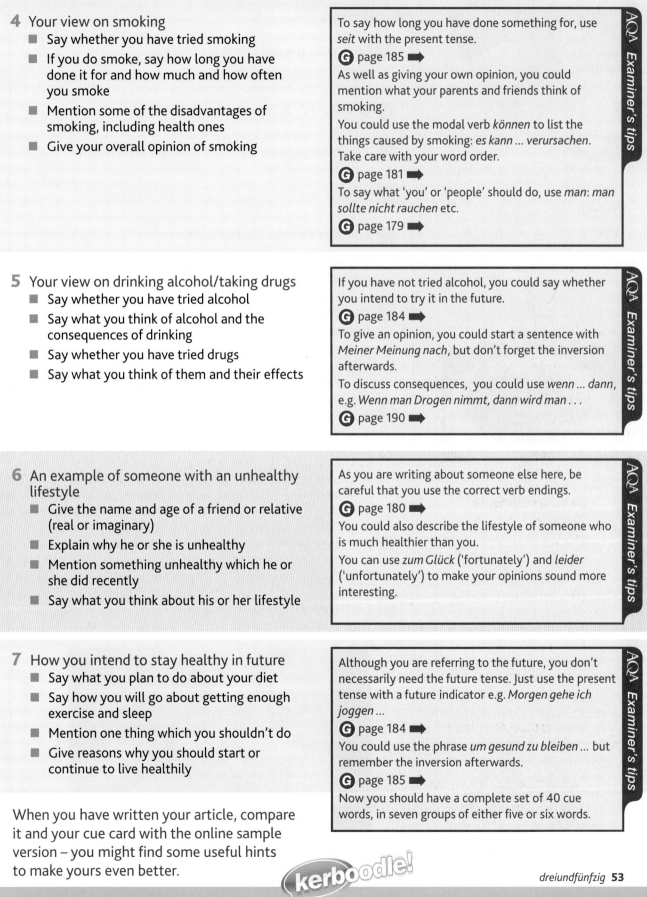

kerboodle!

Context summary

1

Teste dich!

1 Complete the following sentence:

Jeden Tag soll man fünf Stück Obst und _____ essen.

2 What is the 'er' form of *laufen*?

3 Give the German for three examples of *Fleisch*.

4 What is another way of saying *Ich will relaxen*?

5 Complete the following statement:

Um gesund zu bleiben, soll man _____ pro Nacht schlafen.

6 Complete the following statement with the correct form of *dürfen*:

Meine Schwester ist 12 Jahre alt und sie _____ nicht zu spät ausbleiben.

7 What is a synonym (another word) for the verb *reden*?

8 Complete the following statement with a suitable conjunction:

Es ist nötig, _____ Frauen und Männer den gleichen Lohn bekommen.

9 Translate the following statement into English:

Er arbeitet ehrenamtlich.

10 Translate the following statement into German:

I can't stand my brother as he is too loud.

Wussten Sie schon ???

- Laut einer internationalen Studie hat Großbritannien die zweifelhafte Ehre, das dickste Land in der EU zu sein. 56,4% der Frauen und 65,1% der Männer in England sind übergewichtig. Deutschland liegt aber nicht weit hinten – 51,4% der Frauen und 67,7% der Männer in diesem Land sind zu dick. (Quelle: IASO)

- Trotz der wachsenden Bedeutung alternativer Familienformen machen Ehepaare mit Kindern immer noch knapp drei Viertel (73,9 Prozent) der Familien in Deutschland aus. Ihr Anteil an allen Familien variiert aber in den Ländern von 53,0 Prozent in Berlin bis 80,1 Prozent in Baden-Württemberg. (Quelle: bpb)

kerboodle!

2 Leisure

Free time and the media

▢ Sports and leisure, clothes

Erik: Ich spiele gern Fußball. Ich spiele jedes Wochenende. Ich spiele nicht gern Basketball. Ich finde es schrecklich.

Jana: Ich gehe gern schwimmen. Kraulen mag ich am liebsten.

Frauke: Mein Bruder spielt Gitarre, aber ich bin nicht musikalisch. Ich gehe oft einkaufen.

Tobias: Ich faulenze jeden Abend und sehe meistens fern. Ich treibe nicht gern Sport.

Lisa: Ich sehe selten fern. Das finde ich langweilig. Ich gehe aber oft ins Kino, weil ich das besser finde. Am liebsten lese ich. Ich lese drei bis vier Bücher pro Monat.

1a 📖🎧 Read the texts above and note down in English what each person likes doing, adding any extra details.

Beispiel: Erik – football, …

1b ✏️ Write down answers to the following questions, using the texts above to help you.

- Was machst du gern in deiner Freizeit?
- Wie oft machst du das?
- Was machst du nicht gern?
- Warum nicht?

2a 📖🎧 Match the statements below to the items of clothing.

Beispiel: a 7

- a   Ich trage einen Rock.
- b   Ich trage eine Jacke.
- c   Ich trage ein Hemd.
- d   Ich trage Schuhe.
- e   Ich trage eine Hose.
- f   Ich trage ein Kleid.
- g   Ich trage einen Hut.
- h   Ich trage Socken.

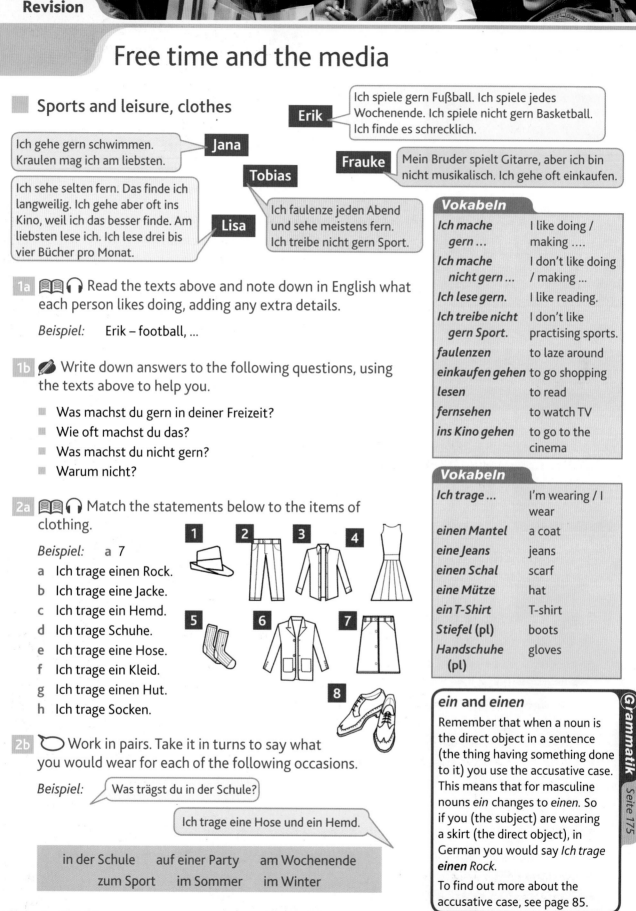

2b 🗨️ Work in pairs. Take it in turns to say what you would wear for each of the following occasions.

Beispiel: Was trägst du in der Schule?

Ich trage eine Hose und ein Hemd.

| in der Schule | auf einer Party | am Wochenende |
| zum Sport | im Sommer | im Winter |

Vokabeln

Ich mache gern …	I like doing / making ….
Ich mache nicht gern …	I don't like doing / making …
Ich lese gern.	I like reading.
Ich treibe nicht gern Sport.	I don't like practising sports.
faulenzen	to laze around
einkaufen gehen	to go shopping
lesen	to read
fernsehen	to watch TV
ins Kino gehen	to go to the cinema

Vokabeln

Ich trage …	I'm wearing / I wear
einen Mantel	a coat
eine Jeans	jeans
einen Schal	scarf
eine Mütze	hat
ein T-Shirt	T-shirt
Stiefel (pl)	boots
Handschuhe (pl)	gloves

ein and *einen*

Remember that when a noun is the direct object in a sentence (the thing having something done to it) you use the accusative case. This means that for masculine nouns *ein* changes to *einen*. So if you (the subject) are wearing a skirt (the direct object), in German you would say *Ich trage einen Rock*.

To find out more about the accusative case, see page 85.

Grammatik   Seite 175

Transport, places in town

Ich wohne in München. Das ist im Südosten von Deutschland. Im Zentrum gibt es viele Kaufhäuser und Geschäfte. Man kann dort vor allem Klamotten kaufen. Es gibt hier auch Kinos und Cafés. Im Norden von München gibt es ein berühmtes Stadion – das Olympiazentrum. Dort gibt es auch die neue Allianz-Arena, wo man Fußballspiele sehen kann. Im Süden gibt es die Bavaria Filmstudios. Dort kann man sehen, wie man Filme macht. In nur einer Stunde ist man im Osten in den Alpen. Im Winter kann man da Ski fahren.

Jochen

das Stadtzentrum Münchens

Grammatik — Seite 175

es gibt ...

To say what there is in a place use *es gibt*:

Es gibt einen Bahnhof / ein Postamt / ein Museum.

To say what there isn't, you still use *es gibt*, but instead of *ein*, use *kein*:

Es gibt keinen Bahnhof / kein Postamt / kein Museum.

Remember that whatever comes after *es gibt* will be in the accusative case.

1a 📖 🎧 Read the text about Jochen's home town. Read the following statements and for each, write T (true), F (false) or ? (Not in the Text).

Beispiel: a T

a Joachim lives in the southeast of Germany.
b You can shop for clothes in the centre of Munich.
c In the north of Munich is the Olympic stadium.
d The film studios are in west Munich.
e It only takes an hour to get to the mountains.
f In winter you can go skating in the Alps.

1b ✏️ Using Jochen's text as a model, write about what there is and isn't in your area.

2a 📖 🎧 Read the statements below. For each find a matching picture. Note down any additional details in English.

Beispiel: a 2 – normally goes by bike to school

a Ich fahre normalerweise mit dem Rad zur Schule.
b Ich fliege jedes Jahr mit dem Flugzeug nach Spanien.
c Ich fahre meistens mit der U-Bahn in die Stadt.
d Ich gehe zu Fuß zu meiner Freundin.
e Ich fahre am Wochenende mit dem Auto zu meinen Großeltern.

2b 💬 Work in pairs. One person asks the following questions and the other answers. Then swap roles.

- Wie fährst du zur Schule?
- Wie fährst du zu deinen Freunden?
- Wie fährst du zum Einkaufen?
- Wie fährst du in die Stadt?

Vokabeln

im Norden	in the north
im Süden	in the south
im Westen	in the west
im Osten	in the east
der Bahnhof (-höfe)	train station
der Berg (-e)	mountain
der See (-n)	lake
das Kaufhaus (häuser)	department store
das Geschäft (-e)	shop
das Kino (-s)	cinema
das Stadion (-s)	stadium
das Museum (Museen)	museums

Vokabeln

Ich fahre mit ...	I travel by ...
...dem Rad / Bus / Schiff / Zug.	... bike / bus / ship / train.
...der U-Bahn / Straßenbahn.	...underground / tram.
Ich fliege mit dem Flugzeug	I fly by plane.
Ich gehe zu Fuß.	I go on foot.

kerboodle!

Was hast du gestern gemacht?

Startseite | Index | Hilfe | Kontakt | Textversion

Jetzt chatten!

Karim:
Hi. Alles klar? Ich habe gestern den neuen Indiana Jones Film gesehen. Ich habe ihn echt gut gefunden. Was hast du gestern gemacht?

Hannah:
Ich habe nichts gemacht. Ich habe kein Geld gehabt, weil ich letzte Woche alles ausgegeben habe. Ich habe zu viel eingekauft – Klamotten, Make-up und noch anderes Zeug. Es gab eine Menge Sonderangebote und dann haben Tamara und ich noch in einer Pizzeria gegessen. Jetzt bin ich pleite.

Karim:
Mann, das ist schade. Ich wollte fragen, ob du heute Abend in die Disko gehen möchtest. Wir haben schon lange nichts mehr zusammen gemacht.

Hannah:
Zu teuer. Ich habe wirklich kein Geld mehr. Ich habe mich letztes Wochenende mit Frederick getroffen und wir haben ein paar Spiele für meine Playstation gekauft. Das hat auch viel gekostet. Aber möchtest du zu mir kommen? Wir können die neuen Spiele ausprobieren.

Karim:
Prima Idee. Bis später.

Homepage
Kontakt
Sitemap
Neues
Forum
Shop

---

1 📖 🎧 Copy the sentences and fill in the gaps with one of the words on the right.

Beispiel: **a** Kino

a Karim war gestern im _____ .
b Der Indiana Jones Film hat ihm gut _____ .
c Hannah hat kein _____ mehr.
d Karim möchte heute Abend in die _____ gehen.
e Letztes Wochenende hat sich Hannah mit einem anderen _____ getroffen.
f Die Computerspiele, die Hannah gekauft hat, waren sehr _____ .
g Hannah möchte, dass Karim zu ihr nach _____ kommt.
h Karim findet, dass Hannahs Plan für heute Abend eine gute _____ ist.

Hause	gefallen
Disko	Freund
Idee	Geld
Kino	teuer

---

2 🎧 What did these people do last week? Did they enjoy it or not?

	🙂 ?	🙁 ?
Anna		saw film
Stefan		
Michaela		
Nuri		
Maik		

Tipp

🎧 Listen out for the verbs to work out what each person has done. You might not have encountered the past participles before, but don't worry – you can often work them out from the stem:

ge**spiel**t
ge**mach**t
an**gesehen** etc.

3 **G** Copy the sentences and fill in the gaps with the correct form of *haben*.

Beispiel: **a** habe

a Ich _____ am Wochenende meine Hausaufgaben nicht gemacht.

b Wir _____ uns letzten Montag in der Stadt getroffen.

c Paul und Bernhard _____ im neuen Einkaufszentrum eingekauft.

d _____ du schon das Buch ‚Tintentod' gelesen?

e Er hatte so viel Durst, dass er das ganze Glas auf einmal ausgetrunken _____ .

f Guten Tag, Frau Schubert _____ Sie schon gehört? Diebe _____ gestern bei mir eingebrochen.

4 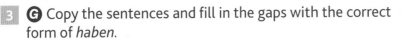 Practise dialogues about what you did and give opinions.

| Was hast du | gestern | gemacht / getrunken / |
| letztes Wochenende | gegessen … ? |
| letzten Monat |
| gestern Abend … |

Ich habe … gemacht / getrunken / gegessen.

Wie hast du das gefunden?

| Ich habe das | gut | gefunden. |
| interessant |
| spannend |
| langeweilig |
| nutzlos… |

Using the perfect tense with *haben*

The perfect tense is used to talk about the past. It is made up of two parts – an auxiliary verb (*haben*) and a past participle:

ich habe	gemacht
du hast	
er/sie/es hat	gespielt
wir haben	
ihr habt	getroffen
sie haben (plural)	
Sie haben (formal)	

Also learn how to use separable verbs with the perfect tense.

See page 70 ➡️

Grammatik *Seite 182*

Reusing questions when giving answers

When giving an answer work out how you can reuse the question you were asked.

*Was hast du **letztes Wochenende gegessen?***

*Ich habe **letztes Wochenende** Pizza und Pommes **gegessen**.*

You can also reuse the question and then extend your answer.

*Was hast du **letztes Wochenende gemacht?***

*Ich habe **letztes Wochenende** viel **gemacht**. Ich habe zum Beispiel einen Freund getroffen.*

Strategie

---

5 You are describing last weekend to friends. Write down what you did following the prompts:

- what you did last weekend
- who else took part in the activity
- how you found the weekend

Now describe what someone else did.

Ich habe	letztes Wochenende	Sport …	gemacht.
	dann	Musik …	gespielt.
	später	einen Film …	gesehen.
	danach	Freunde …	getroffen.
		Pizza …	gegessen.
			eingekauft. ferngesehen.
	das	mit meinen Freunden mit meiner Familie allein	gemacht.
Ich habe	das Wochenende	gut / schlecht / interessant …	gefunden.

Ich bin in die Stadt gegangen

Ich bin in die Stadt gefahren

Kornelia

Ich bin in die Stadt gefahren. Ich wohne außerhalb des Zentrums und bin deshalb mit dem Zug gefahren. In der Stadt bin ich einkaufen gegangen. Ich bin mit dem Zug um 17 Uhr wieder nach Hause gefahren.

Natascha

Am Wochenende bin ich zu Hause geblieben, weil am Freitag Feiertag war und ich am Donnerstagabend mit Freunden in die Disko gegangen bin. Wir sind nach der Disko mit dem Taxi nach Hause gefahren. Ich hatte deshalb am Wochenende kein Geld.

Ich bin Mitglied im Schwimmverein. Ich gehe also sehr oft schwimmen. Ich bin schon um halb sechs aufgestanden und mit Freunden zu einem Wettkampf gefahren, wo wir geschwommen sind. Ich habe schon an vielen Wettkämpfen teilgenommen und oft gewonnen. Ich hoffe bei den Olympischen Spielen in London 2012 zu schwimmen.

Erika

Ich mache gern Sport im Freien. Vorgestern bin ich in den Skatepark gegangen und bin mit ein paar Freunden Skateboard gefahren. Ich bin zum ersten Mal in einer Halfpipe gefahren und über Hindernisse gesprungen und bin ein paar Mal vom Skateboard gefallen. Und dann ist es passiert – ich habe mein Bein gebrochen.

Andreas

Kai

Ich bin am Wochenende mit meinen Freunden in die Stadt gegangen. Wir haben uns den neuen James-Bond-Film angesehen. Nach dem Film sind ein paar meiner Freunde nach Hause gegangen und mit den anderen bin ich noch ein bisschen in der Stadt herumgelaufen.

1 📖🎧 Read what the teenagers say about their weekends then answer the following questions:

Beispiel: **a** Natascha

a Wer ist am Wochenende nicht ausgegangen?
b Wer macht gern draußen Sport?
c Wer wohnt nicht in der Stadtmitte?
d Wer ist sehr früh aufgestanden?
e Wer ist ins Kino gegangen?
f Wer ist um 5 Uhr Nachmittag wieder zurückgefahren?
g Wer ist oft Sieger bei Sportwettkämpfen gewesen?
h Wer ist während der Woche beim Tanzen gewesen?
i Wer hat einen Unfall gehabt?

2 **G** Copy and complete each sentence, using the correct form of *sein*. If you need extra help, look for the different examples of *sein* elsewhere on the page.

Beispiel: **a** bin

a Ich _____ am Wochenende ins Kino gegangen.
b Am Samstag _____ wir in die Stadt gefahren.
c Peter und Angelika _____ jeden Tag im Hallenbad geschwommen.

Grammatik Seite 182

Using the perfect tense with *sein*

Certain verbs, mainly verbs of motion, form their perfect tense using *sein* rather than *haben* as the auxiliary verb. Common examples of these include:

	past participle
gehen	*gegangen*
fahren	*gefahren*
kommen	*gekommen*
laufen	*gelaufen*
schwimmen	*geschwommen*
fliegen	*geflogen*

Ich bin ins Kino gegangen.
'I went to the cinema.'

Wir sind nach Österreich geflogen.
'We flew to Austria.'

All of these verbs have irregular past participles. Learn more about these. See page 70 ▶

d Katja _____ erst um Mitternacht nach Hause gekommen.

e Frau Schiller, ich höre Sie _____ vom Rad gefallen. Das tut mir sehr Leid.

f Armin, _____ du nach Spanien geflogen oder mit dem Auto gefahren?

The past participle is often formed by adding *ge-* at the beginning and *-en* or *-t* at the end. A lot of verbs, however, are irregular and change more than that. Look out for examples of these in the text on the previous page and make sure you learn them.

Tipp

3 🎧 Listen to the following interviews and write down the correct letters for Fabian, Max, Charlotte and Denise. You need to listen for where they went, when, with whom and, for three of them, how they got there.

Beispiel: Fabian c, d …

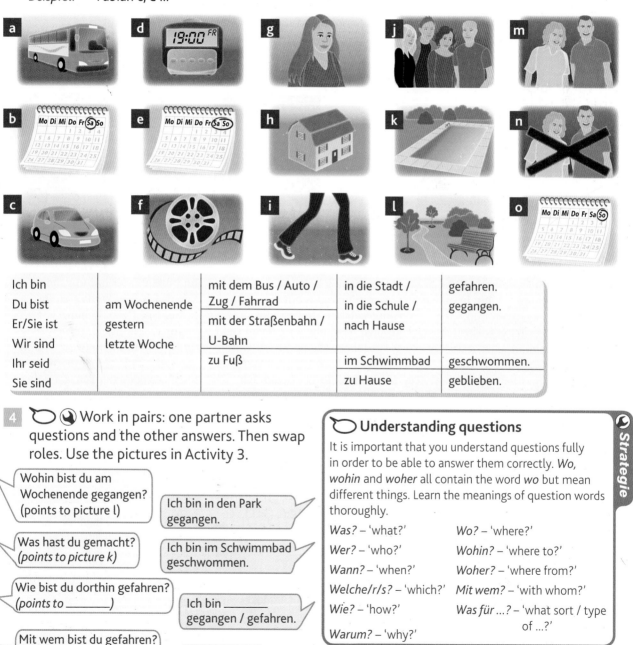

Ich bin		mit dem Bus / Auto / Zug / Fahrrad	in die Stadt /	gefahren.
Du bist	am Wochenende		in die Schule /	gegangen.
Er/Sie ist	gestern	mit der Straßenbahn / U-Bahn	nach Hause	
Wir sind	letzte Woche			
Ihr seid		zu Fuß	im Schwimmbad	geschwommen.
Sie sind			zu Hause	geblieben.

4 🗨️ 🌐 Work in pairs: one partner asks questions and the other answers. Then swap roles. Use the pictures in Activity 3.

> Wohin bist du am Wochenende gegangen? (points to picture l)

> Ich bin in den Park gegangen.

> Was hast du gemacht? *(points to picture k)*

> Ich bin im Schwimmbad geschwommen.

> Wie bist du dorthin gefahren? *(points to _____)*

> Ich bin _____ gegangen / gefahren.

> Mit wem bist du gefahren? *(points to _____)*

> Ich _____

🗨️ **Understanding questions**

It is important that you understand questions fully in order to be able to answer them correctly. *Wo, wohin* and *woher* all contain the word *wo* but mean different things. Learn the meanings of question words thoroughly.

Was? – 'what?'   *Wo?* – 'where?'

Wer? – 'who?'   *Wohin?* – 'where to?'

Wann? – 'when?'   *Woher?* – 'where from?'

Welche/r/s? – 'which?'   *Mit wem?* – 'with whom?'

Wie? – 'how?'   *Was für …?* – 'what sort / type of …?'

Warum? – 'why?'

Strategie

Wir bekommen nicht genug Taschengeld!

1 **V** Identify the items below. Match them up with the correct shop.

1 **2** **3** **4** **5** **6**

a Obst- und Gemüseladen	c Schreibwarengeschäft	e Metzgerei
b Juweliergeschäft	d Elektrogeschäft	f Konditorei

Mein Geld

Ich bekomme € 10 pro Woche von meinen Eltern. Ich finde, das ist genug. Ich habe mein Geld ein paar Monate gespart und dann habe ich letzte Woche einen MP3-Spieler gekauft. Ich bin in einige Geschäfte gegangen und habe auch im Internet gesucht. Ich habe ein Schnäppchen gemacht, weil ich einen billigen MP3-Spieler im Kaufhaus gefunden und gekauft habe. Er war im Sonderangebot. Ich habe dann auch sofort im Internet Musik heruntergeladen, aber das hat relativ viel gekostet.

Nina

Ich bekomme € 20 im Monat. Ich finde, das ist nicht genug. Meine Eltern sagen, ich muss mein Geld sparen. Letzten Monat habe ich ziemlich viel Klingeltöne auf mein Handy runtergeladen und zu viel gesimst. Da habe ich zu viel Geld ausgegeben. Meine Eltern waren ziemlich wütend. Jetzt bekomme ich weniger Taschengeld. Ich finde das recht unfair, aber ich habe jetzt gelernt, dass ich mit meinem Geld vorsichtiger umgehen muss.

Saed

Meine Eltern sind geschieden. Meine Mutter gibt mir € 20 pro Monat und mein Vater auch. Das reicht mir, weil ich nicht viel kaufen muss. Meine Mutter hat mir letzte Woche zum Beispiel eine neue Hose gekauft und mein Vater hat mir meine Schulsachen gekauft – Hefte, Stifte usw. Deshalb hatte ich genug Taschengeld, um DVDs und ein neues Handy zu kaufen. So etwas kaufen meine Eltern nicht, weil sie denken, dass das nicht wichtig ist. Ich habe auch schon etwas für meine Ferien gespart, weil ich nächstes Jahr reisen möchte.

Christian

2a 📖 🎧 Read the paragraphs above and decide whether the statements are True (T), False (F) or not in the text (NT).

Beispiel: a T

a Saed has sent too many text messages.
b Nina's MP3 player was expensive.
c Christian's mother bought him a pair of new trousers last week.
d Saed has a new mobile phone.
e Nina bought a new MP3 player on the Internet.
f Christian would like to travel next year.

2b 📖 🎧 Now do the same with the sentences in German.

   a Nina meint, dass ihr Taschengeld reicht.
   b Saeds Eltern waren sauer auf ihn.
   c Christian kauft sich selbst Hosen und Schulsachen.
   d Christian fährt nächstes Jahr nach Spanien.

3 🎧 Listen to the interviews and complete the table.

Name	Pocket money received	Spent on...? Saved?	Enough?	Extra details
Ahmet	10 Euros per week	trainers	No	

4a Ⓖ 🌐 Copy out the sentences and choose the correct auxiliary verb to go in the gaps.

   Beispiel: **a** bin

   a Ich (habe / bin) mit meinen Freunden in die Stadt gefahren.
   b In der Stadt (haben / sind) wir ins Kino gegangen.
   c Im Kino (haben / sind) wir einen Film gesehen.
   d Mein Bruder (hat / ist) zu Hause geblieben.
   e Meine Eltern (haben / sind) ihm kein Taschengeld gegeben.

4b Ⓖ 🌐 Now add the correct form of *haben* or *sein*.

   a Mein Bruder _____ aber trotzdem in die Stadt gegangen.
   b In der Stadt _____ er noch mehr Geld für Computerspiele ausgegeben.
   c Ich _____ am Wochenende Karten für ein Fußballspiel gekauft.

5 🗨️ ✏️ Carry out a pocket money survey in class. Ask the questions below and use the box to help you with your answers. Then write up the results of your survey, using the worksheet to help you (you will need to use verbs in the third person!).

Ⓖ **Grammatik** · *Seite 182*

Using the perfect tense with *haben* or *sein*

Remember that some past participles take *haben* as the auxiliary in the perfect tense and some take *sein*. Normally verbs of motion or change of state take the auxiliary verb *sein*.

Make sure you know which past participles take which and learn the different forms of *haben* and *sein*. Use pages 192–195 to check which verbs take *haben* and which verbs take *sein*.

Also learn to recognise the imperfect tenses of *haben* and *sein*. See page 71 ➡️

🌐 **Strategie**

Ⓖ Checking auxiliary verbs

As well as using the right auxiliary verb (*haben* or *sein*), you need to make sure that the form of the auxiliary verb agrees with the person you are talking about (*ich habe, er/sie hat* etc.). Always check your written work after you have completed it, to ensure that you have followed this rule.

Tipp

It's good to gain confidence in switching between tenses. In Activity 5 you will use the present and perfect tenses.

Taschengeldumfrage:
• Wieviel Taschengeld bekommst du?
• Was machst du mit deinem Taschengeld?
• Was hast du kürzlich mit deinem Taschengeld gemacht/gekauft?
• Wofür sparst du?

Ich bekomme	... Euro / Pfund / kein Taschengeld	pro Woche / Monat.
Ich kaufe	Makeup / Zeitschriften / CDs / DVDs / Guthaben fürs Handy / Schmuck / Kleidung / Klamotten	.
Ich gebe mein Geld für		aus.
Ich habe		gekauft.
Ich habe mein Geld für		ausgegeben.
Ich spare auf	die Ferien / ein Geschenk für ... / einen MP3-Spieler / ein Handy.	

Wir waren im Einkaufszentrum

Ich kaufe Klamotten

Katharina, 16

Ich war im KaDeWe. Das ist ein großes Kaufhaus in Berlin. Gestern war mein Geburtstag und ich hatte etwas Geld. Ich habe eine neue Jeans und ein grünes Top dazu gekauft. Ich bin ganz zufrieden, obwohl es keine Jacke gab, die mir passte. Ich muss morgen noch einmal schauen.

Selima, 17

Ich hatte kein Glück. Ich war in einer Boutique. Ich habe nichts gefunden, was mir gefallen hat. Es war Sommerschlussverkauf, aber die Qualität der Klamotten war echt schlecht. Ich wollte einen Rock kaufen, aber die waren wirklich alle ätzend.

Lars, 16

Ich war mit ein paar Freunden in der Stadt unterwegs. Wir waren in ein paar Sportgeschäften. Ich wollte eigentlich nichts kaufen, aber ich schaute mich ein bisschen um und habe diese tollen Turnschuhe gesehen. OK, sie waren ein bisschen teuer, aber ich kaufte sie dann doch, nur darf ich das nicht meinen Eltern sagen.

Uli, 16

Ich stehe auf Markenwaren und gehe normalerweise in Designerläden. Da weiß ich, dass die Qualität gut ist. Meine letzte Hose war aus dem Billigladen. Einmal und nie wieder. Die war sofort kaputt und passte nach dem ersten Waschen nicht mehr. Ich muss sie jetzt umtauschen.

Frau Peters, 56

Ich kaufe jetzt nicht mehr so viel Kleidung, aber als ich jünger war, kaufte ich sehr viel. Ich investierte mein ganzes Geld in Hüte, Kleider und Schuhe. Ich kann mir das jetzt nicht mehr leisten. Ich bestelle jetzt meistens aus dem Katalog.

---

1 📖🎧 Put the correct name in each of the gaps.

a _____ war eigentlich nur zum Herumschauen in der Stadt.

b _____ war gar nicht zufrieden beim Einkaufen und fand alles furchtbar.

c _____ findet, dass Designer-Kleidung besser ist.

d _____ kauft jetzt weniger als früher.

e _____ kaufte etwas, obwohl es nicht billig war.

f _____ hat zwei Kleidungsstücke gekauft.

2 **G** Fill in the gaps with the correct form of the imperfect.

Beispiel: **a** war

a Ich _____ ('was') gestern mit Freunden in der Stadt.

b Das Geschäft _____ ('had') leider keine blauen Hosen.

c Meine Freunde _____ ('bought') alle eine Kappe.

d Wir _____ ('were') acht Stunden in der Stadt.

e Peter _____ ('had') kein Geld.

f Du _____ ('said'), dass du diesen Rock magst?

3 🎧 Listen to the recordings. Note down where each person went, what they bought and whether there were any problems. Include any extra details you pick up.

Beispiel: **a** department store, yellow jacket …

4 ✏️ 🌐 Write an email to a friend about a shopping trip. Mention:

- ◾ where you went and what you bought
- ◾ what the item looked like
- ◾ whether the item was expensive or cheap
- ◾ any problems with the item

If you're able to work on a computer, find pictures of the items you bought to send as attachments. Refer to page 194 to find the correct German characters on your keyboard.

Using the imperfect tense

(Grammatik — Seite 180)

The imperfect tense is another way of talking about the past. It is often used in written texts such as newspapers and sometimes in spoken language. To form the imperfect tense for regular verbs, take the infinitive of the verb, remove the *-en* and add the following endings to the stem:

ich kaufte

du kauftest

er/sie/es kaufte

wir kauften

ihr kauftet

sie kauften

Sie kauften

The most common irregular forms of the imperfect tense are *sein*, *haben* and *geben*.

haben – to have		**sein** – to be	**geben** –to give (*es gibt* – 'there is')
ich	hatte	war	gab
du	hattest	warst	gabst
er/sie/es	hatte	war	gab
wir	hatten	waren	gaben
ihr	hattet	wart	gabt
sie	hatten	waren	gaben
Sie	hatten	waren	gaben

Also revise modal verbs in the present tense.

See page 71 ➡️

✏️ 💬 **Paraphrasing**

(Strategie)

If you don't remember a particular phrase or word you can use alternatives. For example, if you can't remember *es passte mir nicht*, you can say *es war zu groß / klein / eng / weit* etc.

Ich war Wir waren	gestern / letzten Samstag / am Wochenende	in der Stadt / im Einkaufszentrum.
Ich kaufte Wir kauften	einen Pulli / eine Jacke / ein T-Shirt / CDs.	
Er / Sie / Es	war	neu / blau / billig.
		zu teuer / zu klein / zu altmodisch.
Er / Sie / Es	kostete / kosteten	… Euro / Pfund.

(Tipp)

In order to say 'there was' or 'were', use the expression *Es gab*.

Es gab wenig Auswahl. – 'There was little to choose from.'

Ich lebe im Internet

Surfen, chatten und SMSen

Ich simse gern
Es is praktisch,
schnell und billig.

Benny

BACK   REPLY

Name: Antonia

Alter: 16

Hi Leute, ich weiss nicht, wann ich abhängig geworden bin, aber ich bin total süchtig nach dem Internet. Gestern war ich nach der Schule 9 Stunden im Internet zum Chatten. Heute chatte ich schon seit 8 Uhr morgens im Internet und es ist jetzt schon 4 Uhr nachmittags. Wer kann mir helfen? Antonia X

Von: Martina@gcsegerman.de

An: EmailfreundeInternational

Hallo, ich heiße Martina. Ich finde das Internet und E-Mail super. Ich habe viele E-Mail-Freunde in anderen Ländern und auf verschiedenen Kontinenten, zum Beispiel Afrika und Südamerika. Ich kann schnell etwas recherchieren und wenn man zum Beispiel Freunde in anderen Ländern hat, kann man kostenlos Bilder schicken. Ich habe zum Beispiel gestern meine Ferienbilder gemailt. Ich suche jetzt einen Freund oder eine Freundin in Griechenland.

Thema: Wie findest du soziale Netzwerke?

Ich hatte eine Seite bei Nettheadz. Als ich sie zum ersten Mal ausprobierte, fand ich soziale Netzwerke positiv und glaubte, dass man dort viele Freunde findet. Dann haben meine „Freunde" begonnen, über mich negativ zu chatten. Sie haben mich total gemobbt. Später dann auch mit dem Handy. Ich weiß nicht warum, aber jetzt finde ich die neue Technologie ziemlich gefährlich.

Simon

Ich habe schon lange keine CDs mehr gekauft. Als ich noch CDs kaufte, fand ich sie immer sehr teuer. Ich lade jetzt immer Musik runter. Das kostet weniger und ich kann sie auf CD brennen, wenn ich will, oder mit meinem i-Pod synchronisieren. **Karina**

---

1 📖🎧 Read the texts above. Copy and complete each sentence, using the words below.

Beispiel: a Benny findet simsen nicht teuer.

a Benny findet simsen nicht _____.

b Antonia chattet jeden Tag viele _____.

c Antonia sucht _____.

d Martina findet, dass man schnell Informationen _____ kann.

e Martina hat gestern _____ geschickt.

f Simon _____, dass Chatten auf sozialen Netzwerken gut war.

g Simons „Freunde" _____ später sehr unsympathisch.

h Karina _____ schon lange keine CDs mehr gekauft.

teuer	Stunden	Hilfe	finden	schickt	hattest
	Fotos	glaubte	waren	war	hat

2 **G** Re-read the texts on page 66 and for each person, identify and note down the verbs and tenses he or she uses.

Beispiel:

	Present	Imperfect	Perfect	Infinitive
Benny	simse, ist			

3 🎧 Listen to the conversation between Norbert and his grandmother. Choose the correct answers from the options below:

Beispiel: **a** 2

a Norbert ist jetzt schon
   1 3   **2** 4   **3** 5 Stunden im Internet.

b Norberts Großmutter hatte als Kind
   1 kein Telefon   **2** ein Telefon
   3 ein Telefon vor dem Haus.

c Sie findet, Norbert sollte
   1 seine Freunde treffen   **2** seine Freunde anrufen
   3 seinen Freunden eine E-mail schreiben.

d Sie meint es kostet
   1 nicht viel   **2** ein bisschen zu viel   **3** viel zu viel.

e Norbert
   1 hat seine Hausaufgaben noch nicht gemacht   **2** hat seine Hausaufgaben schon gemacht
   3 möchte seine Hausaufgaben später machen.

f Er übt
   1 Tippen   **2** Mathe   **3** Fremdsprachen.

g Norbert sagt
   1 seine Oma soll etwas über das Internet lernen
   2 seine Oma ist altmodisch
   3 seine Oma soll ihn in Ruhe lassen.

4 ✏️ 💬 🔊 Make a presentation on the advantages or disadvantages of modern technology. Choose one particular item (mobile phone, MP3 player etc). Make notes then present your arguments to the class or a partner.

Ich finde	das Internet / E-Mails / soziale Netzwerke / MP3-Spieler / chatten / simsen	lehrreich / praktisch / langweilig / doof / nützlich / teuer / gefährlich.
Meiner Meinung nach ist / sind		
Das Internet / Chatten	macht	süchtig / abhängig / Spaß.
E-Mails / soziale Netzwerke	machen	
Ich mache mir Sorgen, dass … Ich bin sicher, dass …		

Grammatik **Seite 180**

Using different tenses (past and present)

Whenever you can, try to use different tenses. When talking about something in the past you can use the perfect tense or the imperfect tense. In spoken German the perfect tense is used more widely, while the imperfect tense is used very often in written texts. To revise forming these tenses see the following:

present tense   page 18

perfect tenses   pages 59, 60, 63

imperfect tense   page 65

Also learn how to distinguish between *als* and *wenn*.   *See page 71* ➡️

Tipp

When preparing to answer multiple-choice questions in a listening activity, read through all the options first. Some of them may be quite similar so you'll need to know what to listen out for!

Strategie

✏️ 💬 Using notes when making a presentation

If you don't want to just read from a sheet:

■ Plan out what you are going to say and in what order.

■ Decide on and practise the structures you are going to use.

■ Note down key words and give yourself visual clues.

■ Don't worry if you get stuck – if you have the main vocab, you can always use simpler structures to get your point across.

Free time and the media

Tokio Hotel

„Tokio Hotel" – Das ist eine Band aus Deutschland und ein Phänomen. Wenn sie auftritt, werden die Fans ganz verrückt und schreien. Sie sind anders. Ihr Sound authentisch und sehr eindrucksvoll. Und sie sehen exotisch aus.

Aber wer sind „Tokio Hotel"?
„Tokio *Hotel*" sind vier Freunde aus Magdeburg im Osten von Deutschland – Bill, Tom, Gustav und Georg. Sie haben schon 2002 unter dem Namen „Devilish" begonnen, Musik zu machen, heißen aber erst seit 2003 „Tokio Hotel". Bill ist der Leadsänger und der Zwillingsbruder von Tom, der Gitarre spielt. Gustav spielt Schlagzeug und Georg spielt Bassgitarre.

Hier sind ein paar Informationen über die Bandmitglieder:

Name:	Bill
Spitzname:	keinen
Geburtsdatum:	01.09.89
Geburtsort:	Leipzig
Geschwister:	Zwillingsbruder Tom
Wohnort:	Loitsche
Sternzeichen:	Jungfrau
Größe:	1,83 m
Augenfarbe:	braun
Haarfarbe:	schwarz

Name:	Tom
Spitzname:	keinen
Geburtsdatum:	01.09.89
Geburtsort:	Leipzig
Geschwister:	Zwillingsbruder Bill
Wohnort:	Loitsche
Sternzeichen:	Jungfrau
Größe:	1,80 m
Augenfarbe:	braun
Haarfarbe:	dunkelblond

Name:	Gustav
Spitzname:	Juschtel
Geburtsdatum:	08.09.88
Geburtsort:	Magdeburg
Geschwister:	eine ältere Schwester
Wohnort:	Magdeburg
Sternzeichen:	Jungfrau
Größe:	1,70 m
Augenfarbe:	braun
Haarfarbe:	dunkelblond

Name:	Georg
Spitzname:	die anderen Bandmitglieder nennen ihn manchmal Moritz
Geburtsdatum:	31.03.87
Geburtsort:	Halle
Geschwister:	keine
Wohnort:	Magdeburg
Sternzeichen:	Widder
Größe:	1,78 m
Augenfarbe:	grau-grün
Haarfarbe:	braun

Wann kam die erste CD auf den Markt?
Die erste Single kam 2005 auf den Markt. Sie hieß „Durch den Monsun" und war sofort an der Spitze der deutschen Charts. Das erste Album wurde im gleichen Jahr veröffentlicht. Der Titel des ersten Albums war „Schrei" und es war Nummer 1 in Deutschland und Österreich. In der Schweiz war das Album auf dem 3. Platz. Auch in Amerika schaffte es „Schrei" in der englischen Version in die Top 40.

Und was war euer letzter großer Erfolg?
2007 kam dann das zweite Album, „Zimmer 483", auf den Markt. Die erste Single aus dem Album war sofort Nummer 1. Gerade haben „Tokio Hotel" bei den „MTV Video Music Awards 2008" in den Paramount Studios in Los Angeles die Auszeichnung Best Newcomer bekommen! Und damit haben sie Geschichte gemacht, denn die Auszeichnung ist das erste Mal an eine deutsche Band gegangen. 2008 sind sie auch in den USA auf Tournee gewesen. Wer weiß, vielleicht kann eine deutsche Band den englischsprachigen Markt doch noch erobern.

1a 📖🎧 Read the article about the group "Tokio Hotel" and answer the questions below, giving the name of the correct person each time.

a Wer ist der Zwillingsbruder von Bill?

b Wer ist das älteste Mitglied der Band?

c Wer singt meistens in der Band?

d Wer ist am kleinsten?

e Wer hat im März Geburtstag?

Vokabeln

auftreten	to perfom
verrückt	crazy
eindrucksvoll	impressive
das Mitglied	member
der Erfolg	success
erobern	to conquer

1b 📖🎧 Read the article again, then read the following sentences. For each sentence write T (true), F (false) or ? (Not in the Text).

a „Tokio Hotel" kommen aus Deutschland.

b „Tokio Hotel" hatten früher einen anderen Namen.

c Die Mitglieder kommen alle aus derselben Stadt.

d „Tokio Hotel" lieben Tokio.

e Es haben schon viele deutsche Bands die MTV Auszeichnung gewonnen.

f 2010 werden „Tokio Hotel" wieder in Amerika spielen.

Grammatik *Seite 182*

The article on "Tokio Hotel" mentions events which happened in the past, using the following tenses:

a Perfect tense

*Sie **haben begonnen**, Musik zu machen.*

*Sie **sind** auf Tournee **gewesen**.*

b Imperfect tense

*Die erste Single **kam** 2005 auf den Markt.*

*Der Titel des ersten Albums **war** „Schrei".*

Look for further examples of these tenses in the article.

2a 🎧 Listen to the interviews, then answer the following questions in English.

Part 1

a What sort of music do "Juli" make?

b When were they founded?

c How many members are there in "Juli"?

d What is the name of the lead singer?

Part 2

e How does the name of the rap group translate into English?

f What is special about them?

g What year did they start performing together?

h What year saw their last hit?

Part 3

i Where and when was Marlene Dietrich born?

j In which other two countries did she live?

k Apart from being a singer, what else did she do?

l What happened in 1930?

AQA Examiner's tip

When listening, don't worry if you don't understand a particular word. It is unlikely that you would understand every word in an authentic listening situation, but you will often be able to work things out through context.

2b 🎧 Listen to the report about a special event for a member of "Tokio Hotel". Choose the correct answers.

a The party for Bill will be in

1 London 2 Berlin 3 Bremen

b The party will take place on

1 13th September 2 23rd September 3 30th September

c You get free entry if you

1 bring a present for Bill 2 dress like Bill 3 dye your hair like Bill

d The party will start at

1 9 o'clock 2 9.30 3 9.50

e At the party you will find

1 only Bill 2 Bill and his brother 3 all the band members

Vokabeln

einziehen in + acc.	to move into
die Enthüllung	unveiling

kerboodle!

G Free time and the media

1a 📖✏️ Unjumble the sentences below. Sentences a–c are in the present tense and sentences d–f are in the perfect tense.

a Ich mein mache zu Buch.

b macht Sie auf ihr Geschenk.

c richtig hört selten zu Ihr.

d Er hat Spielen mitgemacht bei nie.

e im Kaufhaus eingekauft Sie hat.

f die ganze Nacht Sie ferngesehen haben.

1b 🗨 Work in pairs. You will need a dice. Roll the dice once to pick a pronoun and a second time to pick an activity. Then say the sentence in either the present or perfect tense.

> **Separable verbs**
>
> Some verbs in German are in two parts. They consist of the normal verb and a separable prefix. Some common examples are **fern**sehen (to watch television), **aus**geben (to spend), **auf**machen (to open) and **an**sehen (to look at).
>
> When you use separable verbs in the present tense you need to move the prefix (*fern-, aus-, auf-* etc.) to the end of the sentence:
>
> *ausgeben* Ich **gebe** viel Geld **aus**. – I spend a lot of money.
>
> When you use separable verbs in the perfect tense the prefix comes before *ge*:
>
> *ausgeben* Ich **habe** viel Geld **ausgegeben**. – I spent a lot of money.

Grammatik Seite 181

Beispiel: 1 + 4 = Ich rufe an / Ich habe angerufen.

= ich / *fernsehen*

= du / *das Fenster aufmachen*

= er/sie / *das Licht ausschalten*

= wir / *anrufen*

= ihr / *Geld ausgeben*

= sie / *einkaufen*

2a 📖 Read the following sentences. Either using your knowledge or referring to the verb table on pages 191–194, correct the mistakes in the past participles.

a Er ist in den Ferien im Meer geschwimmt.

b Wir haben von Madrid viele Postkarten geschreiben.

c Manchmal sind wir am Abend ins Kino gegangt.

d Die Familie Peters ist wie jedes Jahr nach Mallorca gefliegen.

e Als ich jünger war, habe ich in einem Chor gesingt.

f Ich bin heute morgen sehr spät aufgestehen.

2b ✏️ After your teacher has checked your answers, write six sentences of your own using the irregular past participles.

> **The perfect tense with irregular verbs**
>
> Some verbs in the perfect tense don't follow the normal pattern. Very often the vowels in the middle change e.g. *schreiben* → *geschrieben*, *trinken* → *getrunken*. Sometimes an additional letter is added e.g. *essen* → *gegessen*. Occasionally the vowel changes and an additional letter is added e.g. *nehmen* → *genommen*. Irregular past participles always end in *–en*. You need to learn them off by heart.

Grammatik Seite 182

3 📖 Choose the correct imperfect forms of *haben* and *sein* in each sentence.

Beispiel: a Wo warst du letztes Wochenende? Hattest du gutes Wetter?

a Wo hattest / warst du letztes Wochenende? Hattest / Warst du gutes Wetter?

b Ich hatte / war gestern im Park und meine kleine Schwester hatte / war dabei.

c Wir hatten / waren wenig Zeit, als wir letztes Wochenende beim Einkaufen hatten / waren.

d Peter und Angelika hatten / waren sehr enttäuscht (*disappointed*), dass es zu spät fürs Kino hatte / war.

e Hattet / Wart ihr in den Ferien? Hattet / Wart ihr gutes Wetter? Ihr seht so braun aus.

4a 📖 Translate the following sentences into English.

a Ich muss mein Geld auf einen MP3-Spieler sparen.

b Er darf nicht zu lange ausgehen.

c Wir können uns am Wochenende in der Stadt treffen.

d Wir sollen meine Oma nächstes Wochenende besuchen.

4b ✏ Now translate these sentences into German.

a I want to buy new trainers.

b We must not stay out too late.

c She cannot understand me.

d Can you (*ihr*) visit grandmother at the weekend?

5a ✏ Read the sentences and fill in the gaps with *wann, wenn* or *als*.

a _____ kommst du nach Hause?

b Ich mache immer die Hausaufgaben, _____ ich nach Hause komme.

c _____ du deine Arbeit nicht machst, bekommst du kein Taschengeld.

d Ich hatte einen Teddybär, _____ ich jünger war.

e Er weiß nicht, _____ er einen neuen Computer bekommt.

f Es war alles viel schwieriger, _____ es noch keine Computer gab.

5b ✏ Now write five sentences of your own using *wann, wenn* and *als*.

Grammatik Seite 183

The imperfect tenses of *haben* and *sein*

The imperfect tenses of *haben* and *sein* are used very often. They are a useful way to add a past tense to your writing and speaking, too. Refer to page 65 for the correct forms.

Grammatik Seite 181

Modal verbs (revision)

Modal verbs are *können* (can, to be able to), *mögen* (to like), *sollen* (should), *dürfen* (may, to be allowed to), *wollen* (to want to) and *müssen* (must, to have to). They usually go together with a second verb in the infinitive, which goes at the end of the sentence or clause e.g. *Ich darf heute in die Stadt gehen.* For all the forms of the modal verbs in the present tense, see pages 23 and 25

Grammatik Seite 180

Using *wann, wenn* and *als*

The words *wann, wenn* and *als* all translate into 'when' in English. However, they are not interchangeable.

Wann means 'at what time':

Wann surfst du im Internet?

Ich weiß nicht, wann ich ankommen werde.

Wenn is a conjunction like *dass* and *weil* and sends the verb to the end. It can also be translated as 'whenever' or 'if':

Ich chatte gern im Internet, wenn mir langweilig ist.

Als refers to the past (either single points in time or uninterrupted periods):

Ich war noch nicht fertig, als er ankam.

Ich habe oft im Internet gespielt, als ich jünger war.

Free time and the media

Was hast du gestern gemacht? ➡ Seite 58–59

	amüsieren (sich)	to enjoy (oneself)
	anrufen	to telephone
	ansehen (sich etwas)	to see, to watch
	anstrengend	exhausting
	ausgehen	to go out
	begleiten	to accompany
das	Computerspiel	computer game
	fernsehen	to watch TV
der	Film	film
die	Freizeit	free time
	gefallen (+ dat)	to please
	Hausaufgaben (pl)	homework
das	Interesse	interest
das	Konzert	concert
	lesen	to read
	Lieblings-	favourite
das	Lied	song
die	Lust	desire, pleasure
	Musik hören	to listen to music
	quatschen	to chat
die	Sendung	TV programme
der	Spaß	fun
das	Spiel	game
	spielen	to play
	treffen (sich mit)	to meet (with)
	unterhalten (sich)	to talk
	unternehmen	to undertake, to do

Ich bin in die Stadt gegangen ➡ Seite 60–61

das	Freibad	open-air swimming pool
der	Fußball	football
	gehen	to go
	gewinnen	to win
das	Hallenbad	indoor swimming pool
der	Handball	handball

	herumlaufen	to run or go around
	kegeln	to bowl
das	Kino	cinema
	klettern	to climb
der	Klub	club
die	Mannschaft	team
	mitgehen	to go with somebody
das	Mitglied	member
	mitkommen	to come with somebody
	Rad fahren	to go cycling
	schwimmen	to swim
	segeln	to go sailing
	Skateboard fahren	to go skateboarding
	tanzen	to dance
	turnen	to do gymnastics
der	Verein	club, society
der	Wettkampf	competition

Wir bekommen nicht genug Taschengeld! ➡ Seite 62–63

	ausgeben	to spend
das	Bargeld	cash
	bekommen	to receive
	geben	to give
das	Geld	money
das	Geschäft	shop
das	Handy	mobile phone
	kaufen	to buy
das	Kaufhaus	department store
die	Konditorei	cake shop
	kosten	to cost
die	Kreditkarte	credit card
der	Laden	shop
der	MP3-Spieler	MP3 player
	pleite	skint
	reichen	to be enough

der	Schmuck	jewellery
ein	Schnäppchen machen	to pick up a bargain
	sparen	to save
der	Tante-Emma-Laden	corner shop
das	Taschengeld	pocket money

Wir waren im Einkaufszentrum ➡ Seite 64–65

	altmodisch	old-fashioned
das	Angebot	offer
die	Anprobe	changing room
	anprobieren	to try on
	ätzend	lousy
	ausverkauft	sold out
die	Auswahl	selection, range
	beschweren (sich)	to complain
	bestellen	to order
	billig	cheap
	einkaufen	to shop, to buy
das	Einkaufszentrum	shopping centre
	es passt dir	it fits you
	es steht dir	it suits you
	günstig	reasonable, at a good price
die	Kappe	baseball cap
	Klamotten (pl)	clothes
das	Kleid	dress
die	Kleidung	clothes
	kostenlos	free
	leisten	to afford
die	Marke	brand
der	Markt	market
die	Mode	fashion
	modisch	fashionable
	passen	to fit
die	Qualität	quality
die	Quantität	quantity
die	Quittung	bill
der	Rabatt	reduction

	schauen	to look
	schick	stylish, chic
der	Sommerschlussverkauf	end of summer sales
das	Sonderangebot	special offer
	teuer	expensive
	umschauen	to look around
	umtauschen	to exchange
	unterwegs	on the move

Ich lebe im Internet ➡ Seite 66–67

	abhängig	dependent
	brennen	to burn
	chatten	to chat (on the internet)
der	Computer	computer
	drücken	to push, to press
die	E-Mail	e-mail
	herunterladen	to download
	hochladen	to upload
die	Internetseite	internet site
der	Klingelton	ringtone
	lehrreich	educational
	mailen	to send (by e-mail)
	mobben	to bully
	nützlich	useful
	praktisch	practical, practically
	recherchieren	research
das	Satellitenfernsehen	satellite TV
	schicken	to send
	simsen	to send text messages
die	SMS	text message
das	soziale Netzwerk	social networking site
	speichern	to save (files on a computer)
die	Technologie	technology
die	Webseite	webpage

2.6 Ich möchte mal nach ...

Lernziele

Talking about holiday preferences and experiences

Using correct word order (time – manner – place)

Recognising information presented in different ways

Urlaubsgrüsse

Liebe Karina,

ich bin im Moment in Österreich in den Alpen. Ich bin hier mit Mutti, Vati und Erik, meinem Bruder. Wir haben eigentlich mit dem Wetter ziemlich viel Glück, aber gestern war es sehr windig und viel zu kalt. Heute scheint die Sonne und meine Eltern und ich waren beim Skifahren. Erik ist zu Hause geblieben, weil er nicht Skifahren wollte. Er sagt, sein Bein tut weh, aber meistens ist er nur zu faul. Ich fahre sehr gern Ski und morgen möchte ich einen Snowboardingkurs beginnen. Du weißt ja, dass ich in den Ferien gern aktiv bin. Deshalb ist im Winter ein Skiurlaub in den Alpen für mich ideal. Ich möchte in den nächsten Ferien nach Amerika zum Skifahren gehen, weil der Schnee in Kalifornien so toll ist. Was machst du diese Ferien?

Deine Katja

> **Tipp**
>
> In the postcards you will find *ich möchte* to say what you would like to do. Where might you have heard it before?

Lieber Matthew,

hallo aus Sylt. Du fragst dich vielleicht, wo Sylt ist. Also, Sylt ist eine Insel im Norden von Deutschland in der Nordsee. Ich komme jeden Sommer hierher und ich liebe es. Meistens fahre ich mit einer Jugendgruppe und wir übernachten auf einem Zeltplatz. Wir haben meistens Glück mit dem Wetter und wir können im Meer schwimmen. Ab und zu regnet es aber, und dann ist es relativ kühl. Im Allgemeinen finde ich Sylt aber toll. Nächstes Jahr möchte ich aber woanders hinfahren, zum Beispiel nach Afrika auf eine Safari. Wo bist du dieses Jahr?

Dein Knut

1 📖🎧🌐 Match up the two sentence halves.

Beispiel: **a 3**

a Katja fährt dieses Jahr in ...
b Gestern war es nicht ...
c Erik hatte wahrscheinlich keine ...
d Morgen möchte Katja ...
e Sylt liegt ...
f Wenn das Wetter gut ist, ...
g Manchmal kann das Wetter auf Sylt ...
h Nächstes Jahr möchte Knut ...

1 in der Nordsee.
2 auch schlecht sein.
3 den Alpen Ski.
4 Lust zum Skifahren.
5 geht Knut schwimmen.
6 Snowboarden lernen.
7 warm genug, um ski zu fahren.
8 wilde Tiere, wie zum Beispiel Giraffen, Zebras und Löwen, sehen.

> 📖 **Recognising information presented in different ways**
>
> **Strategie**
>
> Remember that the same pieces of information may be presented in different ways:
>
> *Es ist nicht warm genug zum Schwimmen. = Es ist zu kalt, um schwimmen zu gehen.*

2 🎧 Listen to the five people discussing holidays. For each person, choose three pictures to illustrate any of the following: destination, season, length of stay, transport, which people he or she went with. Each person will only mention three of the five things, but there may be additional details for you to note down.

Beispiel: Felix i, k, ...

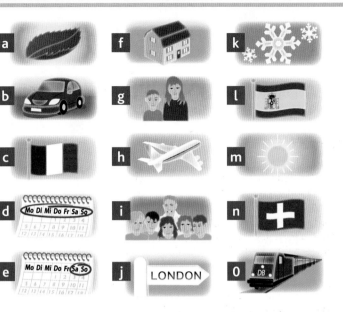

3a ⓖ Put the words in each sentence in the correct order.

Beispiel: **a** In den Ferien fahre ich nach Spanien mit dem Auto.

a fahre ich   In den Ferien   nach Spanien   mit dem Auto

b Meine Eltern   im Sommer   reisen   alleine   nach Italien

c in die Schweiz   möchte ich   Nächstes Jahr   fliegen   mit Freunden

d mit dem Zug   Mein Bruder und ich   möchten   im Winter   nach Holland   fahren

e im Sommer   Er ist   mit seiner Schulklasse   gefahren   nach Deutschland

3b ⓖ Now write some sentences of your own using the time – manner – place rule.

> **Using correct word order (time – manner – place)** ⓖrammatik Seite 186
>
> When you mention when (time), how (manner) and where (place) you do something, you give the time first, then the manner and then the place. This is called the Time, Manner, Place rule and it applies in all tenses. The conjugated verb still remains the second idea.
>
> Example:
>
> *Ich fahre jedes Jahr mit meinen Eltern nach Frankreich.*
>
> *Jedes Jahr fahre ich mit meinen Eltern nach Frankreich.*
>
> Also learn the use the different forms of *ich möchte* etc.
>
> See page 84 ➡

Ich möchte	in den nächsten Ferien / nächstes Wochenende / so bald wie möglich	mit meiner Familie / mit einer Gruppe / mit dem Auto	in die Berge / ans Meer / irgendwohin	fahren.
	jeden Tag / abends / regelmäßig	mit meinen Freunden / alleine	im Meer	schwimmen.
			im Restaurant	essen.
			in den Bergen	skifahren.
Ich war	schon oft / ein paar Mal / ab und zu / noch nie		auf dem Land. / in Amerika. / in einer Großstadt.	

4 🗨 Work in pairs. You are at a travel agent's. One of you plays the role of the client explaining what your holiday preferences are, while the other plays the role of the agent trying to find the perfect holiday. Include the following questions, using the *Sie* form of address:

Wohin möchten Sie fahren?   Was möchten Sie dort machen?   Wo waren Sie schon in den Ferien?

The person playing the agent should make a suggestion before you swap roles:

Ich kann Ihnen ... empfehlen.

kerboodle!

Das werde ich machen

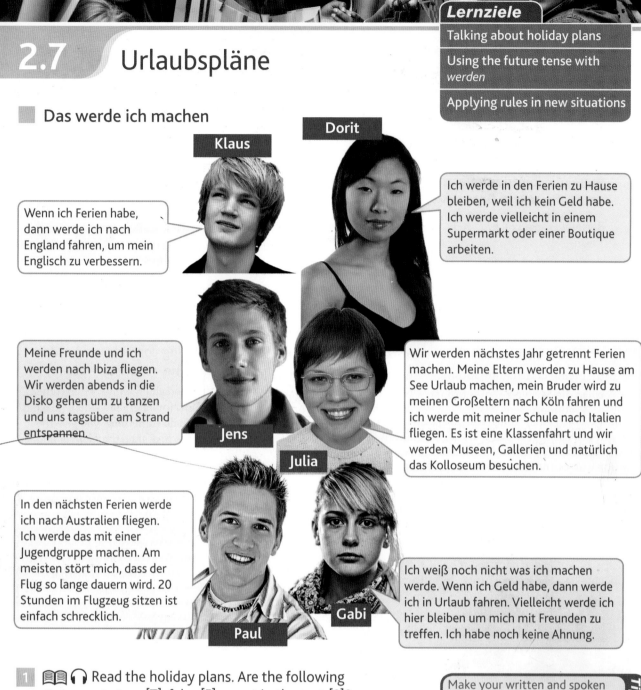

Klaus

Wenn ich Ferien habe, dann werde ich nach England fahren, um mein Englisch zu verbessern.

Dorit

Ich werde in den Ferien zu Hause bleiben, weil ich kein Geld habe. Ich werde vielleicht in einem Supermarkt oder einer Boutique arbeiten.

Jens

Meine Freunde und ich werden nach Ibiza fliegen. Wir werden abends in die Disko gehen um zu tanzen und uns tagsüber am Strand entspannen.

Julia

Wir werden nächstes Jahr getrennt Ferien machen. Meine Eltern werden zu Hause am See Urlaub machen, mein Bruder wird zu meinen Großeltern nach Köln fahren und ich werde mit meiner Schule nach Italien fliegen. Es ist eine Klassenfahrt und wir werden Museen, Gallerien und natürlich das Kolloseum besuchen.

Paul

In den nächsten Ferien werde ich nach Australien fliegen. Ich werde das mit einer Jugendgruppe machen. Am meisten stört mich, dass der Flug so lange dauern wird. 20 Stunden im Flugzeug sitzen ist einfach schrecklich.

Gabi

Ich weiß noch nicht was ich machen werde. Wenn ich Geld habe, dann werde ich in Urlaub fahren. Vielleicht werde ich hier bleiben um mich mit Freunden zu treffen. Ich habe noch keine Ahnung.

1 📖🎧 Read the holiday plans. Are the following statements true [T], false [F] or not in the text [?]?

a Klaus möchte nächstes Jahr lernen eine Fremdsprache besser zu sprechen.

b Dorit will zuerst etwas Geld verdienen.

c Jens wird nicht nach Ibiza fliegen.

d Julia wird nächstes Jahr mit ihren Eltern Ferien machen.

e Julia wird mit anderen Schülern und Schülerinnen nach Italien fahren.

f Paul war schon einmal in Australien.

g Paul findet lange im Flugzeug sitzen furchtbar.

h Gabi hat schon Pläne für ihren Urlaub.

Tipp

Make your written and spoken presentations more fluent by adding *wenn ... dann ...* ('if' ... 'then' ...) and *um ... zu ...* ('in order to' ...). Watch out where the verbs go in the sentences:

Wenn es mir meine Eltern erlauben, dann werde ich nach Portugal fahren.

Ich fahre nach Portugal, um Portugiesisch zu lernen.

Can you find further examples in the speech bubbles?

2 🅖 Write the correct form of *werden* and add the infinitive in German of the word in brackets.

Beispiel:　**a** Ich werde nach Frankreich reisen.

a Ich _____ nach Frankreich _____ . (travel)

b Wir _____ meine Oma und meinen Opa _____ . (visit)

c Lara und Tobias _____ mit dem Flugzeug _____ . (fly)

d _____ du mit mir nach Amerika _____ ? (come)

e Sie (she) _____ sich am Strand _____ . (relax)

---

3 🎧 Listen to Lukas talking about his holiday plans and fill in the gaps.

Grüß Gott. Ich heiße Lukas. Ich habe schon viele **a** _____ für meine Sommerferien. Ich werde in der ersten **b** _____ meiner Ferien zu meinen **c** _____ gehen. Dann in der zweiten Woche werden meine Eltern und ich mit dem **d** _____ nach **e** _____ fahren. In Italien **f** _____ wir zuerst in Venedig mit einer Gondel auf den Kanälen **g** _____ . Dann fahren wir weiter und verbringen noch **h** _____ Wochen an der Küste. Wenn das **i** _____ gut ist, werde ich im Meer **j** _____ , Beachvolleyball **k** _____ und am **l** _____ viel Pizza essen.

---

4 🗨️ 🔊 Work in pairs. You are planning a holiday. Tell your partner your plans, using the future tense with *werden*. Use the following questions as a starting point:

▪ Wohin wirst du in den Ferien fahren?

▪ Was wirst du in den Ferien machen?

---

5 ✏️ Write up both your plans and your partner's.

Using the future tense with *werden*

The future tense is formed with the present tense of *werden* plus the infinitive at the end of the clause:

Ich werde nach Berlin fahren.

Wir werden die Sehenswürdigkeiten besichtigen.

ich werde	I will	
du wirst	you will	
er/sie/es wird	he/she/it will	
wir werden	we will	+ infinitive
ihr werdet	you will (plural)	
sie werden	they will	
Sie werden	you will (formal)	

Also learn more about using *ohne … zu …*, *anstatt … zu …* and *um … zu …* .

See page 84 ➡️

Grammatik · Seite 184

🗨️ Applying rules in new situations

When you're working with new topics and tenses, it's easy to forget the grammar rules you've already learnt. For instance, when talking about your holiday plans using the future tense with *werden*, don't forget to apply the time – manner – place rule if you want to say when, how and where you will do something.

Strategie

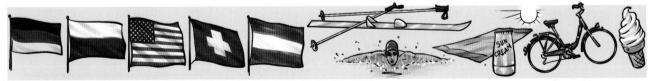

Ich werde	nächstes Jahr / in den Sommerferien	mit meinen Eltern / mit meinen Freunden / allein	in die Schweiz / nach Österreich	fahren.
Dort werde ich	jeden Tag / morgens / abends		im Meer	baden.
			am Strand	Eis essen.
			in den Alpen	skifahren.

Daniels Urlaub

das Bundestagsgebäude

Berlin Zoo

Ich heiße Daniel. Ich bin ein richtiger Stadtmensch und möchte nie auf dem Land wohnen. Ich wohne in Berlin und finde es einfach total klasse. Es ist jetzt August und, obwohl ich auch gerne in andere Länder reise, bin ich diese Ferien in Berlin, weil ich auf einen großen Urlaub nächstes Jahr spare. Man kann in Berlin viel unternehmen, es gibt überall etwas Interessantes zu sehen. Wenn das Wetter gut ist, kann man nach Wannsee fahren. Das ist ein Stadtteil von Berlin und dort gibt es auch Seen, wo man schwimmen, surfen und segeln kann. Meine Freunde und ich sind schon mindestens 8 Mal dorthin gefahren, weil das Wetter bis jetzt wirklich super war. Aber in Berlin kann man auch viel unternehmen, wenn die Sonne nicht scheint. Es gibt viele Kinos, wo man die neuesten deutschen und internationalen Filme sehen kann. Natürlich kann man auch gut einkaufen in großen Kaufhäusern, aber auch kleineren Boutiquen. Am Dienstag waren wir im Berliner Zoo. Er ist sehr berühmt und liegt im Zentrum Berlins. Leider hat es an diesem Tag geregnet und viele Tiere haben sich deshalb versteckt. Dieses Jahr habe ich mich auch entschlossen, mal das „touristische Berlin" zu sehen – etwas Kulturelles. Ich bin zum Beispiel letzten Freitag zum Bundestagsgebäude gegangen. Dort kann man manchmal Politiker bei Sitzungen sehen. Morgen werde ich dann zum Museum am Checkpoint Charlie gehen. Dort kann man sehen, wo bis 1989 die Berliner Mauer war, und am Mittwochabend werden ich und ein paar Freunde grillen. Das wird bestimmt Spaß machen.

Checkpoint Charlie

1a 📖 🎧 🌐 Read Daniel's article then choose the correct answers for each question.

a Wo wohnt Daniel?   **1** auf dem Land   **2** in einer Stadt   **3** am Meer

b Welche Ferien hat Daniel im Moment?   **1** Sommerferien   **2** Osterferien   **3** Weihnachtsferien

c Was wird Daniel nächstes Jahr machen?
  1 Er wird in die Ferien fahren.   **2** Er wird zu Hause bleiben.   **3** Er weiß es noch nicht.

d Was hat Daniel schon oft gemacht, wenn das Wetter gut war?
  1 Er hat ferngesehen.   **2** Er hat geschlafen.   **3** Er ist nach Wannsee gefahren.

e Wo war Daniel am Dienstag?   **1** am See   **2** im Tierpark   **3** im Kino

1b 📖 🎧 🌐 Read the article again and answer these questions in German:

a Was hat Daniel letzten Freitag gemacht?

b Was wird Daniel am Mittwochabend machen?

c Was kann man sonst noch in Berlin machen?

2 🎧 Five teenagers are being interviewed on holiday. They each mention what they are doing, what they have done and what they are going to do. Copy and complete the table.

	macht	schon gemacht	wird machen
Jutta	b	d, f	d

a eine Bootsfahrt machen

b ein Museum besuchen

c in einem Restaurant essen

d einkaufen gehen

e Sehenswürdigkeiten besichtigen

f sich sonnen

g im Meer schwimmen

3 🗨️ Throw a dice and, using the pictures from the previous activity, practise the present tense, perfect tense and future tense (blue = present tense, orange = perfect tense, green = future tense).

Anfang	1 e) h)	2 a) f)	3 c) e)	4 b) f)	5 d) g)	6 h) c)
13 h) a)	12 f) e)	11 freie Wahl	10 b) d)	9 g) f)	8 freie Wahl	7 freie Wahl
14 e) c)	15 f) d)	16 a) e)	17 freie Wahl	18 f) a)	19 d) g)	Ende

> Du hast eine Vier.

> Also, vier … Ich werde ein Museum besichtigen und ich werde mich sonnen.

> Prima! Jetzt bin ich dran …

Ich mache	eine Bootsfahrt	.
Ich habe		gemacht.
Ich werde		machen.
Ich gehe	einkaufen	.
Ich bin		gegangen.
Ich werde		gehen.

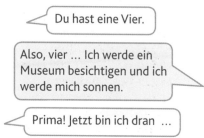

Using different tenses (past, present and future)

When speaking and writing, remember to include different tenses. Refer to what you did yesterday or last week, what you are doing at the moment and what you will do in future. To revise forming these tenses see the following:

present tense ➡️   *see page 18*

perfect tense ➡️   *see pages 59, 61, 63*

imperfect tense ➡️   *see page 65*

future tense ➡️   *see page 77*

Grammatik   *Seite 180*

4 Ⓖ Where do the sentences start and finish? Are the sentences in the perfect tense, present tense or future tense?

ichfahreindenFerienoftnachAmerikaletztesJahrbinichauch nachAmerikagefahrenwirsindnachOrlandogeflogenichliebe OrlandomeinBruderundichliebendieVergnügungsparksund Wasserparkswirsindvielschwimmengegangenundhabeoftin Fastfood-RestaurantsgegessenwirwerdennächstesJahrnicht nachAmerikafliegenichwerdemeinenBrieffreundinder TürkeibesuchenundmeineElternwerdenhierbleiben.

Revise different time indicators for the past, present and future: gestern, letztes Jahr, heute, in Zukunft, nächstes Jahr etc. Add them to your writing and speaking to add fluency and interest.

Tipp

kerboodle!

2.9 Auf Achse

Lernziele

Talking about travel

Asking questions using interrogatives

Making vocab lists

1 **V** You see the following signs at a train station. Where would you go if you wanted to:

a   leave your suitcase
b   have a snack
c   exit the station
d   get some information
e   reserve a ticket for a later journey
f   wait for your train

Ausgang

Auskunft

Bahnsteig

Gepäckaufbewahrung

Imbiss

Reservierungen

2 📖🎧 Read what these people have to say about different modes of transport. For each, note down:

■ the mode of transport
■ whether their experiences are positive or negative, and why
■ any extra details

Beispiel: Herr und Frau Schiller: car / hire car, positive …

Olaf

Ich war letztes Jahr in Südamerika mit meiner Familie. Wir wollten zuerst ein Auto mieten, aber dann haben wir uns entschlossen drei Wochen mit dem Reisebus zu fahren. Einmal und nie wieder. Wir haben das viel zu anstrengend gefunden. Ich bleibe nächstes Jahr zu Hause und gehe an den See.

Herr und Frau Schiller

Wir haben letztes Jahr im Urlaub einen Leihwagen gemietet, weil wir die Umgebung erkunden wollten. Wir haben das ausgezeichnet gefunden, weil wir unabhängig waren. Wir wollen das in Zukunft wieder machen.

Esther

Ich werde dieses Jahr mit meiner Schwester ein paar Länder in Osteuropa bereisen. Weil wir beide keinen Führerschein haben, werden wir uns eine Interrailkarte kaufen und mit dem Zug fahren. Das ist relativ billig für Jugendliche.

Tatjana

Ich will nächstes Jahr in Europa herumreisen, aber ich möchte Fliegen vermeiden, weil ich die Umwelt schützen möchte und der CO_2-Ausstoß so hoch ist. Ich bin ziemlich aktiv in meiner Umweltschutzgruppe in der Schule.

Karsten

Ich sammle dieses Jahr Geld für einen guten Zweck. Deshalb werde ich eine gesponserte Radtour in den Alpen machen. Ich muss dafür 500 Euro sammeln. Ich trainiere viel und bin schon ziemlich fit. Gesund bleiben und gleichzeitig etwas für einen guten Zweck tun finde ich prima.

3 🎥 Watch and listen to the dialogues. Where does each person want to go? How will they get there? Note down any extra information you pick up.

Beispiel: **a** main railway station, walk, only five minutes away …

4a Ⓖ Fill the gaps with the correct question word.

a _____ kommt der Zug aus Salzburg an?

b _____ finde ich bitte einen Supermarkt?

c _____ fährt dieser Bus – nach Augsburg oder Nürnberg?

d _____ kostet eine Karte für einen Erwachsenen?

4b Ⓖ Now try to ask the correct question for the underlined part of each sentence.

a Eine Karte für Jugendliche kostet <u>vier Euro.</u>

b Die Bushaltestelle ist <u>neben dem Verkehrsamt.</u>

c Der Zug fährt <u>nach Hamburg.</u>

d Der Zug kommt <u>aus Wien.</u>

5a 💬 🌍 You and a friend are planning a trip. It could be a weekend trip or a journey around the world. Answer your friend's questions.

- Wohin fahren wir?
- Wie reisen wir dorthin?
- Wann fahren wir los?
- Wie lange dauert die Reise?
- Wo werden wir übernachten?
- Was werden wir dort machen?
- Wie viel wird die Reise kosten?

5b ✏️ Now write about your plans.

Grammatik   *Seite 187*

Asking questions using interrogatives

Question words or interrogatives go at the start of a question. German interrogatives start with *w*:

Wer?	Who?	*Was?*	What?
Wo?	Where?	*Welche(r/s)*	Which?
Womit?	What with?	*Wie?*	How?
Wohin?	Where to?	*Warum?*	Why?
Woher?	Where from?	*Wie viel(e)?*	How much/ many?
Wann?	When?	*Wie lange?*	How long?

Also revise different cases (nominative and accusative).

See page 85 ➡

Strategie

💭 **Making vocabulary lists**

Use creative tasks as an opportunity to expand your vocabulary. Make a list of five nouns, five verbs and five adjectives that will come in useful. Don't waste too much time trying to translate particularly difficult expressions, though – if you're unsure, you can always paraphrase or think up alternatives.

Tipp

Remember that you can reuse questions when giving answers. See page 59.

Wir	fliegen	nach Südamerika / auf eine karibische Insel.	
	fahren	mit dem Bus / mit dem Flugzeug / mit dem Schiff.	
Die Reise beginnt	in zwei Tagen / nach den Prüfungen.		
Die Reise dauert	eine Stunde / zwei Tagen / eine Woche.		
Wir werden	in einem Hotel / in einer Jugendherberge	übernachten.	
	wilde Tiere sehen / jeden Abend ausgehen / am Strand liegen.		
Die Reise wird	600 Pfund / 3000 Euro	kosten.	

Holidays

Zell am See und Kaprun

Startseite | Index | Hilfe | Kontakt | Textversion

Zell am See und Kaprun im Winter

Willkommen in Österreich. Ob Skianfänger oder Profi – 138 Kilometer Abfahrten und 57 Pisten machen jedem Wintersportler Spaß. Die leichten Pisten sind blau markiert und sind besonders gut für Anfänger. Wenn Sie schon ein besserer Skifahrer sind, dann wählen Sie eine von den 49 Kilometer langen roten Pisten oder die schwierigen Pisten der schwarzen Kategorie.

Sie sind noch nie Ski gefahren? Dann haben unsere Skilehrer die richtigen Tipps für Sie. Wir haben Englisch, Französisch, Italienisch, Polnisch und natürlich Deutsch sprechende Skilehrer. Wählen Sie zwischen einem halben Tag Unterricht von 10 bis 13 Uhr oder 13.30 bis 16.30 Uhr, oder den ganzen Tag. Wir bieten ihnen Einzelunterricht oder Unterricht in Gruppen bis maximal zehn Personen.

Sie wollen Snowboarden? Die drei Snow-Parks auf dem Kitzsteinhorn sind der richtige Ort dafür. Die sechs Meter hohe Superpipe ist nur eine der vielen Highlights im 30 000 Quadratmeter großen Mellow Park. Man kann hier immer üben, denn Schnee liegt hier auf dem Gletscher garantiert das ganze Jahr.

Zell am See und Kaprun im Sommer

Wozu das Meer, wenn wir einen See mit Trinkwasserqualität haben.... Wandern, Mountainbiken, Gleitschirmfliegen – Vieles ist möglich in der Europa-Sportregion. Hier kann man wandern oder Wassersport treiben, wie schwimmen, surfen, segeln oder Wasserski fahren.

Ein Rundflug durch die Alpen, Sommerskifahren auf dem Gletscher des Kitzsteinhorns oder Canyoning sind nur einige der Alternativen aus einem Programm mit über 40 Sportarten. In der Europa-Sportregion finden Familien mit Kindern, Paare und Singles jeden Alters ihr ganz persönliches Erholungsparadies.

Die idyllische Bergstadt Zell liegt 758 Meter über dem Meeresspiegel. Im Tal liegt der berühmte, vier Kilometer lange und 1,3 Kilometer breite Zeller See.

Kaprun liegt in der Nähe von Zell und auch in Kaprun gibt es viel zu unternehmen. Kaprun gehört zu den besten Adressen im europäischen Tourismus. Gäste aus 70 Nationen schätzen das Angebot. Seit 1966 bildet man zusammen mit Zell am See die Europa-Sportregion. Vierzig verschiedene Sportarten werden mit Hilfe intensiver Kooperation der Nachbarorte angeboten. Von Wandern und Biken bis zu Extremsportarten wie Canyoning und Raften – Kaprun hat alles.

1a 📖 🎧 Read the texts on Zell am See and Kaprun, then answer the following questions in English.

a Which country are Zell am See and Kaprun in?

b What colour slope is recommended if you are a beginner skier?

c What languages do the skiing instructors speak?

d What is the maximum number of people who can learn to ski in one group?

e What four types of water sports are mentioned?

f How long and wide is lake Zell?

g How many different varieties of sporting activities are offered in Kaprun?

1b 📖 🎧 Read the texts again and match up the sentence halves.

a Wenn man ein guter Skifahrer ist, ...

b Ein halber Tag Skiunterricht dauert ...

c Auf dem Gletscher gibt es ...

d Man kann im Sommer mit dem Flugzeug ...

e Zell am See hat ein Programm ...

f Nach Kaprun kommen Touristen aus ...

g Zusammen mit Zell am See wird Kaprun ...

1 ... über die Alpen fliegen.

2 ... die Europa-Sportregion genannt.

3 ... kann man auf einer roten oder schwarzen Piste fahren.

4 ... 365 Tage im Jahr genug Schnee um Ski zu fahren.

5 ... siebzig verschiedenen Ländern.

6 ... für jeden.

7 ... drei Stunden.

2a 🎧 Listen to the interview with Herr Weber and answer the following questions in English.

a What are the two traditional greetings which are used in this part of Austria?

b Where does Herr Weber work?

c What three means of transport does Herr Weber suggest you should take to get to Zell am See?

2b 🎧 Listen to the next part of the interview and answer the following questions in English.

a How many inhabitants does Zell am See have?

b How deep is Lake Zell?

c What does Herr Weber say about the highest mountain in Austria?

d How much does a night in a youth hostel cost?

e Name three of the facilities you can find at the youth hostel Herr Weber mentions.

Vokabeln

die Abfahrt	slope
die Anfänger	beginners
wählen	to choose
der Unterricht	lesson
der Gletscher	glacier
das Gleitschirmfliegen	hanggliding
der Rundflug	a sightseeing tour by plane or helicopter
das Kitzsteinhorn	name of a mountain
die Erholung	relaxation, recovery
das Tal	the valley
verschieden	different
das Angebot	offer

AQA *Examiner's tip*

Use your understanding of grammar to help you with activity 1b. Here you have, for example, a conjunction at the beginning of a sentence, *Wenn man ein guter Skifahrer ist* ... The second half of the sentence needs to start with a verb. Which of options 1)–7) starts with a verb and therefore has to be the correct answer?

Grammatik *Seite 187*

Man sagt doch „Grüß Gott" in dieser Gegend, oder? is the first question the interviewer asks Herr Weber. By adding *oder?* or *nicht wahr?* to a statement, you make it into a question by inviting confirmation – it's the equivalent of "isn't it?" in English.

What other ways of asking questions does the interviewer use? Note down the question words you hear. It's a good idea to learn lots of different ways of asking questions, not only so you understand others, but because you may want to use questions yourself to keep conversations going.

kerboodle!

(G) Holidays

1a 🗨 Work in pairs. Ask your partner the following questions about a future holiday. He or she answers. Then swap roles.

Beispiel:

> Wohin möchtest du fahren?

> Ich möchte nach Spanien fahren.

- ▥ Wohin möchtest du fahren?
- ▥ Mit wem möchtest du fahren?
- ▥ Wie möchtet ihr fahren?
- ▥ Wo möchtet ihr übernachten?
- ▥ Was möchtest du machen?
- ▥ Was möchte deine Freundin/dein Freund machen?
- ▥ Wie viel Geld möchtest du ausgeben?

1b ✏🗨 Using your work in the previous activity as a starting point, write up your holiday plans. Present your plans to the class (using pictures to illustrate, if wished).

2a 📖✏ Put the second half of the following sentences into the right order.

Beispiel: **a** Ich werde nach Italien fahren, um Italienisch zu lernen.

- **a** Ich werde nach Italien fahren, zu um Italienisch lernen zu.
- **b** Ich werde nach Paris fahren, ohne zu den Eiffelturm sehen.
- **c** Wir werden meine Großmutter besuchen, ihren Geburtstag zu feiern um
- **d** Sie wird dieses Jahr ans Meer fahren, in die Berge zu anstatt gehen.
- **e** Sie werden eine Weltreise machen, das Geld anstatt sparen zu.
- **f** Er wird mit Freunden nach Spanien fahren, seine Eltern ohne zu fragen.

2b ✏ Now complete the following sentences, using *um ...
zu ...* , *ohne ... zu ...* or *anstatt ... zu ...*. Use as many words
as possible from the box (but you can also add your own
ideas!).

> *ansehen   besuchen   Chinesisch
> Dublin   eine DVD   eine Pizza
> essen   im Meer   kaufen   lernen
> schwimmen   sehen   Souvenirs*

a Ich werde nach Irland fahren, ...

b Ich werde zu Hause bleiben, ...

c Wir werden ins italienische
Restaurant gehen, ...

d Wir werden nach China fliegen, ...

e Sie werden ins Geschäft gehen, ...

f Sie werden an den Strand gehen, ...

3a ✏ Translate the following phrases into German.

Beispiel: a etwas Großes

a something big

b something bigger

c nothing interesting

d nothing blue

e little of interest ('little
interesting')

f much good

g everything modern

**Using adjectives after *etwas,
nichts, viel, wenig* and *alles***

When you add an adjective after
etwas (something), *nichts* (nothing),
viel (much) or *wenig* (little) the
adjective gains a capital letter
(becomes a noun) and you add *–es*
to the end of it:

*etwas Interest**es***

After *alles* (everything) you just add
an *–e*:

*alles Interessant**e***

Grammatik Seite 178

3b ✏ Once your teacher has checked your work on the
previous activity, write six sentences, each one containing
one of the phrases you have translated.

Beispiel: Ich habe diese Stadt besucht, aber es gab
nichts Interessantes dort.

4a 📖 Choose the correct accusative article in each of the sentences below.

Beispiel: a den

a Er hat den/die/das Bus genommen.

b Es gibt einen/eine/ein tolles Museum in der
Stadt.

c Wir haben keinen/keine/kein Plan für
nächstes Jahr.

d Ich hatte einen/eine/ein tolle Woche in Berlin.

e Wir möchten bald einen/eine/ein Ausflug
aufs Land machen.

**The nominative and accusative cases
(revision)**

In German you need to be aware of the different
cases because these affect how words are spelled and
spoken (for instance articles and adjective endings).
A noun is in the nominative case if it is the subject or
'doer' of an action, for example after the word 'is':

Der Bahnhof *ist groß.*

A noun is in the accusative case if it is the object of an
action:

*Ich sehe **den Bahnhof**.*

Endings for definite and indefinite articles in the
nominative and accusative cases are as follows:

	masc.	fem.	neut.	pl.
nom.	*der / ein*	*die / eine*	*das / ein*	*die*
acc.	*den / einen*	*die / eine*	*das / ein*	*die*

You will notice that only masculine singular articles
change their spelling.

Grammatik Seite 175

4b ✏ Fill in the gaps with the correct forms of
the articles in the nominative and accusative
cases.

a Hier ist endlich _____ (*the*) Hotel (n).
Ich bin froh, dass wir _____ (*the*) Hotel
gefunden haben.

b Das war _____ (*the*) beste Urlaub (m)
meines Lebens. Ich werde _____ (*the*)
Urlaub nie vergessen.

c Das war wirklich _____ (*a*) lange Fahrt
(f). _____ (*the*) Fahrt hat 9 Stunden gedauert.

d _____ (*the*) Schule (f) macht mir _____ (*no*) Spaß (m).

Holidays

Ich möchte mal nach ... ➡ *Seite 74–75*

die	Alpen	the Alps
	bleiben	to stay
	fahren	to travel
die	Ferien	holidays (time)
	fliegen	to fly
	Frankreich	France
die	Insel	island
das	Land	country
das	Meer	sea
die	Niederlande	the Netherlands
die	Nordsee	the North Sea
	Österreich	Austria
die	Ostsee	the Baltic Sea
	Polen	Poland
	Russland	Russia
	Schottland	Scotland
die	Schweiz	Switzerland
	Ski fahren	to go skiing
	Spanien	Spain
die	Türkei	Turkey
	übernachten	to stay the night
der	Urlaub	holiday (trip)
	verbringen	to spend (time)
	woanders	somewhere else
das	Zelt	tent
	zelten	to camp

Urlaubspläne ➡ *Seite 76–77*

der	Aufenthalt	stay
	baden	to bathe
die	Broschüre	brochure
	dauern	to last (time)
das	Flugzeug	plane
die	Galerie	gallery
das	Gasthaus	guesthouse

der	Kanal	canal
	keine Ahnung haben	to have no idea
die	Klassenfahrt	school trip
die	Küste	coast
das	Museum	museum
die	Pension	guesthouse
der	Plan	plan
	reservieren	to reserve
die	Rezeption	reception
der	See	lake
die	See	sea
	stören	to bother, to disturb
der	Strand	beach
die	Touristeninformation	tourist information
	unterbringen	to accommodate
die	Unterkunft	accommodation
	Venedig	Venice
	verbessern	to improve
das	Verkehrsamt	tourist information
die	Vollpension	full board
der	Wohnwagen	caravan
der	Zuschlag	supplement (to pay)

Berlin ist cool! ➡ *Seite 78–79*

	berühmt	famous
	besichtigen	to see (while sightseeing)
	bestimmt	definitely
das	Boot	boat
	Bundestagsgebäude	German parliamentary buildings
	Checkpoint Charlie	Checkpoint between former East and West Berlin
der	Dom	cathedral
	dorthin fahren	to go / travel there
	entscheiden (sich)	to decide
das	Erlebnis	experience

	führen	to lead, to guide
	grillen	to have a barbeque
	kulturell	cultural
die	*Landschaft*	landscape
die	*Oper*	opera (house)
	reisen	to travel
das	*Schiff*	ship
	sehenswert	worth seeing
die	*Sehenswürdigkeit*	sight (thing worth seeing)
die	*Sitzung*	meeting, session
	sonnen (sich)	to sunbathe
das	*Souvenir*	souvenir
der	*Stadtmensch*	town / city person
der	*Stadtteil*	part of town
	surfen	to surf
der	*Tourismus*	tourism
	überall	everywhere
	verstecken (sich)	to hide
das	*Zentrum*	centre
der	*Zoo*	zoo

Auf Achse ➡ *Seite 80–81*

der	*Ausgang*	exit
	ausgezeichnet	excellent, excellently
die	*Auskunft*	information
der	*Bahnhof*	railway station
der	*Bahnsteig*	platform
der	*Fahrkartenautomat*	ticket machine
der	*Fahrkartenschalter*	ticket counter
die	*Fahrt*	trip, journey
der	*Führerschein*	driver's licence
die	*Gepäckaufbewahrung*	left luggage
	geschlossen	closed
	gleichzeitig	at the same time
die	*Haltestelle*	bus stop
	Haupt-	main, central
	herumreisen	to travel around
der	*Imbiss*	snack
die	*Imbissstube*	snack bar

die	*Jugendherberge*	youth hostel
die	*Karte*	ticket
die	*Kirche*	church
der	*Leihwagen*	hire car
die	*Linie*	route, line
	mieten	to rent
	Osteuropa	Eastern Europe
das	*Postamt*	post office
die	*Reise*	journey
der	*Reisebus*	coach
die	*Reservierung*	reservation
die	*Richtung*	direction
	sammeln	to collect
die	*Straßenbahn*	tram
die	*Umgebung*	surrounding area
	umsteigen	to change (trains, buses etc)
	unabhängig	independent
die	*Verbindung*	connection
	vermeiden	to avoid
	wunderschön	gorgeous, very beautiful
der	*Zoll*	customs
der	*Zweck*	cause, goal

Extra!   Question words

wann?	when?
warum?	why?
was?	what?
welche(r/s)?	which?
wer?	who?
wie?	how?
wie lange?	how long?
wie viel(e)?	how many?
wo?	where?
woher?	where from?
wohin?	where to?
womit?	what with?

2 ⬭ Einkaufen ist toll!

You are in the home of your Austrian exchange partner. He or she wants to take you on a shopping trip in Vienna and wants to know what kind of things you like spending money on.

Your teacher will play the role of your exchange partner. He or she could ask you the following:

1 how much pocket money do you get?
2 what do you like buying?
3 where do you like to go shopping?
4 what have you bought recently?
5 what are the best and worst things you ever bought?
6 what would you buy if you won a lot of money?
7 !

Remember you will have to respond to something that you have not yet prepared.

1 How much pocket money do you get?
- ▨ Say how much pocket money you get
- ▨ Say how often you receive it
- ▨ Say whether you think it is enough
- ▨ Mention if you get any money from elsewhere

2 What do you like buying?
- ▨ Mention the kind of things you like buying
- ▨ Describe them
- ▨ Say how often you buy them
- ▨ Explain why you like them

3 Where do you like to go shopping?
- ▨ Say which town you usually shop in
- ▨ Say whether you prefer large or small shops
- ▨ Explain your preference, giving advantages and disadvantages
- ▨ Mention a place you would like to shop (even if you've never been there!)

Remember that you are allowed to have prepared notes consisting of a total of up to 40 words for the whole task. You could use six words for five of the sections and five for the remaining two, but you will know which sections need the most support.

You must not include full sentences or phrases in your notes. Verbs have to be written in the infinitive.

> *AQA Examiner's tips*

Now start your notes. Write five or six words for each of the seven sections:

1 *bekommen, Pfund, Woche …*

Remember that *bekommen* is a false friend – *ich bekomme* means 'I receive', not 'I become'.

Make sure you can remember your numbers in German. Sometimes candidates forget how to say them because they are nervous!

> *AQA Examiner's tips*

Be as specific as you can be. If you like buying clothes, say what sort of clothes you prefer – *modisch, sportlich, nur schwarz …* etc.

When giving descriptions, don't forget to use qualifiers to make your language more expressive.

G See page 179 ➡

You can use adverbs of frequency (e.g. *oft, selten* etc.) to say how often you do something.

G See page 178 ➡

> *AQA Examiner's tips*

Use as many different ways of expressing opinions as you can e.g. *ich finde / ich mag / Am liebsten gehe ich … etc.*

If you use the phrase *Ich gehe lieber in … als in …* you will need to use the preposition *in* plus the accusative case (as you are describing movement towards somewhere).

G See page 177 ➡

Use *ich möchte* to say what you would like to do.

G See page 184 ➡

> *AQA Examiner's tips*

4 What have you bought recently?
- Mention an item which you recently bought
- Describe the item
- Say how much it cost
- Say why you bought it and whether you are still happy with it

Use the perfect tense to say what you have bought.

G See page 182 ➡

Use the imperfect tense (*Er/Sie/Es war...*) to describe the item.

G See page 182 ➡

Be imaginative with the adjectives you use to describe your item. Remember that adjectives in front of the noun need different endings.

G See page 177 ➡

5 What are the best and worst things you ever bought?
- Describe the best thing you have ever bought
- Explain why it was such a good buy
- Describe the worst thing you have ever bought
- Explain why it was such a bad buy

As you can only use 40 words in total you have to be very selective in what you write down for each section. Don't waste words!

You could memorise the following phrase: *Das Beste / Schlimmste, was ich gekauft habe, ist ...*

When giving reasons and justifications, don't always use *weil*. You could, for instance, use *denn* (the verb remains the second idea) or *da* (the verb is sent to the end of the sentence or clause).

6 What would you buy if you won a lot of money?
- Say what items you would buy with your money
- Explain why you would like them
- Mention other things (e.g. trips) you would spend your money on
- Say whether you would buy things for other people

This question gives you the opportunity to really use your imagination. You might want a car (*ein Auto*) or a luxury holiday (*eine Luxusreise*), or perhaps you would prefer to donate the money (*Geld spenden*).

To say what you would do, use *ich würde* plus an infinitive e.g. *ich würde ein Auto kaufen*.

G See page 184 ➡

It is easy to get nervous when tasks are open-ended. Don't forget there is no wrong or right answer, but make sure you give reasons for your choices.

7 ! At this point you will be asked a question which you don't know in advance. However, you can try to guess what it might be and prepare various options:
- Give your view on internet shopping
- Say whether you think some people shop too much
- Say whether you think money can make people happy
- Say whether you think young people should work for their pocket money

Try to collect three ideas for each of the bullet points. For instance, for internet shopping you might think about convenience, prices and not being able to try things out.

You may not be asked specifically about any of the options you prepare for, but your preparation will still give you extra vocab to use in other situations and make you more fluent.

Now you should have a complete set of 40 cue words, in seven groups with either five or six words in each.

You should now have completed your plan and prepared your answers. Give your plan to your teacher for feedback. Compare your answers to the online sample version – you might find some useful hints to make yours even better.

2  Meine Ferien

You are on holiday and are posting about it on your blog to keep everyone back home up to date. You could include:

1 location and weather
2 your journey there
3 food and accommodation
4 local sights
5 holiday activities
6 a comparison with past holidays
7 your future holiday plans

AQA Examiner's tips

Start off with a greeting to your friends and family at home e.g. *Hallo! ... hier!*

You can write about a real holiday location you have visited, or somewhere you would really like to go.

Writing a blog is a very immediate way of communicating. You can make your writing more sophisticated by adding time indicators. When you write about where you are you could say *ich bin zur Zeit / im Moment / gerade in ...*

---

1 Location and weather

- ▦ Say which country and/or town you are in at the moment
- ▦ Give details on where the country and/or city is
- ▦ Mention why you chose this destination
- ▦ Say what the weather is like at the moment

AQA Examiner's tips

Now start your notes. Write five or six words.
1 *Spanien, besuchen, südlich, Landschaft, Küste, sonnig*
2 ....

When giving information about where your location is you can use points on the compass (*im Norden / Süden / Westen / Osten*) or mention a more famous place that is nearby (*Das ist in der Nähe von ...*).

If you feel confident you could mention what the weather has been like in previous days, using the imperfect tense.

G See page 182 ➡

---

2 Your journey there

- ▦ Say how you travelled to your destination, and what the journey was like
- ▦ Give some advantages and/or disadvantages about the way you travelled
- ▦ Say where your journey was from and how long it took
- ▦ Mention what you did during your journey

AQA Examiner's tips

You will need to use the perfect tense to talk about how you travelled and what you did. Make sure you know which verbs take *haben* and which take *sein* as their auxiliary verb.

G See page 182 ➡

You are not allowed to take full sentences into your final assessment but you are allowed to take up to 40 words. If you include verbs they must either be infinitives or past participles.

---

3 Food and accommodation

- ▦ Say what type of accommodation you are staying in
- ▦ Mention some of the facilities there
- ▦ Say what kind of food is available
- ▦ Mention whether you like it or not and give a reason why

AQA Examiner's tips

When you mention some of the facilities you could also extend and link your sentences by adding what there isn't e.g. *es gibt ein Schwimmbad, aber das Zimmer hat keinen Balkon.*

Remember to use the accusative case after *es gibt*.

G See page 175 ➡

Build on language you have learnt at Key Stage 3. You will have talked about different types of accommodation and facilities.

4 Local sights
- Say what the local sights are
- Say what sights you have already seen
- Mention what your favourite sight has been so far and why
- Mention what else you plan on seeing

The sights you mention can be famous but don't have to be. You could mention a particularly nice beach or a very high mountain. You can draw on language from the Home and local area topic for describing places.

You have the opportunity to use an impressive mix of tenses here – the present tense (to say what sights there are), the perfect and imperfect tenses (to say what sights you have already seen) and the future tense (to say what you plan on seeing).

Present tense: **G** See page 180 ➡

Perfect tense: **G** See page 182 ➡

Imperfect tense: **G** See page 182 ➡

Future tense: **G** See page 184 ➡

5 Holiday activities
- Say what you are currently doing
- Mention what you have done already
- Say what you are going to do tomorrow
- Suggest something for your friends or family to do if they came to the area

This is another great opportunity for you to show you can handle present, past and future tenses.

To say what else you can do in the area, you could use *man kann* … Remember that the next verb needs to go to the end of the sentence.

G See page 180 ➡

Here you can draw on vocab you have learnt for the Free time and the media topic (free time activities, shopping) and the Health topic (food, healthy activities).

6 A comparison with past holidays
- Mention another holiday you went on previously
- Say what is better about this holiday
- Mention anything that was better about the last holiday
- Give an overall judgement on which holiday you prefer, stating why

Show that you can use some more advanced adjectives to give an opinion and describe your holiday. Ones to add to your list could be *aufregend, anstrengend, erlebnisreich*.

Make sure you know how to use comparative adjectives correctly in order to make your comparisons e.g. *Dieser Urlaub ist **billiger** als der Letzte. Ich habe den letzten Urlaub **besser** gefunden, weil er **erlebnisreicher** war.*

G See page 178 ➡

7 Your future holiday plans
- Say where you would next like to go on holiday
- Give reasons
- Mention what you would like to do on this holiday
- Say where you will stay

You could use *ich möchte* to say what you would like to do, or *ich werde* to say what you are going to do. If you are going to travel with another person, remember to use *wir möchten* and *wir werden*.

möchte: **G** See page 184 ➡

Future tense: **G** See page 184 ➡

Now you should have a complete set of 40 cue words, in seven groups with either five or six words in each.

When you have written your blog, compare it and your cue card with the online sample version – you might find some useful hints to make yours even better.

kerboodle!

2

Teste dich!

1 Fill in the gaps in the following sentence:

Was _____ du gestern gemacht? Ich _____ zuerst ferngesehen und dann _____ meine Eltern und ich zu Abend gegessen.

2 Translate the following sentence into English:

Meine Schwester hat viel in der Stadt eingekauft, aber ich habe nicht genug Geld gehabt.

3 Fill in the gaps in the following sentence:

Meine Freunde und ich _____ in die Stadt gegangen, aber mein Bruder _____ nicht mitgekommen.

4 Write a question which could prompt the following answer:

Ich bin letztes Jahr mit dem Flugzeug nach Italien geflogen.

5 Write a suitable ending for the following sentence:

Mein Taschengeld reicht mir, weil _____.

6 Fill in the gaps in the following sentence:

Er _____ nach Amerika geflogen und _____ viel eingekauft, obwohl er nicht genug Geld _____.

7 Translate the following sentence into German:

I tried on the new trousers but I am not allowed to keep them because they are too expensive.

8 What is another way of saying *Es passt mir nicht*?

9 Put the words and punctuation mark below into the correct order to make a sentence:

mit dem Auto / fährt / Ute / nächstes Jahr / . / nach Italien

10 Fill in the gaps in the following sentence:

Meine Eltern hatten kein Handy _____ sie Teenager waren, aber _____ Kinder heute Geburtstag haben, wollen sie oft ein neues Handy.

kerboodle!

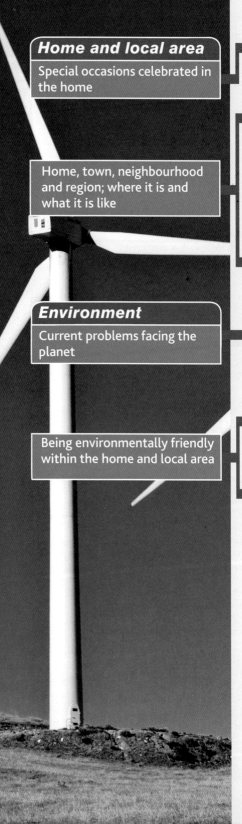

3 Home and Environment

Home and local area

■ **Rooms in the house, items of furniture**

1a 📖🎧 Read the descriptions below, then note down the German room being referred to in each case.

Beispiel: **a** das Wohnzimmer

a In diesem Zimmer gibt es bequeme Sessel und ein altes Sofa.

b Hier haben wir einen kleinen Kleiderschrank neben dem Fenster. Es gibt auch eine Kommode.

c Hier steht die Spülmaschine und daneben steht der Herd.

d Die Badewanne hier ist sehr modern, aber leider gibt es keine Dusche.

e Es gibt viele Bücher in diesem kleinen Zimmer und auch einen Computer.

f Hier hänge ich meinen Mantel auf, wenn ich nach Hause komme.

g Ein Tisch und vier Stühle sind in diesem Zimmer.

1b 💬 Work in pairs. Take it in turns to talk about different rooms in your house, using the prompts below to help you. Include adjectives if you are confident about adding the endings.

Beispiel: **a** Mein Haus hat ein kleines Badezimmer. Im Badezimmer gibt es eine weiße Toilette und einen kleinen Spiegel.

a Badezimmer / Toilette / Spiegel

b Küche / Herd / Spülmaschine

c Wohnzimmer / Fernseher / Sofa

d Esszimmer / Tisch / Stühle

2a 📖🎧 Read Lisa's email. What does she have in her room? Note down the items, then draw a plan of the room.

2b ✏️ Using Lisa's email as a model, write a description of your own bedroom.

> ### Grammatik   *Seite 175 & 177*
>
> **In diesem Zimmer gibt es …**
>
> Remember that you use the accusative case after *es gibt*:
>
> *Es gibt **einen Herd**.*
>
> You should also note that when you are describing where things are, you use the dative case after *in*. For the definite article, *der* and *das* change to *dem*, and *die* changes to *der*:
>
> *In **der Küche** gibt es einen Herd.*
>
> To find out more about the dative case after *in*.

> ### Vokabeln
>
> | | |
> |---|---|
> | *das Arbeitszimmer* | study |
> | *der Flur* | hall |
> | *das Bücherregal* | bookcase |
> | *das Kopfkissen* | pillow |
> | *der Herd* | cooker |
> | *der Sessel* | armchair |
> | *die Badewanne* | bathtub |
> | *die Spülmaschine* | dishwasher |

◄ | ◯ | 🔍 Suche

Startseite | Index | Hilfe | Kontakt | Textversion

Mein Schlafzimmer ist klein, aber sehr schön. Die Wände sind rosa und ich habe bunte Vorhänge. Es gibt natürlich ein Einzelbett und einen Kleiderschrank. Ich möchte einen Computer hier im Zimmer haben, aber das geht im Moment nicht. Ich habe Bilder von meiner Lieblingsgruppe an der Wand. Auf meinem Nachttisch steht eine Lampe. In der Ecke gibt es ein Radio, aber keinen Fernseher. Ich habe ein paar Bücher, aber leider kein Bücherregal. Meine Oma hat mir neulich ein paar Kopfkissen gekauft. Sie sind auf meinem Bett.

Lisa

Lisa

House types and locations

Mein Haus ist ein Doppelhaus am Stadtrand. Das gefällt mir nicht so gut, weil meine Freunde in der Stadtmitte wohnen. Das Haus ist groß, hat aber leider keinen Garten. Wenn ich viel Geld hätte, würde ich in einer großen Wohnung in einer Großstadt wohnen. Es gibt viele Geschäfte, zum Beispiel ein Warenhaus, eine Buchhandlung und eine Konditorei, aber mein Lieblingsgeschäft ist ein Modegeschäft. Meine Eltern möchten ein kleines Haus auf dem Lande, aber ich finde das zu langweilig.

Anke

1a 📖🎧 Read Anke's description of her home then read the following statements. For each write T (True) or F (False).

a   Ankes Haus ist im Stadtzentrum.

b   Anke wohnt gern dort.

c   Das Haus hat einen Garten.

d   Anke mag Kleidung kaufen.

e   Anke möchte auf dem Lande wohnen.

1b 💬 Work in pairs. Practise asking and answering the following questions.

■   In was für einem Haus wohnst du?

■   Wo liegt das Haus?

■   Wie ist das Haus?

■   Was gibt es in der Nähe?

■   Wo möchtest du wohnen? Warum?

2a 📖🎧 Read Stefan's letter then complete the gaps in the text below, using the words from the box.

Stefan wohnt in einem **a** _____ am **b** _____ . Das Haus ist **c** _____ von einem Wald. Er **d** _____ das Haus besser als die Wohnung, weil die Wohnung zu **e** _____ war. Auch haben ihm die Möbel nicht **f** _____ , weil sie nicht **g** _____ waren. Die Küche ist **h** _____ in diesem Haus. Er ist **i** _____ , dass er sein Zimmer nicht **j** _____ muss.

> Doppelhaus   findet   froh   gefallen   größer
> klein   Meer   modern   nicht weit   teilen

2b ✏️ Write a short piece about where you live, using Anke and Stefan's texts as models. Mention:

■   the type of house you live in

■   how many rooms there are

■   what area it is in

■   what else there is nearby

Mein Haus liegt an der Küste in der Nähe von einem Wald. Es ist ein Doppelhaus mit fünf Zimmern – einem Wohnzimmer, einem Esszimmer und drei mittelgroßen Schlafzimmern. Früher haben wir in einer Wohnung gewohnt, was mir nicht so gut gefallen hat. Die Wohnung war nicht groß genug und die Möbel waren altmodisch, aber hier haben wir sogar eine Waschküche, und die Küche hat Platz für mehr Geräte. Auch habe ich endlich mein eigenes Zimmer.

Stefan

Grammatik Seite 177

Avoiding adjective endings

When an adjective is not used in front of the noun, no ending is needed. If you find it hard to remember the correct endings, this is a useful way of avoiding the problem.

See page 105 ➡

kerboodle!

Home and local area

■ Daily routine

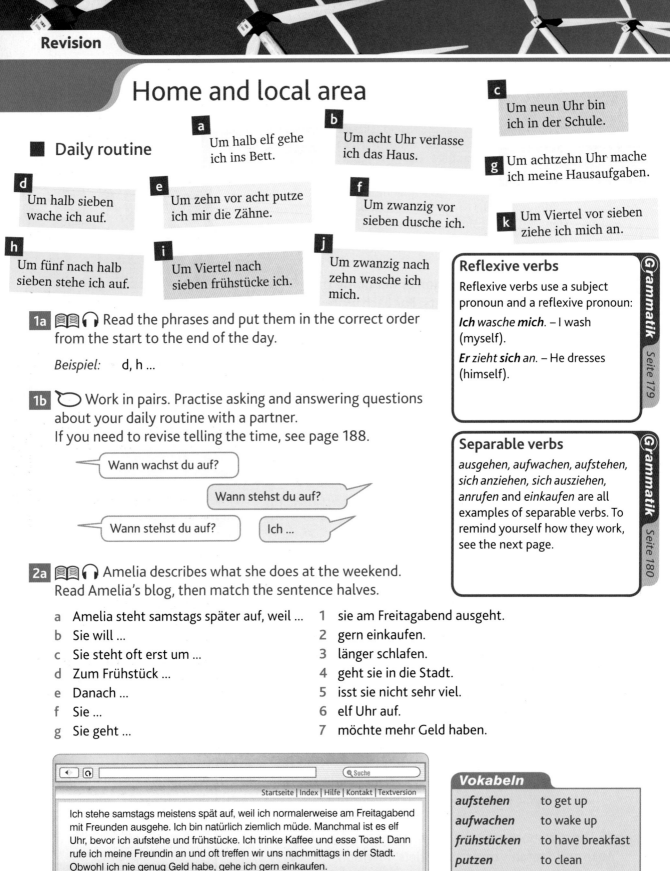

a Um halb elf gehe ich ins Bett.

b Um acht Uhr verlasse ich das Haus.

c Um neun Uhr bin ich in der Schule.

g Um achtzehn Uhr mache ich meine Hausaufgaben.

d Um halb sieben wache ich auf.

e Um zehn vor acht putze ich mir die Zähne.

f Um zwanzig vor sieben dusche ich.

k Um Viertel vor sieben ziehe ich mich an.

h Um fünf nach halb sieben stehe ich auf.

i Um Viertel nach sieben frühstücke ich.

j Um zwanzig nach zehn wasche ich mich.

1a 📖🎧 Read the phrases and put them in the correct order from the start to the end of the day.

Beispiel: d, h …

1b 🗩 Work in pairs. Practise asking and answering questions about your daily routine with a partner.
If you need to revise telling the time, see page 188.

> Wann wachst du auf?

> Wann stehst du auf?

> Wann stehst du auf?
> Ich …

2a 📖🎧 Amelia describes what she does at the weekend. Read Amelia's blog, then match the sentence halves.

a Amelia steht samstags später auf, weil …
b Sie will …
c Sie steht oft erst um …
d Zum Frühstück …
e Danach …
f Sie …
g Sie geht …

1 sie am Freitagabend ausgeht.
2 gern einkaufen.
3 länger schlafen.
4 geht sie in die Stadt.
5 isst sie nicht sehr viel.
6 elf Uhr auf.
7 möchte mehr Geld haben.

Grammatik Seite 179

Reflexive verbs

Reflexive verbs use a subject pronoun and a reflexive pronoun:

Ich wasche mich. – I wash (myself).

Er zieht sich an. – He dresses (himself).

Grammatik Seite 180

Separable verbs

ausgehen, aufwachen, aufstehen, sich anziehen, sich ausziehen, anrufen and *einkaufen* are all examples of separable verbs. To remind yourself how they work, see the next page.

🔊 ⭕ [   ] 🔍 Suche

Startseite | Index | Hilfe | Kontakt | Textversion

Ich stehe samstags meistens spät auf, weil ich normalerweise am Freitagabend mit Freunden ausgehe. Ich bin natürlich ziemlich müde. Manchmal ist es elf Uhr, bevor ich aufstehe und frühstücke. Ich trinke Kaffee und esse Toast. Dann rufe ich meine Freundin an und oft treffen wir uns nachmittags in der Stadt. Obwohl ich nie genug Geld habe, gehe ich gern einkaufen.

Vokabeln

aufstehen	to get up
aufwachen	to wake up
frühstücken	to have breakfast
putzen	to clean
sich anziehen	to get dressed
sich ausziehen	to get undressed
sich waschen	to get washed
verlassen	to leave

2b ✏️ Using Amelia's blog as a model, write an account of your daily routine either on a school day or at the weekend.

Helping at home

> Ich putze die Fenster und manchmal sauge ich Staub. Am Abend mache ich oft das Abendessen, weil meine Mutter arbeiten muss. Auch wasche ich ab. Jeden Tag mache ich auch mein Bett.
> **Jürgen**

> Ich passe auf kleine Kinder auf, um Geld zu verdienen. Zu Hause mache ich auch viel: ich bügel und räume mein Zimmer auf. Abwaschen tue ich aber nie. Ich soll auch im Garten helfen, aber ich habe keine Zeit dafür, deshalb mäht mein Bruder den Rasen.
> **Tina**

1a 📖 🎧 Read what Tina and Jürgen say they do to help at home, then match each picture to the correct name.

Beispiel: a   Jürgen

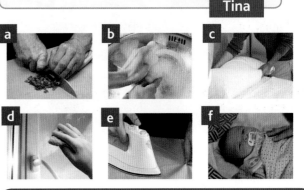

1b 💬 Work in pairs. Take it in turns to ask each other if you do a particular household job. If you don't do the one your partner picks, mention one which you do do.

> Trocknest du

> Nein, aber ich wasche das Auto.

2a 📖 🎧 Read the magazine extract, then answer the questions, giving the name of the correct person each time.

Separable verbs

Separable verbs consist of two bits – the main verb and the separable prefix (usually a preposition). For instance, with *aufräumen*, *auf* is the separable prefix. In the present tense this goes to the end of the sentence:

*Ich räume **auf**.*

In the perfect tense, the separable prefix comes at the start of the past participle:

*Ich habe **auf**geräumt.*

For more practice in using separable verbs,

see page 70 ➡

Grammatik Seite 181

Wir haben letzten Monat unseren Lesern die Frage gestellt: „Was machst du im Haushalt?". Hier sind einige Antworten:

Andreas, Dortmund: „Ich bin immer müde, weil ich auf meine kleine Schwester aufpassen muss. Sie ist süß aber nie still."

Anna, Ulm: „Ich mähe den Rasen. Das ist wenigstens besser als das Auto waschen."

Paul, Bremen: „Normalerweise muss ich abwaschen und abtrocknen, aber im Moment mache ich das nicht, weil ich bald Prüfungen habe."

Michael, München: „Was für eine dumme Frage! Ich habe nie im Haus geholfen und werde einfach nie anfangen, das zu machen."

a   Wer arbeitet gewöhnlich in der Küche?
b   Wer macht gar nichts?
c   Wer macht sehr viel im Haus?
d   Wer findet Gartenarbeit nicht so schlecht?

2b ✏ You decide to write in to the magazine to say what you do to help in the home. Include:

■ Several things you do to help and how often you do them

■ One thing you should do, but do not and why

■ Your opinion on having to help in the home

Vokabeln	
abwaschen	to wash up
abtrocknen	to dry the dishes
aufpassen (auf + accusative)	to look after
aufräumen	to tidy up
bügeln	to iron
den Rasen mähen	to mow the lawn
staubsaugen	to vacuum
das Bett machen	to make the bed

kerboodle!

3.1 Feier mit uns!

Traditionelle Feste

Karneval oder Fasching feiert man meistens im Rheinland und in Süddeutschland. Das beginnt am elften November, aber das große Fest findet vor Ostern statt. Am Rosenmontag gibt es Straßenumzüge und viele Leute gehen verkleidet durch die Straßen.

Zu Ostern isst man viel Schokolade, wie in England. Der Osterhase bringt Eier für kleine Kinder. Oft verstecken die Eltern diese Eier im Garten.

Das Oktoberfest in München ist das größte und vielleicht das bekannteste Volksfest der Welt und die Besucher trinken in den zwei Wochen viel Bier. Auch ohne Bier kann man viel Spaß haben, weil es auch eine Achterbahn und ein Riesenrad gibt. Wenn man Hunger hat, kann man überall Würste und Bretzeln kaufen.

Vor Weihnachten gibt es Weihnachtsmärkte, wo man zum Beispiel Lebkuchen kaufen kann. Weihnachten ist anders als in England: Die Kinder müssen nur bis zum vierundzwanzigsten. Dezember warten, bevor sie ihre Geschenke öffnen können. Am Heiligabend liegen sie schon unter dem Weihnachtsbaum. Viele Leute gehen in die Kirche. Am fünfundzwanzigsten Dezember isst man Gans, Pute oder manchmal auch Fisch.

Silvester ist am einunddreißigsten Dezember und in Deutschland feiert man das oft mit Feuerwerken. Man trinkt auch oft Sekt.

Silvester in Berlin

Tipp

Remember phrases with *man* can be very useful when describing what people in general do e.g. *Zu Weihnachten isst man oft zu viel*.

📖 Completing gap-fill exercises

Strategie

When using words to fill gaps, in addition to understanding the gist, it helps if you can make use of your knowledge of grammar:

a *Ich _____ mit dem Bus nach München.*

b *Er hat keine _____, das Oktoberfest zu besuchen.*

gefahren   gute   Zeit   fahre   das

For (**a**), it is clear you need a verb. As the gap is straight after *ich* it cannot be a past participle, so the answer is *fahre*.

keine is the clue in (**b**). It shows that you need either a feminine or plural noun in the gap, so the answer here is *Zeit*.

1 📖🎧 Copy the sentences and fill in the gaps with one of the words in the boxes.

Beispiel: a Karneval
a Fasching ist ein anderes Wort für _____ .
b Während der Karnevalszeit feiern viele Leute auf den _____ .
c Kinder suchen ihre Ostereier _____ .
d Im Oktober kann man sich in München gut _____ .
e Weihnachten in Deutschland ist _____ wie in England.
f Am 24. Dezember _____ die Kinder Geschenke.
g Man _____ viele Feuerwerke am 31. Dezember.

| draußen | Karneval | hört | bekommen |

| amüsieren | Straßen | nicht |

2 🎧 Listen to the young people (a–g) talking about special occasions. Copy and complete the table, using occasions from the list below. Note down extra details if you can!

Person	Occasion	Enjoy it (✓) or not (✗)
a	National holiday	✓
b		
c		

Christmas Eve   Karneval   Easter   Birthday   Wedding   New Year
Name day   National holiday   Munich beer festival

3a **G** Copy the sentences and fill in the gaps with the correct form of the definite article – *den*, *die* or *das*.

Beispiel: **a** das

a   Ohne _____ Auto kann ich nicht zum Oktoberfest im München fahren.

b   Die größten Bierzelte finden Sie um _____ Ecke.

c   Wir haben ein Schiff für _____ Karneval dekoriert.

d   An Silvester kann die Polizei nichts gegen _____ Alkoholkonsum tun.

e   Der Rosenmontagszug geht langsam durch _____ Stadt.

3b **G** Now add the correct accusative preposition as well as the correct article.

a   Du wirst die Schokoladeneier vielleicht _____ Baum im Garten finden.

b   Du musst _____ 24. Dezember warten, bevor du deine Geschenke öffnen kannst.

4 💬✏️ Prepare a presentation on a special occasion of your choice. Mention:

■ when the occasion is celebrated

■ what people traditionally do (in your family / country / elsewhere)

■ what people eat and drink

■ whether you like or dislike the occasion, and why

Make notes using the table below to help you, then give your presentation, first to a partner then to the whole class. If you don't mention the name, you can make people guess what it is!

Heiligabend / Diwali / Ramadan / Chanukah	findet	am ____	statt.
	feiert man	im Februar / März …	.
Normalerweise / Bei uns / In England	singen / tanzen / beten / fasten		wir.
	gibt es	einen Umzug / Geschenke / Feuerwerke.	
	essen wir	Truthahn / Gans / Schokolade / Wurst.	
	trinken wir	Sprudel / Wein / Bier / Tee.	
Es gefällt mir (nicht),	weil … [verb to the end]		
	da / denn … [verb to the end]		

Grammatik *Seite 176*

Prepositions taking the accusative

Prepositions are small words, such as *in* and *für*, usually placed before nouns. Few prepositions are always followed by the accusative, but you do need to know the main ones.

bis	'until', 'as far as'
durch	'through'
für	'for'
gegen	'against'
ohne	'without'
um	'around'

It is important to remember that masculine singular articles change after the accusative: *der* → *den* and *ein* → *einen*. If you need a reminder about the accusative case, see page 28.

Also learn about or revise reflexive verbs.

See page 108 ➡️

---

kerboodle!

3.2 Bei mir, bei dir

Lernziele

Comparing homes

Using prepositions taking the dative case

Using knowledge of social and cultural differences

Wie sieht die ideale Wohnung aus?

Unsere Reporterin hat Folgendes für unsere Leser herausgefunden.

- Genug Zimmer! Die Kinder wollen ein eigenes Schlafzimmer mit Platz für einen Fernseher, einen Computer, ein Bücherregal usw. Die Farbe möchten sie natürlich selbst wählen.
- Eine moderne Küche mit einer Mikrowelle, einem Tiefkühlschrank und einer Spülmaschine.
- Ein ruhiges Wohnzimmer, wo man sich nach der Arbeit entspannen kann. Das Sofa ist vielleicht aus Leder und es gibt auch bequeme Sessel, einen Farbfernseher und noch viel mehr.
- Ein Balkon, wo man sich sonnen kann, und hoffentlich auch eine Grünanlage oder einen Spielplatz in der Nähe. Wenn man Glück hat vielleicht auch Gartenbenutzung (leider nicht möglich, wenn man in einem Wohnblock wohnt).
- Das Badezimmer soll eine Dusche haben und es ist besser, wenn die Toilette nicht im Badezimmer ist, besonders bei einer großen Familie. Im Moment sind Farben wie türkis, weiß und lila modisch.

Und das ideale Haus?

Natürlich hat es auch einen schönen Garten, eine Sonnenterrasse und vielleicht auch einen Wintergarten. Es gibt wahrscheinlich auch einen Dachboden und einen Keller.

1a 📖 🎧 Read the article and find the German words to match the English ones below.

Beispiel: a   Platz für einen Fernseher

a   room for a TV
b   dishwasher
c   where you can sunbathe
d   a play area nearby
e   use of the garden
f   colours such as turquoise
g   an attic

1b 📖 🎧 Look at the article again and decide whether these statements are true (T) or false (F):

Beispiel: a   F

a   Die Kinder haben nichts dagegen, ein Schlafzimmer zu teilen.
b   Die richtige Farbe ist sehr wichtig für sie.
c   Viele Leute möchten aktiv sein, wenn sie abends nach Hause kommen.
d   Gartenbenutzung ist für alle möglich.
e   Eine separate Toilette ist nicht so wichtig für große Familien.
f   Das ideale Haus soll viele Zimmer haben.

> 🎧 **Using knowledge of cultural and social differences** — *Strategie*
>
> It is important to remember that the way of life in other countries is not always the same as in Britain. This is particularly true of housing. Far more Germans, for example, choose to rent a flat (*eine Mietwohnung*), rather than buy one (*eine Eigentumswohnung*) or a house. Being aware of this is useful in various skill areas e.g. when listening to someone from Germany describe their home, it is likely to be a flat (*Wohnung*) as part of a larger house (*Mehrfamilienhaus*) rather than a semi-detached house.

2 🎧 Listen to the young people talking about their homes. Do they like where they live (✓) or not (✗)? Give reasons.

Beispiel: a   Martin, ✓, small but comfortable

a Martin   b Olivia   c Henrik
d Anna   e Michael   f Udo

3 **G** Complete the sentences by using *dem*, *der* or *den*.

Beispiel: a   dem

a   Das Sofa ist gegenüber _____ Fenster.

b   Ich wohne im Moment bei _____ Familie meiner Freundin.

c   Das Haus mit _____ großen Garten ist sehr schön.

d   Was machst du nach _____ Schule?

e   Der Kleiderschrank steht links von _____ Bett.

f   Wir wohnen seit _____ Sommerferien in diesem Haus.

4 🖊️ You have just got back from a visit to Germany and are writing to your German friend about what your home is like and how it is different from your friend's. Mention:

- ▪ your house and what it is like
- ▪ your room and what it is like
- ▪ your friend's house and room (you can make this up – it can be as perfect or horrible as you like!)
- ▪ which you prefer

You will need to use a mix of tenses – past and present!

Prepositions taking the dative

Grammatik   *Seite 176*

Some prepositions are always followed by the dative. If you need a reminder about the dative case, see page 176.

aus	'out of', 'made of'
bei	'at someone's house', 'with'
mit	'with', 'by' (transport)
nach	'after'
seit	'since', 'for' (a length of time)
von	'from', 'by', 'of'
zu	'to'
gegenüber	'opposite' (this preposition often comes after the noun)

You often see shortened versions of *bei*, *von* and *zu*: *beim = bei dem*, *vom = von dem*, *zum = zu dem* and *zur = zu der*.

Wie komme ich zur Stadtmitte?

Der Wald liegt nicht weit vom Dorf.

Also learn how to compare things.

See page 108 ➡️

Tipp

When comparing things, phrases such as the following can be useful:

*Bei mir ist die Küche ziemlich klein, **während** bei dir ist sie viel größer.*

'The kitchen at my house is quite small, **whilst** yours is a lot bigger.'

*Mein Haus gefällt mir **besser als** dein Haus, weil es ruhiger ist.*

'I like my house **better than** yours because it's quieter.'

Im Vergleich zu = 'in comparison with'

Remember to use the dative after *zu*!

Ich finde	mein Haus meine Wohnung mein Zimmer	gut, schlecht, okay,	weil es / sie	(zu) groß (zu) klein bequem	ist.
Meiner Meinung nach ist		mein Haus …		(zu) neu (zu) alt wunderschön	.
Ich habe	dein Haus deine Wohnung dein Zimmer	gut schlecht okay	gefunden, weil es / sie	typisch Deutsch / Englisch	ist.
Dein Haus …	hat mir (nicht) gefallen, weil es / sie				ist.

3.3 Meine Gegend, deine Gegend

Lernziele

Comparing neighbourhoods

Using *in* with the dative or accusative

Using grammar to work out meaning

1 🟣 Unscramble the names of these towns in Germany, Austria or Switzerland.

a nBre

c cüZihr

e zgeiLpi

b lrnBei

d tfrnFuakr

f alSzrugb

Beispiel: a *Bern*

Nils

Die Landschaft um mein Dorf herum ist schön, aber die Jugendlichen hier wissen nicht, was sie mit sich anfangen sollen. Das Beste hier ist die Kneipe, aber ich bin noch zu jung, um dorthin zu gehen. Es gibt keine guten öffentlichen Verkehrsmittel und das neue Hallenbad ist immer noch nicht fertig. Die Luft ist aber sehr sauber und man hat die schönste Aussicht auf den See. Der Wald in der Nähe ist auch wunderschön.

Martina

Ich wohne in einer Großstadt im Rheinland. Die Einkaufsmöglichkeiten sind sehr gut, und für sportliche Leute gibt es Tennisplätze, Schwimmbäder und vieles mehr. Erst abends geht es hier richtig los, was ich toll finde! Es gibt so viele Restaurants, Diskos und drei Kinos. Meine Freunde und ich gehen am liebsten am Samstagabend in die Stadt.

Axel

Ich wohne erst seit drei Monaten in dieser Industriestadt und es gibt Vorteile und Nachteile. Die Stadt ist nicht sehr schön und auch ziemlich schmutzig, aber man kann viel unternehmen. Man kann sehr billig mit dem Bus ins Stadtzentrum fahren. Das ist wichtig für mich, da ich im Stadtzentrum arbeite.

> **📖 Using grammar to work out meaning** — *Strategie*
>
> *Man hat die schönste Aussicht auf den See.*
>
> What does the above sentence mean? *See* can mean 'sea' (*die See*) or 'lake' (*der See*). Which is it here?
>
> If you remember that the masculine version (*der*) means 'lake' and that the accusative follows *auf* (*der → den*), then it's clear that the house has a view of the lake.

2 📖 🎧 🌐 Read what these people are saying about where they live, then read the statements below. For each statement, write T (True), F (False), or ? (Not in the Text).

Beispiel: a T

a Nils darf noch nicht in die Kneipe gehen.

b Nils findet es einfach, in die nächste Stadt zu fahren.

c Nils mag die Landschaft.

d Es gibt Geschäfte in Marinas Stadt.

e Marina geht abends gern aus.

f Axel hat schon immer in seiner Stadt gewohnt.

g Er mag seine Stadt.

h Er findet die öffentlichen Verkehrsmittel gut.

Now correct the statements which are false.

> **Using *in* with the dative or accusative** — *Grammatik   Seite 177*
>
> In the reading text, Axel says the following things about where he lives:
>
> *Man kann sehr billig mit dem Bus ins Stadtzentrum fahren.*
>
> *Das ist wichtig für mich, da ich im Stadtzentrum arbeite.*
>
> What do you notice about his use of the preposition *in* when he is talking about the town centre?
>
> In the first sentence, he uses *in* followed by the accusative case (*in das = ins*). This is because there is movement following the preposition (he goes into the town centre). In the second, he uses *in* followed by the dative (*in dem = im*). This is because there is no movement following the preposition (he is already in the town centre).
>
> Also learn about superlative adjectives.
>
> *See page 109* ➡

3 **ⒼＧ** Complete the sentences with *in* + accusative or *in* + dative. Remember to decide whether there is movement or not!

> **Tipp**
> There are some shortened (contracted) versions of *in* + the definite article:
> *in das = ins*
> *in dem = im*

Beispiel: **a**   in dem (im)

- **a**   Ich wohne _____ Haus.
- **b**   Ich darf noch nicht _____ Kneipe gehen.
- **c**   Willst du heute Abend _____ Kino gehen?
- **d**   Das Sofa _____ Wohnzimmer ist sehr alt.
- **e**   Mein Bruder geht lieber _____ Hallenbad schwimmen, aber ich gehe gern _____ Nordsee schwimmen.
- **f**   Treffen wir uns _____ Restaurant?
- **g**   Ich gehe lieber _____ Stadt, aber mein Freund geht lieber _____ Park.
- **h**   Meine Schwester fährt mit dem Bus _____ Stadtzentrum.

4a 🎧 Listen to Christa, Theo, Mary and Heiko talking about what there is to do where they each live. Note down the letters of each thing available in their town. Take care – they will also mention things which aren't there!

Beispiel: Christa a, d …

4b 🎧 Now decide whether each person likes living in their town or village. Add a tick or a cross for each.

5 🗨️ Work in pairs. Practise giving information about where you live. One partner asks questions and the other answers. Then swap roles. Talk about:

- ▦ location (*Wo …?*)
- ▦ the type and size of your town or village (*Was für eine Stadt ist …/ Wie groß ist …?*)
- ▦ what there is to do (*Was gibt es …?*)
- ▦ opinions (*Wie findest du …?*)

Use the table below to help you structure your answers.

Ich wohne in	einem Dorf / einer Stadt / einer Großstadt	im	Norden / Osten / Süden / Westen.
		nördlich / östlich / südlich / westlich	von …
Es Sie	ist	sehr / ziemlich / nicht	groß / klein / langweilig / amüsant.
		größer / kleiner / anders	als …
Dort	gibt es	einen Zoo / eine Wiese / ein Museum / viele Geschäfte.	
	kann man	einkaufen gehen / sich entpannen / spazieren gehen / ins Kino gehen.	

Ein Vorteil Ein Nachteil	der Stadt des Dorfs	ist	der Tourismus.	Das gefällt mir.
			die Ruhe.	Das gefällt mir nicht.
			die Landschaft.	Ich mag ihn / sie / es.
			die Industrie.	Ich hasse ihn / sie / es.
			das Einkaufszentrum.	

3.4 Kommen Sie nach Baden-Württemberg!

Lernziele

Comparing geographical regions

Using adjective endings

Using knowledge from other topic areas

Entdecken Sie Baden-Württemberg!

Baden-Württemberg liegt in Südwestdeutschland und ist das drittgrößte Bundesland mit 10,7 Millionen Einwohnern (fast so viele wie Belgien).

Man kann sich auf das Klima hier verlassen: im Sommer schön warm und meistens sonnig, und im Winter kälter mit Schnee, aber nicht zu viel!

Wer das Bundesland Baden-Württemberg besucht, muss unbedingt Städte wie Freiburg, Tübingen, Ulm und Ravensburg besuchen. Warum diese Städte? Sie sind nicht so groß wie zum Beispiel Stuttgart oder Heidelberg, aber sie bieten trotzdem viel für den Besucher.

Freiburg

Es gibt so viel zu sehen und zu tun. Die Landschaft ist abwechslungsreich: der Bodensee im Süden, die Berge im Schwarzwald, wo man schöne Wanderungen oder Radtouren machen kann, und es gibt auch viel für die Leute, die sich für Geschichte interessieren: In Tübingen kann man das alte Rathaus und das Schloss besuchen. Die Uni dort ist außerdem eine der ältesten in Deutschland.

Natürlich sind die Einkaufsmöglichkeiten auch sehr gut – Kaufhäuser gibt es viele. In Freiburg in der Fußgängerzone gibt es eine Menge Geschäfte und in der alten Marktstraße in Ravensburg kann man, wenn Markt ist, frisches Gemüse und Obst kaufen.

Industrie gibt es auch – zum Beispiel „Ravensburger AG", eine Firma, die Kinderspiele macht. Diese Spiele kann man überall in der Welt kaufen. Jeden Sommer kann man neue Spiele im „größten Spielzimmer der Welt" ausprobieren.

> **Strategie**
>
> 📖 **Recognising familiar words**
>
> If you are careful to learn the vocabulary for each topic really thoroughly as you go along, you are more likely to encounter familiar words in new topics. Where might you have already come across language relating to different regions and countries?

1 📖 🎧 🌐 Read the article about Baden-Württemberg. Which of the sentences below are backed up by the article? Write down the letters of the five that are.

Beispiel: a …

a Tübingen liegt in Baden-Württemberg.

b Das Wetter in dieser Gegend ist nicht besonders gut.

c Ravensburg ist kleiner als Stuttgart.

d Baden-Würtemberg ist so groß wie Belgien.

e Diese Gegend ist gut für Leute, die gern Wanderungen machen.

f Es gibt historische Sehenswürdigkeiten in dieser Gegend.

g Die Einkaufsmöglichkeiten kann man nicht empfehlen.

h Man kann die Kinderspiele spielen, ohne sie zu kaufen.

2 🎧 Listen to these people responding to questions about their region, country or city. Match each person with the correct place from the box. There are more places than people, so be careful! Try also to note down one extra detail each time.

Beispiel: Jessica – South West Germany (weather warmer than in the north)

| Jessica | Lana | Andreas | Johannes | Bernd | Christina | Anna |

| South West Germany | East of England | Northern Scotland | South America | South West England |
| Austria | Munich | Northern Germany | France | South Africa | Switzerland | London |

3 🎧 Peter is talking about life in Switzerland. Listen carefully and answer the questions in English.

a What do most people assume about Switzerland?

b What example does he give to prove that this is not the case?

c What is important for many inhabitants?

d Why do tourists like Switzerland? Give 2 reasons.

e What does Peter think of sport?

f What is his overall opinion of Switzerland?

Grammatik   Seite 177

Using adjective endings

If you use an adjective in front of the thing it describes, you will need to add an ending.

> *Das Rathaus ist alt.*

BUT   *Man kann das alte Rathaus besuchen.*

When using an adjective with the definite article ('the') to describe something, use the following endings:

	masc.	fem.	neut.	pl.
Nom.	*der schöne Park*	*die schöne Stadt*	*das schöne Haus*	*die schönen Blumen*
Acc.	*den schönen Park*	*die schöne Stadt*	*das schöne Haus*	*die schönen Blumen*
Dat.	*dem schönen Park*	*der schönen Stadt*	*dem schönen Haus*	*den schönen Blumen*

You also use these endings with *dieser* and *jeder*. If you get stuck, remember that the endings are either *-e* or *-en*.

Also learn how to use adjective endings after the indefinite article ('a').

See page 109 ➡️

---

4 Ⓖ Add the correct adjective endings to this brochure advertising a German town.

Beispiel: **a** die schönste Stadt

Besuchen Sie **a** die schönst _____ Stadt Süddeutschlands! **b** Das wunderschön _____ Schloss und **c** die mittelalterlich _____ Pauluskirche mit **d** dem hoh _____ Turm sind weltberühmt.

Sie können auch **e** die renoviert _____ Altstadt besuchen. Dort gibt es **f** den alt _____ Brunnen und **g** das historisch _____ Museum.

Im Sommer gibt es **h** das regional _____ Schützenfest und unsere Stadt hat auch **i** die best _____ Geschäfte in **j** der ganz _____ Gegend.

---

5 🖊️ Produce a brochure for German-speakers visiting your home region. Include details on:

■ location

■ climate

■ activities for tourists

> **Tipp**
> Remember to include opinions and justifications – you need to sound convincing!

Use the phrases here to help you.

Kommen Sie nach Besuchen Sie	[meine Gegend] !		
[Meine Gegend]	bietet	viele Geschäfte eine schöne Landschaft	für den Besucher.
Wer [meine Gegend] besucht, muss unbedingt		die schönen Dörfer besichtigen. das alte Rathaus sehen.	
Es gibt auch viel für Leute, die sich für		Geschichte / Musik / Kunst	interessieren.
Wir freuen uns auf Ihren Besuch!			

Home and local area

▪ Umzug in ein neues Haus in Freiburg

Das Bundesland Baden-Württemberg in Süddeutschland ist ein beliebtes Ziel für Touristen aus aller Welt. Jedes Jahr gibt es mehr als 40 Millionen Übernachtungen und der Tourismus ist sehr wichtig für die Einwohner: Mehr als 200 000 Menschen haben Arbeitsplätze, die direkt vom Tourismus abhängig sind.

Nicht nur Touristen kommen nach Baden-Württemberg. Auch würden viele Einwohner die schöne Landschaft, die Kultur, die Feste und das Essen empfehlen. Wir haben mit einer Familie gesprochen, die neulich nach Freiburg umgezogen ist.

Können Sie unseren Lesern sagen, warum Sie umgezogen sind, Herr Biber?

Ja. Wir haben 10 Jahre lang in einem Vorort von Frankfurt gewohnt. Ich habe neulich eine neue Arbeitsstelle hier in Freiburg bekommen und wir mussten deswegen umziehen.

Sie wohnen jetzt in einem Doppelhaus, nicht wahr?

Ja, was uns sehr gefällt. Jetzt wo unsere Kinder älter sind, wollten wir unser eigenes Haus. Die alte Wohnung war im dritten Stock eines modernen Wohnblocks, aber sie war sehr klein für eine Familie.

Wie war der Umzug nach Freiburg?

Sehr anstrengend! Obwohl ich die neue Stelle schon hatte, dauerte es ewig, bevor wir das richtige Haus gefunden hatten. Wir haben uns viele Häuser angesehen, aber oft war der Preis einfach zu hoch oder der Garten zu klein usw.

Was machen Sie im Moment?

Wir räumen auf und fangen an, die Zimmer in Ordnung zu bringen. Leider müssen wir noch vier Wochen warten, bevor unsere neue Küche fertig sein wird. Den Kindern gefällt es gut, Imbisse usw. zu essen oder ins Restaurant zu gehen, aber meine Frau ist damit nicht zufrieden.

Haben Sie Zeit gehabt, die Nachbarn kennenzulernen?

Ja. Sie sind sehr hilfsbereit und recht freundlich. In der alten Wohnung haben wir die Nachbarn kaum gesehen.

Eine letzte Frage. Wie finden Sie die Stadt Freiburg?

Ich bin wirklich froh, dass wir nach Freiburg umgezogen sind, obwohl hier vieles teurer ist.

1a 📖 🎧 Read the article, then read the following sentences. For each sentence write T (true), F (false) or ? (Not in the Text).

a Baden-Württemberg is in Northern Germany.
b Over 200,000 people visit the area every year.
c Herr Biber lived alone in Frankfurt.
d The new house is very large.
e The family is still waiting for their new kitchen.
f Herr Biber prefers Freiburg to Frankfurt.

1b 📖 🎧 Read the article again and answer the following questions in English.

a What does the number 40 million refer to?
b Why did the Biber family move?
c Why was having their own house important?
d How did they find the move? Give one reason to support your answer.
e What is the family busy with at present?
f What is Herr Biber's view of the former neighbours? Give one reason to support your answer.

2a 🎧 Listen to the descriptions of where each person lives. Copy and complete the table, noting down one advantage or disadvantage of each person's location.

Person	Location	Advantage / Disadvantage
Anna	old part of town	advantage – it's quiet
Georg		
Monika		
Erik		
Andrea		
Mark		

2b 🎧 Listen to Max talking about where he lives then answer the following questions in English.

a Give one reason why Max likes Ravensburg.
b In Max's opinion what makes the Rutenfest different?
c Name one of the two festival activities he mentions.
d In what way is the Rutenfest similar to the Munich Oktoberfest?
e How exactly does the festival rate compared to Karneval?

Vokabeln

der Umzug	(house) move
umziehen	to move house
würden ...	would
empfehlen	recommend ...
die Arbeitsstelle	job, post
ansehen	to look at, to view

Grammatik Seite 177

The article on Freiburg uses many grammatical features you have just learnt about. If you are unsure about how these work, why not look them up?

a Adjective endings after the indefinite article

*Ich habe neulich **eine neue Arbeitsstelle** hier in Freiburg bekommen.*

See page 109 ➡

b Adjective endings after the definite article

***Die alte Wohnung** war im dritten Stock eines modernen Wohnblocks.*

See page 105 ➡

c Prepositions taking the dative or accusative cases

*Den Kindern gefällt es gut, **ins Restaurant** zu gehen.*

See page 102 ➡

AQA Examiner's tip

Make sure you can recognise the different tenses, so that you select the right information for your answers. If the perfect tense is being used, there will be two verbs: the auxiliary (*haben* or *sein*) and the past participle, which is normally at the end of the sentence.

Vokabeln

weder ... noch ...	neither ... nor ...
jahrhundertalt	centuries-old
der Schützenzug	parade of riflemen
der Trommler	drummer
trotzdem	nevertheless

(G) Home and local area

1 ✏ Complete the following sentences using one of the reflexive verbs given in the box below.

a Ich _____ _____ auf Weihnachten, weil es so lustig ist.

b Mein Bruder _____ _____ , weil ich seinen Geburtstag vergessen habe.

c _____ _____ , sonst kommen wir zu spät zur Party!

d Jedes Jahr _____ _____ mein Onkel auf dem Oktoberfest.

e Als ich jünger war, ging ich immer auf den Karneval, aber ich kann _____ nicht mehr daran _____ .

f Wenn ich _____ nicht _____ , beginnt der Karneval am 11. November.

> sich ärgern   sich beeilen   sich besaufen (to get drunk)
> sich erinnern   sich freuen   sich irren

2a 💬 With a partner practise comparing your home/home area using both methods explained on the right. Use the pictures below as prompts. Some adjectives are given in the box below, but try thinking of your own!

Beispiel: Mein Garten ist kleiner als dein Garten.
Mein Garten ist nicht so groß wie dein Garten.

der Garten

die Küche

das Badezimmer

das Schlafzimmer

die Stadt

das Dorf

> bunt   gemütlich   groß   klein   ruhig
> schmutzig   schön

2b ✏ Now write up your conversations. Remember to use the correct possessive adjectives (ihr = her, sein = his). Remember to add an extra e to the possesive adjective when the noun is feminine.

Beispiel: Mein Garten ist kleiner als sein/ihr Garten, aber seine/ihre Küche ist schmutziger als meine Küche.

Reflexive verbs (revision)

Grammatik Seite 179

Reflexive verbs use a subject pronoun and a reflexive pronoun:

Ich erinnere **mich**. – I remember (I remind myself).

Usually the reflexive pronoun is accusative. The accusative reflexive pronouns are as follows:

> *ich erinnere **mich***
> *du erinnerst **dich***
> *er/sie/es erinnert **sich***
> *wir erinnern **uns***
> *ihr erinnert **euch***
> *sie erinnern **sich***
> *Sie erinnern **sich***

For dative reflexive pronouns and their use, see **page 180** in the grammar reference section.

Comparing things

Grammatik Seite 178

If you want to make comparisons in German, you can use comparative adjectives. Usually you need to add *–er* to the end of the adjective you are using (as also often happens in English):

> *klein – klein**er** – Mein neues Haus ist kleiner.*
> small – small**er** – My new house is smaller.

Some comparatives add an umlaut:

> *alt – **ä**lter*

Others are irregular:

> *gut – besser*
> *hoch – höher*
> *viel – mehr*

To compare something with something else use the word *als*:

> *Mein neues Haus ist **kleiner als** das alte Haus.*

You can also compare things by saying that something is 'not as … as' – *nicht so … wie*:

> *Das alte Haus ist **nicht so groß wie** mein neues Haus.*

3 🗩✏️ Using comparative and superlative adjectives make sentences comparing the following items. Work in pairs, deciding how the items should compare, then write up your answers.

Beispiel: Das Schlafzimmer ist größer als das Badezimmer, aber das Wohnzimmer ist das größte Zimmer.

a das Zimmer: das Schlafzimmer – das Badezimmer – das Wohnzimmer (groß)

b die Stadt: Bonn – Berlin – Wien (schön)

c das Haus: das Doppelhaus – das Reihenhaus – das Einfamilienhaus (klein)

d das Gebäude: die Kirche – der Dom – das Schloss (alt)

e der Fluss: die Themse – die Donau – der Rhein (lang)

f die Straße: die Poststraße – die Hauptstraße – die Bergstraße (breit)

g der Berg: Ben Nevis – Mont Blanc – der Brocken (hoch)

4 📖 Read what Ralf tells you about his family and his friend, Karl, and pick out the indefinite adjective endings, stating what gender and case they are. If you can recognise them, it will also help you to use them correctly!

Beispiel: einem kleinen Dorf – neuter, dative

Meine Familie wohnt in einem kleinen Dorf. Es liegt nicht weit von einem schönem Wald. In der Nähe gibt es auch einen kleinen Bauernhof – dort wohnt mein bester Freund Karl. Ich habe eine kleine Schwester. Mein älterer Bruder studiert in Berlin. Berlin ist die Hauptstadt Deutschlands und liegt im Norden.

Ralf

Letztes Jahr habe ich mit meinen Eltern einen kurzen Urlaub im Schwarzwald verbracht. Wir haben in einem bequemen Hotel in der Nähe von schönen Wäldern gewohnt. Die Landschaft war sehr hübsch, aber ich möchte lieber in einer großen Stadt wie München wohnen. Karl hat seinen letzten Urlaub im Ausland verbracht. Seine ältere Schwester arbeitet in England und er hat sie in ihrer neuen Wohnung in York besucht. Er hat eine alte Kirche in der Gegend besucht und hat sie sehr interessant gefunden. Leider gab es keine guten Verkehrsverbindungen und er hat eine lange Reise mit dem Auto machen müssen.

Grammatik Seite 178

Superlative adjectives

To say something is the biggest, smallest, best etc., you need to use superlative adjectives. In German you add *–ste* to the adjective:

*klein – klein**st***
*Mein Schlafzimmer ist das klein**ste** Zimmer im Haus.*

If the adjective ends in *–t* or a vowel, then add *–est*:

*neu – neu**est***

Some superlatives are irregular:

gut – beste
hoch – höchste
nah – nächste
viel – meiste

If the superlative is NOT directly in front of a noun the following form is used:

klein – am kleinsten
Mein Schlafzimmer ist am kleinsten.

Grammatik Seite 178

Adjective endings after the indefinite article

After *ein*, possessive adjectives (*mein, dein* etc.) and the negative article *kein*, you need to use a different set of adjective endings from those used after *der/die/das*.

The endings depend on gender (masc., fem., neut.), case (nominative, accusative, dative) and also whether you are referring to the singular or the plural. Remember that the dative and plural endings are all *–en*.

	masc.	fem.	neut.	pl.
nom.	*–er*	*–e*	*–es*	*–en*
acc.	*–en*	*–e*	*–es*	*–en*
dat.	*–en*	*–en*	*–en*	*–en*

*Ich habe ein rot**es** Sofa.* – accusative, neuter, singular

*Wir wohnen in einer klein**en** Stadt.* – dative, feminine, singular

For general revision of gender and cases,

see page 174–176 ➡️

(V) Home and local area

Feier mit uns! ➡ *Seite 98–99*

die	Achterbahn	rollercoaster
	amüsieren (sich)	to enjoy (oneself)
der	Baum	tree
	besuchen	to visit
	beten	to pray
das	Bier	beer
	erlauben	to allow
der	Fasching	a traditional German celebration
	fasten	to fast
	feiern	to celebrate
der	Feiertag	holiday (one day)
das	Fest	festival, celebration
das	Feuerwerk	firework
die	Gans	goose
der	Geburtstag	birthday
das	Geschenk	present
der	Heiligabend	Christmas Eve
	heutzutage	these days
die	Hochzeit	wedding
der	Karneval	carnival (traditional German celebration between Epiphany and Ash Wednesday)
das	Kostüm	costume
	langweilig	boring
	mitmachen	to join in
	München	Munich
das	Oktoberfest	Munich beer festival in October
	Ostern	Easter
die	Pute	turkey
der	Rhein	Rhine
das	Riesenrad	big wheel
	Rosenmontag	Monday before Ash Wednesday

der	Sekt	sparkling wine, champagne
	Silvester	New Year's Eve
	stattfinden	to take place
	suchen	to look for
die	Tradition	tradition
	typisch	typical
der	Umzug	parade
	verkleidet	dressed-up, disguised
	Weihnachten	Christmas
der	Weihnachtsmarkt	Christmas market
die	Wurst	sausage

Bei mir, bei dir ➡ *Seite 100–101*

der	Abstellraum	storeroom
das	Arbeitszimmer	study
	aussehen	to look like
das	Badezimmer	bathroom
der	Balkon	balcony
	bequem	comfortable
das	Bücherregal	bookcase
der	Dachboden	attic
die	Dusche	shower
das	Einfamilienhaus	detached house
die	Farbe	colour
der	Fernseher	TV set
der	Garten	garden
die	Gartenbenutzung	use of a garden
	geräumig	roomy
die	Grünanlage	green space / area
das	Haus	house
	herausfinden	to find out
der	Keller	cellar
die	Küche	kitchen
das	Leder	leather
das	Mehrfamilienhaus	house for several families
die	Mikrowelle	microwave oven

	neu	new
der	Platz	space, room
	prima	great
das	Reihenhaus	terrace house
	ruhig	calm, peaceful
das	Schlafzimmer	bedroom
der	Sessel	armchair
die	Sonnenterrasse	sun terrace / deck
der	Spielplatz	playground
die	Spülmaschine	dishwasher
der	Tiefkühlschrank	freezer
die	Toilette	toilet
	türkis	turquoise
	umziehen	to move house
	wählen	to choose
die	Waschküche	laundry room
	wichtig	important
der	Wohnblock	block of flats
	wohnen	to live (in a particular place)
die	Wohnung	flat
das	Wohnzimmer	living room
das	Zimmer	room

Meine Gegend, deine Gegend ➡ *Seite 102–103*

	amüsant	fun
die	Aussicht	view
das	Dorf	village
die	Fußgängerzone	pedestrian zone
die	Großstadt	city
die	Industrie	industry
das	Kino	cinema
die	Kneipe	pub
die	Landschaft	landscape
	losgehen	to get going, to get started
der	Marktplatz	market place, market square
	möglich	possible
das	Museum	museum
	nächster/e/es	nearest, next

der	Nachteil	disadvantage
	öffentliche Verkehrsmittel (pl)	public transport
das	Restaurant	restaurant
das	Sportzentrum	sports centre
die	Stadt	town
das	Theater	theatre
der	Tourist	tourist
der	Verkehr	traffic
der	Vorteil	advantage
der	Wald	forest, wood

Kommen Sie nach Baden-Württemberg! ➡
Seite 103–104

	abwechslungsreich	varied
	bieten	to offer
der	Brunnen	fountain, well
der	Einwohner	inhabitant
	empfehlen	to recommend
	entdecken	to discover
die	Firma	company
	freuen (sich auf etwas)	to look forward to something
die	Gegend	area
die	Geschichte	history
das	Klima	climate
	liegen	to be situated in
die	Menge	a lot, plenty
das	Rathaus	town hall
das	Schloss	castle
der	Turm	tower
	verlassen (sich auf etwas)	to rely on something
	verlassen	to leave
	wandern	to hike, to go on walks

Umweltfreundlich oder umweltfeindlich?

1 **V** Look at the vocabulary items below and decide whether they are good or bad for the environment, then put them under the correct heading.

Gut für die Umwelt	Schlecht für die Umwelt

Flugzeug Abgase recyceln Fahrrad zu Fuß gehen

Energiesparlampen Auto Solarenergie FCKWs wegwerfen

Sind wir umweltfreundlich oder umweltfeindlich?

Die Schüler und Schülerinnen des Schiller-Gymnasiums haben neulich eine Umfrage gemacht und hier sind die Ergebnisse.

86% trennen den Müll.

75% würden mit dem Zug fahren, wenn es billiger wäre.

70% schalten Geräte nur ein, wenn man sie braucht.

62% haben zum Beispiel eine Dose auf der Straße weggeworfen.

55% glauben, dass Abgase nicht so umweltfeindlich wie saurer Regen sind.

40% wollen mehr machen, haben aber nicht genug Zeit.

33% benutzen umweltfreundliches Papier.

21% haben in letzter Zeit Energiesparlampen gekauft.

14% sind der Meinung, dass Spraydosen schlechter als Plastiktüten für die Umwelt sind.

Weniger als 10% sparen Wasser.

2 📖📖 🎧 Look at the results of the survey on the environment, and write down the correct percentage for each of the statements.

Beispiel: **a** Less than 10%

a Save water.

b Think that plastic bags harm the environment less than aerosols.

c Have recently bought energy-saving light bulbs.

d Use recycled paper.

e Think that acid rain is more of a problem than exhaust fumes.

f Admit to having dropped litter rather than using a bin.

g Always switch off electrical appliances.

h Sort their rubbish.

i Would use public transport if it was not so expensive.

j Are prevented from doing more because they are too busy.

3 🎧 Listen to these people talking about the environment. For each person, find a corresponding picture. Try to add any extra details.

Beispiel: Johannes, e + better for the environment

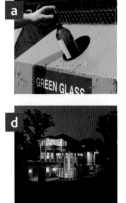
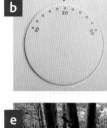

Grammatik   Seite 179

Using qualifiers

Certain words can be used to qualify what you are saying or writing. Although often short words, they can change meanings. Here are some of the most common:

sehr	'very'
ziemlich	'fairly', 'quite'
zu	'too'
ein bisschen	'a little' / 'a bit'
fast	'almost', 'nearly'
oft	'often'
nie	'never'

Die Umwelt ist mir ziemlich wichtig. – 'The environment is quite important to me.'

Ich fahre selten mit dem Auto in die Stadt. – 'I rarely travel by car to town.'

Also learn about prepositions taking the genetive.   *See page 120* ➡️

4a Ⓖ Find the qualifier(s) in these sentences and write down the meaning of each.

Beispiel: a   immer – always

- a   Meine Familie fliegt immer mit dem Flugzeug in den Urlaub.
- b   Am Wochenende bringe ich manchmal Flaschen zum Container.
- c   Seit letztem Monat mache ich ziemlich viel für die Umwelt.
- d   Meine Schwester ist zu faul, zu Fuß zu gehen.
- e   Ich lasse den Fernseher fast nie auf Stand-by.
- f   Müll trennen ist sehr umweltfreundlich.

4b Ⓖ Now translate the sentences into English.

5 💭 ✏️ 🌐 Produce your own survey on how environmentally friendly your class is. You can use the reading survey as a basis for the questions you ask or make up your own. Once you have completed the survey, you can present your results.

Strategie

💬 Making what you say and write more expressive

There are several ways in which you can do this:

Using qualifiers:

Ich bin sehr umweltfreundlich. (see above)

Varying the adjectives you use:

Das finde ich interessant / lustig /amüsant.

Using comparatives or superlatives:

Recyceln ist mir am wichtigsten. (See p.109)

Varying opinion phrases. (see p.133)

Tipp

You can also ask people how long they've been doing things, using *seit* + the dative. Remember that you'll need to use the present tense!

Seit wie lange recycelst du Papier?

'For how long <u>have you been recycling</u> paper?'

Ich recycle Papier seit drei Jahren.

'<u>I have been recycling</u> paper for three years.'

Bist du umweltfreundlich?

Ja, ich bin		sehr / ziemlich / wirklich	umweltfreundlich.
Nein, ich bin	gar nicht / kaum / überhaupt nicht		umweltfreundlich.

Trennst du den Müll? / Fährst du mit öffentlichen Verkehrsmitteln? / Sammelst du Altpapier?

Ja, ich trenne / fahre / sammle	immer / oft / normalerweise		den Müll / mit dem Zug / Altpapier.
Nein, ich trenne		nie / niemals / selten	den Müll.

3.6 Unsere Welt, unsere Umwelt

1 **V** Match the problem to the photo.

Beispiel: 1 c

a Spraydosen

b Müll

c Aussterben von Tieren

d Waldsterben

e Luftverschmutzung

Thema Umwelt

Stefan

„Für mich ist das Thema sehr wichtig, weil ich mein Bestes tun will, um die Umwelt zu retten. Ich interessiere mich sehr für Tiere und hier in Deutschland sind einige Tiere vom Aussterben bedroht, z. B. Fische und Vögel. Die Menschen sind schuld daran, weil wir zu viel Lärm machen und die Vögel können sich nicht mehr in der Nähe von Straßen zwitschern hören. Es gibt auch weniger Wohnraum wie Wälder, Buschland und Wasser für viele Tierarten. Ich möchte mehr Naturschutzgebiete sehen, um die Tiere zu retten. Auch sollten wir alle umweltfreundliche Produkte kaufen und Energie sparen."

Gisela

„Ich finde die Luftverschmutzung am schlimmsten. Ich wohne auf dem Land, aber ich sehe jeden Tag, wie wir die Luft verschmutzen: Autos mit Kohlenmonoxid und anderen Abgasen, und FCKWs aus Spraydosen, verpesten die Luft. Es gibt nicht genug alternative Energiequellen wie Wind und Sonne und wir produzieren zu viel Müll. Öl, Gas und Kohlendioxid fördern den Treibhauseffekt und ich habe Angst, dass es bald zu spät sein wird – die Umweltverschmutzung ist wahrscheinlich schon zu weit fortgeschritten."

2 📖 🎧 Read Stefan's and Gisela's views on environmental issues, then answer the questions in English.

a How important does Stefan feel environmental issues are?

b Which problem does he then go on to talk about?

c In his view, how are humans to blame?

d How would he try to solve the problem?

e Why might it be surprising that Gisela talks about air pollution?

f Name two things that she feels contribute most to the problem.

g Why does she mention oil and gas?

h What is her main fear?

3 🎧 Listen to these young people talking about environmental problems. Fill in the gaps with the words from the box.

Beispiel: a ärgert

Bruno a _____ sich über die Bauern, weil sie zu viele b _____ benutzen. Sie sollten c _____ Produkte verwenden.

Jasmin ist sicher, dass Sonnenbrand durch ultraviolette d _____ verursacht wird.

Ottos Brieffreund wohnt auf dem Land. Die Fische sind wegen Wasserverschmutzung oder e _____ gestorben.

Thomas wohnt in der Nähe von einem f _____ . Das g _____ die Luft und das Wasser.

Im Schwarzwald sterben Bäume durch h _____ Regen.

| ärgert natürliche Atomkraftwerk sauren |
| Pestizide Biomüll Strahlen verschmutzt |

4 **ⓖ** Fill in the gaps using the correct imperative form of the verb given in brackets.

Beispiel: a Fahren Sie

a (Fahren) nicht so schnell, Frau Becker!

b Verena, (bringen) die Flaschen zum Container!

c Martin und Anna, (machen) die Lichter aus!

d (Kaufen) frisches Obst, meine Damen und Herren!

e (Sparen) mehr Wasser, Vati!

f (Wegwerfen) nicht so viel Müll, Herr Biber!

5 🖊 🌐 Produce a poster on an environmental issue that interests you. The poster should include the problem and some slogans using the imperative with either *du*, *ihr* or *Sie*.

SO RETTEN WIR DAS KLIMA

I ❤🌐

MACH MIT bei der Energie [R]evolution!

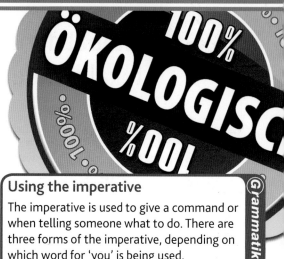

100% ÖKOLOGISC

Grammatik *Seite 185*

Using the imperative

The imperative is used to give a command or when telling someone what to do. There are three forms of the imperative, depending on which word for 'you' is being used.

Talking to an adult or a group of people you don't know very well, you use the *Sie* form of the verb:

Machen Sie das Licht aus!

Talking to someone you know or someone your age, you use the *du* form of the verb without the pronoun and *–st* ending:

Mach das Licht aus!

Talking to a group of people you know you use the *ihr* form of the verb without the pronoun:

Macht das Licht aus!

Also revise cases and articles.

See page 120 ➡

Tipp

Remember that the prefix of a separable verb still goes to the end of the sentence:

Dreh die Heizung herunter!

🖊 **Making German posters**   **Strategie**

Making and displaying posters can help you to remember important expressions but take care – sometimes producing a little language can be as hard as producing a lot, especially if you want it to be punchy! Decide on what your slogan will be and make sure the language is accurate before you finalise your work of art!

Rettet / Retten Sie	die Umwelt!
Spart / Sparen Sie	Wasser!
Trennt / Trennen Sie	Müll!
Macht / Machen Sie	mit!

kerboodle!

Global denken, lokal handeln

UMWELTAKTION: Wie eine Stadt umweltfreundlicher geworden ist!

Sauberstadt hat beschlossen, umweltfreundlicher zu werden. Warum? „Weil die Einwohner das so wollen", sagt der Bürgermeister Herr Brinkmann.

Vor ein paar Jahren gab es viele Probleme hier: Abfall auf den Straßen, Staus auf der Umgehungsstraße, keine Radwege und nicht genug Recyclingcontainer. Viele Leute wollten nicht in die Stadtmitte fahren, weil es nicht genug Parkplätze gab. Die Geschäfte waren oft fast leer und Arbeitslosigkeit war auch ein Problem.

Die meisten Einwohner waren überhaupt nicht umweltbewußt: Sie trennten ihren Müll nicht, kauften viele Produkte in Verpackungen, Einwegflaschen und benutzten immer Plastiktüten. Die Luft in der Stadt wurde durch die Industrie verpestet und es gab keine Fische im Fluss am Stadtrand, da er total verschmutzt war. In den Schulen interessierte sich fast niemand für die Umwelt, und man sah nur wenig Abfalleimer.

Und jetzt? Was hat sich geändert?

Die Stadtmitte wird zu einer Fußgängerzone und die Einwohner sind total dafür. Bei schönem Wetter kann man draußen vor dem Café sitzen. Dieses Jahr wird ein „Park und Ride" gebaut und Kinder und ältere Leute werden zum halben Preis fahren können. Die Geschäfte werden bald mehr Kunden haben, die Straßen werden sicherer für alte Leute und Kinder, und es wird auch ruhiger. In den Schulen sieht man keine Plastikbecher mehr, man macht die Fenster zu und dreht die Heizung herunter, um Energie zu sparen. Eine Bürgerinitiative hat dafür gesorgt, dass es wieder Fische im Fluss gibt.

Vorher

Nachher

1 📖 🎧 🔊 Find the German for the following words or phrases in the text. Be careful, as you may have to alter things such as the word order.

Beispiel: a beschlossen

a decided

b the residents want it that way

c a few years ago

d there weren't enough car parks

e not at all

f separated

g non-refundable bottles

h completely in favour

i safer for children

j you don't see any plastic cups

k a community action group

2 🎥 These people are being interviewed for the local news about the environment in their area. Watch and listen carefully, then answer the questions in English.

Beispiel: a   He thinks everyone should do something

a   What is Jens' attitude towards the environment?
b   What does his family do?
c   What has been done in his village?
d   What is Barbara's opinion of her fellow students' attitude towards the environment?
e   Name two things the 'Greenteams' do in Thomas' town.
f   Why is Thomas in favour of these teams?
g   What would a lot of people in Anke's area like?
h   What is her mother's view and why?

3 Ⓖ Decide whether these sentences need *zu* to make them correct and write out the correct version if they do.

Beispiel: a   Yes. Er hat versucht, Energie zu sparen.

a   Er hat versucht, Energie sparen.
b   Ich will mit dem Bus fahren.
c   Mein Bruder vergisst immer, das Licht ausmachen.
d   Meine Stadt könnte „Park und Rides" einführen.
e   Wir fangen an, umweltfreundlicher sein.
f   Ich hoffe, in der Zukunft nach Amerika fahren.
g   Die Einwohner möchten mehr Radwege.

4 🗨️ Work in pairs: one partner asks the questions about local environmental issues and the other answers. Then swap roles. Include the following questions:

▪️ Was für Probleme gibt es bei dir / in deiner Stadt / in deinem Dorf?

▪️ Was hat man schon für die Umwelt gemacht?

▪️ Was könnte man noch machen?

Grammatik   *Seite 185*

Verbs with *zu*

Some verbs require you to use *zu* + the infinitive of the second verb that follows. The main ones you are likely to need are *versuchen, beschließen, hoffen, beginnen, anfangen, vergessen* and *helfen.*

The sentence can be divided into 2 parts:

Part 1, where you use one of the above verbs followed by a comma;

Part 2, where you need *zu* and the infinitive, which comes at the end.

Sauberstadt hat beschlossen, umweltfreundlicher zu werden.

With a separable verb the *zu* goes in the middle of the infinitive, after the prefix.

Meine Stadt hat neulich begonnen, billigere Busfahrkarten anzubieten.

Also revise the future tense with *werden.*

See page 121 ➡️

Tipp

Remember *zu* is not needed with modals!
Ich versuche, umweltfreundlicher zu werden.
BUT
Ich möchte umweltfreundlicher werden.

Hier / In meiner Stadt / Bei mir	gibt es		zu viel Lärm / nicht genug Busse / Luftverschmutzung.
Man hat (schon)	Recyclingcontainers aufgestellt / Bäume gepflanzt / den Fluss gereinigt.		
Ich versuche	immer, / oft, / täglich,		Müll zu trennen / Altpapier zu benutzen / die Heizung herunterzudrehen.
In der Zukunft könnte man	eine Fußgängerzone bauen / einen autofreien Tag einführen / Umweltaktivitäten für Kinder organisieren.		

Environment

■ Umwelt in Gefahr

Wir haben mit vier Experten gesprochen. Hier sind ihre Meinungen über unsere Umwelt heute.

Zoologin, Frau Meyer

Heutzutage gibt es zwischen zehn und hundert Millionen verschiedene Arten auf der Erde. Früher gab es viel mehr – etwa 99% aller Arten sind schon ausgestorben. Was ist passiert? Vielleicht eine Katastrophe wie eine Supernova? Viele Leute sind der Meinung, dass saurer Regen, ultraviolette Strahlen, Biomüll, Schwefeldioxid, FCKWs und Insektizide dafür verantwortlich sind: aber wer produziert z.B. Insektizide und Biomüll? Wir Menschen!

Wissenschaftler, Herr Dirks

Das Klima hat sich in den letzten Jahren verändert und hat den Treibhauseffekt verursacht – die Temperatur ist seit Beginn der Industrialisierung um 1 Grad gestiegen und seit 1980 hat sich dieser Prozess noch beschleunigt. Man kann in den nächsten fünfzig Jahren mit einem weiteren Anstieg der Temperatur rechnen. Es regnet öfter und der Meeresspiegel steigt jedes Jahr.

Bäuerin, Frau Haag

Bald wird man in Ländern wie Deutschland, Dänemark und Schottland exotische Früchte und Gemüse pflanzen können. Einerseits ist das ein Vorteil, andererseits ein Nachteil, weil andere Pflanzen wegen der Hitze nicht mehr wachsen werden.

Umweltschützer, Herr Marschner

Saurer Regen macht die Wälder krank, wegen Kohlendioxid aus Auspuffgasen wird die Erde wärmer und unser Trinkwasser wird durch Umweltverschmutzung gefährdet. Wir fahren überall mit dem Auto hin, fliegen ins Ausland, kaufen immer mehr elektrische Produkte und werfen zu viel weg, statt unseren Müll zu trennen oder zu recyceln.

Aus Alt mach Neu! Kauf Taschenrechner mit Solarzellen! Verwende nur Flaschen, die man recyceln kann! Die Heizung nicht voll aufdrehen – trag lieber einen warmen Pulli!

1a 📖🎧 Read the article, then read the following sentences. For each sentence write T (true), F (false) or ? (Not in the Text).

a The first expert is a zoologist.
b A natural catastrophe killed lots of animal species.
c Climate change is a recent occurrence.
d It will get even warmer in the next half century.
e Drinking water is not in danger.
f The environmentalist believes we are now doing enough recycling.

1b 📖🎧 Read the article again and answer the following questions in English.

a Apart from insecticides, what are three of the other main causes of the problem raised by the zoologist?
b Other than the rise in temperature, what are two other effects of the changing climate?
c How does the farmer feel about being able to grow exotic fruits in Northern Europe?
d What exactly does the environmentalist think is the main cause of the earth warming up?
e What is the environmentalist's overall advice? Give one specific example he mentions.
f What impression do the experts give overall of the environment today?

2a 🎧 Listen to the different pieces of advice. For each, note down the letter of the matching picture.

2b 🎧 Listen to the radio item on saving the environment and answer the following questions in English.

a What are the benefits of solar energy, according to the speaker?
b What is of the greatest importance to him? Give one reason why.
c Why does he think his ideas might not be popular?
d Give three suggested alternatives to using cars.
e Who does the speaker say can join in with saving the environment?

Vokabeln

die Art	species
der Biomüll	organic waste
das Schwefeldioxid	sulphur dioxide
der Anstieg	rise
der Meeresspiegel	sea level
das Kohlendioxid	carbon dioxide
aufdrehen	to turn up

AQA *Examiner's tip*

When answering questions in English, make sure you give all of the detail required. If the questions contain words such as 'attitude', 'think of' and 'feel about', you are being asked to draw a conclusion, so do not just state facts.

Grammatik Seite 180

In the reading and listening material you will have found examples of the following features. Can you find more examples of each?

a The imperative
Trag lieber einen warmen Pulli!
See page 115 ➡

b Comparative adjectives
Wegen des Anstiegs von Kohlendioxid wird die Erde wärmer.
See page 108 ➡

c Verbs with 'zu'
Versuchen Sie, eine Alternative zu Spraydosen zu finden.
See page 117 ➡

Vokabeln

die Pappe	cardboard
kaum vorstellbar	barely imaginable
mitmachen	to join in

kerboodle!

G Environment

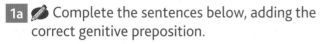

1a ✏ Complete the sentences below, adding the correct genitive preposition.

Beispiel: **a** Trotz

a _____ des starken Verkehrs ist die Luft im Stadtzentrum nicht so schmutzig.

b _____ den hohen Preisen fahren wir nie mit dem Zug.

c Wenn ich mit dem Rad zur Schule fahre, komme ich _____ fünfzehn Minuten an.

d _____ der Stadt ist die Natur wunderschön.

1b 📖 ✏ Complete the following texts by adding the correct definite articles in the genitive case.

Beispiel: **a** der

Ich wohne außerhalb a) _____ Stadt und bin auch umweltfreundlich. Deswegen fahre ich mit dem Bus zur Arbeit. Während b) _____ Reise lese ich. Trotz c) _____ schlechten Wetters im Winter geht mein Bruder zu Fuß zur Schule. Das dauert aber länger.

Karl

Trotz d) _____ kalten Wetters während e) _____ Winters verbrauche ich nicht viel Energie, weil ich warme Kleidung trage, anstatt die Heizung einzuschalten. Innerhalb f) _____ letzten paar Jahre habe ich dadurch viel Geld gespart.

Anna

2a ✏ Choose the correct form of the definite article to complete the following sentences. The gender of each noun is supplied in brackets. In each case state which case is being used.

Beispiel: **a** der   nominative

a _____ Abfall (m) ist furchtbar.

b Ich finde _____ Fahrradwege (m pl) zu schmal.

c In _____ Stadtmitte (f) gibt es zu viel Verkehr.

d _____ Verschmutzung (f) _____ Luft (f) wird immer schlimmer.

Grammatik | Seite 177

Using prepositions with the genitive

The genitive case is normally used to show possession:

Das Haus meiner Mutter – My mother's house.

Some prepositions are followed by the genitive:

(an)statt	instead of
außerhalb	outside of, excluding
innerhalb	inside of, within
trotz	in spite of
während	during
wegen	because of

Articles in the genitive case are as follows:

	masc.	fem.	neut.	pl.
def.	*des*	*der*	*des*	*der*
indef.	*eines*	*einer*	*eines*	–

For masculine and neuter nouns you also add an *–s* to the end of the noun:

Wegen des Wetters fahre ich nicht in die Berge.

Grammatik | Seite 180

Articles and cases (revision)

Remember:

All German nouns have a gender and are either masculine, feminine or neuter.

■ You need to know which gender a noun is in order to use the words for 'the' and 'a' correctly.

■ 'The' is called the definite article and 'a' is called the indefinite article.

■ There are four cases in German – nominative, accusative, genitive and dative.

■ The subject of a sentence takes the nominative case, the direct object takes the accusative and the indirect object takes the dative e.g. *Ich* (nom.) *gebe ihm* (dat.) *ein Geschenk* (acc.).

■ There are particular prepositions which take the accusative, dative or genitive cases.

See page 175 –176 ➡

e Das Problem mit _____ Ozonloch (n) verstehe ich einfach nicht.

f Pestizide schaden _____ Trinkwasser (n).

g Ich mache nicht genug für _____ Umwelt (f).

h _____ Lärm (m) von _____ Disko (f) ist unmöglich.

Grammatik | Seites 175–176

The definite article changes in the following way according to case and gender:

	masculine	feminine	neuter	plural
nominative	der	die	das	die
accusative	den	die	das	die
dative	dem	der	dem	den
genitive	des	der	des	der

See pages 175–176 ➡

2b 🖋 Choose the correct form of the indefinite article to complete the following sentences. Again, the gender of each noun is supplied in brackets. In each case state which case is being used.

Beispiel: a eine accusative

a Es gibt _____ Fußgängerzone (f).

b Wir brauchen _____ Abfalleimer (m) im Klassenzimmer.

c Wegen _____ Unfalls (m) gibt es _____ Stau (m).

d Öltanker (m) war daran schuld.

e Ich habe _____ Alternative (f) zum Deospray gefunden.

f Trotz _____ Problems (m) mit dem Wetter ist der Bus pünktlich angekommen.

g Ich habe _____ Auto (n) gekauft, weil ich in Haus (n) auf dem Lande wohne.

Grammatik | Seite 175–176

The indefinite article changes in the following way according to case and gender:

	masculine	feminine	neuter
nominative	ein	eine	ein
accusative	einen	eine	ein
dative	einem	einer	einem
genitive	eines	einer	eines

3a 🗨 With a partner, take it in turns to practise asking and answering these questions using *werden* correctly.

a Was wirst du morgen für die Umwelt machen?

b Was wird deine Familie am Wochenende machen, um Energie zu sparen?

c Was wird deine Schule nächste Woche machen, um umweltfreundlicher zu sein?

d Was werden deine Freunde in der Zukunft machen, um die Umwelt zu schützen?

e Was wirst du für die Umwelt machen, wenn du das nächste Mal einkaufen gehst?

Grammatik | Seite 180

The future tense with *werden* (revision)

To use the future tense you need to use the present tense of *werden* plus an infinitive.

ich werde + infinitive (*kaufen, recyceln, sparen* …)

   du wirst

   er/sie/es wird

   wir werden

   ihr werdet

   sie werden

   Sie werden

Remember that the infinitive needs to go at the end of the sentence or clause.

3b 🖋 You and your family have good intentions about caring for the environment but have yet to put your plans into action! Change the following text from the present tense to the future tense with *werden*.

Ich bin umweltfreundlicher als meine Freundin. Ich recycle alles. Meine Familie kauft keine Einwegflaschen und bringt Flaschen zum Container. Mein Bruder fährt mit dem Rad zur Schule und mein Vater geht zu Fuß in die Stadtmitte. Ich dusche jeden Tag und ich kaufe keine Spraydosen. Die Stadt hat verschiedene Sammelcontainer und baut umweltfreundliche Häuser.

Environment

Umweltfreundlich oder umweltfeindlich?
➡ *Seite 112–113*

	Abgase (pl)	gas emissions
das	Altpapier	recycled paper
	auf dem Lande	in the country
	ausmachen	to turn off
	benutzen	to use
die	Dose	can
	eigentlich	actually, really
	einfach	simply
die	Energie	energy, power
die	Energiesparlampe	energy-saving lightbulb
das	Ergebnis	result
	fallen lassen	to drop
	faul	lazy
	FCKWs	CFCs
die	Flasche	bottle
	hassen	to hate
die	Heizung	heating
	herunterdrehen	to turn down
	in letzter Zeit	recently
der	Kaugummi	chewing gum
	leer	empty
der	Müll	rubbish
	neulich	recently
das	Plastik	plastic
	recyceln	to recycle
	sauber	clean
die	Solarenergie	solar power
	sparen	to save
die	Spraydose	spray can, aerosol
	stecken	to put
	trennen	to separate
die	Tüte	bag
	überall	everywhere

die	Umfrage	survey
die	Umwelt	environment
	umweltfeindlich	environmentally unfriendly
	umweltfreundlich	environmentally friendly
	wegwerfen	to throw away

Unsere Welt, unsere Umwelt ➡ *Seite 114–115*

	ärgern	to bother, to annoy
das	Atomkraftwerk	nuclear power station
	aussterben	to die out
	bald	soon
der	Bauer	farmer
	bedrohen	to threaten
der	Biomüll	organic waste
das	Düngemittel	fertiliser
der	Fluss	river
	genauso	just as, equally
der	Hautkrebs	skin cancer
das	Insektizid	insecticide
	interessieren (sich für)	to be interested in
die	Kohle	coal
das	Kohlendioxid	carbon dioxide
das	Kohlenmonoxid	carbon monoxide
der	Lärm	noise
die	Luft	air
das	Naturschutzgebiet	conservation area
	neben	next to
das	Öl	oil
	organisch	organic
das	Ozonloch	hole in the ozone layer
die	Ozonschicht	ozone layer
das	Pestizid	pesticide
das	Plakat	poster
die	Quelle	source
	retten	to save

	saurer Regen	acid rain
	schaden	to harm, to damage
	schlimm	terrible, awful
	Schuld an etwas sein	to be to blame for something
	sicher	sure
der	Sonnenbrand	sunburn
	spät	late
der	Strahl	ray
das	Thema	topic
das	Tier	animal
der	Treibhauseffekt	greenhouse effect
	verpesten	to pollute
die	Verschmutzung	pollution
	verursachen	to cause
	verwenden	to use
der	Vogel	bird
	wahrscheinlich	probable, probably
	weit	far
	zwitschern	to twitter

Global denken, lokal handeln ➡ Seite 116–117

der	Abfall	waste, litter
der	Abfalleimer	waste bin
	ändern	to change
	anfangen	to begin
die	Arbeitslosigkeit	unemployment
	aufstellen	to establish
	bauen	to build
der	Becher	cup
	beschließen	to decide
	dafür	in favour, for it
	dagegen	opposed to it, against it
	draußen	outside
	einführen	to introduce
die	Einwegflasche	single-use bottle
	enttäuschend	disappointing
	genug	enough

	hoffen	to hope
die	Idee	idea
der	Kunde	customer
	leben	to live
	leider	unfortunately
	niemand	no one
	organisieren	to organise
der	Parkplatz	car park
	pflanzen	to plant
der	Preis	price
der	Radweg	cycle path
	reinigen	to clean
	sicher	sure, safe
	sorgen für	to ensure
der	Stau	congestion, traffic jam
	studieren	to study
	umweltbewusst	environmentally aware
die	Verantwortung	responsibility
	vergessen	to forget
die	Verpackung	packaging
	verschieden	different
	verschwenden	to waste
	werden	to become
	zumachen	to close

Extra! Qualifiers

	besonders	particularly
ein	bisschen	a little
	fast	almost
	gar / überhaupt nicht	not at all
	immer	always
	kaum	hardly
	sehr	very
	selten	rarely
	wirklich	really
	ziemlich	quite
	zu	too

3 🖊 Mein Wohnort

Your Austrian friend has asked you to write an article about your home and local area for his or her school magazine. The piece is entitled *Mein Wohnort*. You could include:

1 where the town/village is situated and what the weather is like
2 a description of your house
3 a description of the town
4 what there is for tourists and young people
5 something you and your friends recently did there
6 the advantages and disadvantages of living there
7 whether you want to live there in the future

1 **Where the town/village is situated and what the weather is like**
   ▪ Give the geographical location of your town/village
   ▪ Say what type of place it is and its size
   ▪ If it is a small place, say how far it is from the nearest larger town
   ▪ Say what the weather is like in summer and winter

2 **A description of your house**
   ▪ Say where your house is in the town/village
   ▪ Describe the house – size, number of rooms, garden
   ▪ Describe your own room
   ▪ Say whether you like the house, giving reasons

3 **A description of the town**
   ▪ Say what the main buildings in the town are
   ▪ Say where some of them are in relation to each other
   ▪ Say what public transport is like
   ▪ Say how you usually travel and why

AQA Examiner's tips

Start off by giving the name of the town or village. Use the *–t* ending on the verb, as you are referring to something in the third person: *Meine Stadt / Mein Dorf heißt …*
Ⓖ See page 180 ➡
Don't forget, material you learned at Key Stage 3, such as basic weather vocabulary, will come in useful.

AQA Examiner's tips

Now start your notes. Write five or six words.
1 *liegen, Nordengland, klein, Hauptstadt, Klima*
2 …
Remember to include suitable verbs in your notes. They must be in the infinitive form. Make sure you know how to use the correct verb endings.
Take care to use the correct pronouns if you want to say 'it'. *Die Stadt* is *sie*, while *das Dorf* is *es*.
Ⓖ See page 179 ➡

AQA Examiner's tips

You can use *es gibt* to say what is in your house. Remember that the items that follow will take the accusative case.
Ⓖ See page 175 ➡
Try to include adjectives to give a more interesting description. Make sure you get any endings correct e.g. *es gibt einen kleinen Garten*.
Ⓖ See page 177 ➡
When giving opinions, always try to justify them e.g. *ich mag mein Haus, weil es sehr modern ist.*

AQA Examiner's tips

Remember to use the correct case (dative or accusative) after prepositions e.g. *das Sportzentrum liegt nicht weit vom Bahnhof.*
Prepositions taking the accusative:
Ⓖ See page 176 ➡
Prepositions taking the dative: Ⓖ See page 176 ➡
Prepositions taking the dative or accusative:
Ⓖ See page 177 ➡
Vary the way you give opinions e.g. *Mein Dorf gefällt mir, weil es sehr ruhig ist. Ich finde das Museum nicht besonders interessant.*

4 What there is for tourists and young people
- Say what there is for tourists
- Give your opinion of one of the attractions
- Say what there is for young people
- Say which facilities you use and why

You could use *man kann* to say what there is to do e.g. *Man kann die alte Kirche besuchen.* Remember that after a modal verb, the infinitive goes to the end of the sentence.

G See page 181 ➡

When saying which facilities you use and why, you could compare yourself to a friend using *während*, (whereas).

Link sentences using words such as *aber, obwohl* and *weil*, but make sure your word order is correct.

G See page 186 ➡

5 Something you and your friends recently did there
- Say what you did and where
- Say who you did it with and what it cost
- Give your opinion
- Say what you and your friends plan to do next weekend

You will need to use past tenses here (perfect and imperfect) so make sure you can do so correctly.

Perfect tense: **G** See page 182 ➡

Imperfect tense: **G** See page 182 ➡

Remember to change the verb ending when you are talking about more than one person.

If you find the future tense with *werden* difficult, you can use a future time phrase with the present tense to talk about your future plans instead e.g. *Nächstes Wochenende gehen wir ins Kino.*

G See page 184 ➡

6 The advantages and disadvantages of living there
- Give one general advantage of living where you do
- Give one advantage specific to you
- Mention one or two disadvantages
- Give your overall opinion of where you live

Remember just how much you already know and adapt your knowledge appropriately.

Here you could add some interesting adjectives to your notes, to sum up how you feel.

You could use qualifiers here to add depth to your opinions e.g. *Ich finde das Einkaufszentrum viel zu teuer.*

G See page 179 ➡

7 Whether you want to live there in the future
- Say what you would like to do in the future
- Say where you would like to live
- Explain why you want to live there
- Compare where you live now with your future choice

If you start a sentence with a time phrase, remember that the main verb is then the second idea e.g. *In der Zukunft möchte ich in London wohnen.*

G See page 186 ➡

Remember you are trying to impress the examiner with your German abilities. Even if you are not sure about your future plans, make sure you can write something relevant and interesting.

Now you should have a complete set of 40 cue words, in seven groups with either five or six words in each.

When you have written your article, compare it and your cue card with the online sample version – you might find some useful hints to make yours even better.

3 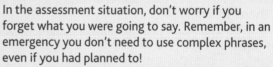 Umweltsumfrage

You have agreed to take part in a survey about environmental issues at your exchange school in Germany.

Your teacher will play the role of the person carrying out the survey. He or she could ask you the following:

1 what environmental problems are there in your area?

2 how does your area compare to other places?

3 what do you think the worst environmental problem is worldwide?

4 what have you done so far to improve the environment?

5 what effect do environmental problems have on health?

6 what could be done in the future?

7 !

Remember you will have to respond to something that you have not yet prepared.

---

1 **What environmental problems are there in your area?**
- Say where you live
- Describe the type of area it is
- Mention two or more environmental problems in the area
- Give your view on the problems

2 **How does your area compare to other places?**
- Mention another place and say where it is
- Briefly describe the area
- Mention one or two good or bad points
- Say whether it is better or worse than your area, giving justifications

3 **What do you think the worst environmental problem is worldwide?**
- Say what you think the worst problem is
- Explain how it affects the environment
- Say who or what you think is to blame
- Say what you think could be done

> **AQA Examiner's tips**
>
> When working on your notes, try to use key words which will help you build whole sentences each time.
>
> You are often being asked to give your personal viewpoint, so make use of the different phrases you know for expressing opinions: *Meiner Meinung nach ..., Ich glaube ..., Ich denke ...* etc.

> **AQA Examiner's tips**
>
> Now start your notes. Write five or six words for each of the seven sections:
>
> 1 *Umwelt, schaden, ...*
>
> When describing where you live, you can use the dative case with *in*: *Ich wohne in einer kleinen Stadt.*
>
> **G** See page 177 ➡
>
> If you use *es gibt* to say what problems there are, remember to use the accusative case afterwards: *Es gibt einen schmutzigen Park.*
>
> **G** See page 175 ➡

> **AQA Examiner's tips**
>
> In the assessment situation, don't worry if you forget what you were going to say. Remember, in an emergency you don't need to use complex phrases, even if you had planned to!
>
> Make sure you can use adjective endings correctly: *Das ist eine industrielle Stadt in Nordengland.*
>
> **G** See page 177 ➡
>
> To make comparisons, use comparative adjectives or, if you forget how to form them, *nicht so schlecht / schmutzig* etc. *wie ...* is a good alternative.
>
> **G** See page 178 ➡

> **AQA Examiner's tips**
>
> The vocabulary you require here is very specific, so make sure you focus on the key words you really need to help you.
>
> You could start off by saying *Das schlimmste Problem ist ...*
>
> You could use the conditional with *könnte* to say what could be done. Make sure your pronunciation and word order are correct!
>
> **G** See page 184 ➡

4 **What have you done so far to improve the environment?**
- Mention one or more things that you have already done
- Explain why these activities are important
- Mention one or more things which your friends do
- Give your opinion on this

Use the perfect tense to say what you have done.

G See page 182 ➡

Be sure to use the plural form when saying what more than one person does: *Meine Freunde* **trennen** *den Müll.*

G See page 180 ➡

Vary the ways in which you say 'why'. You can use *weil* the first time, then *denn,* but remember to use the correct word order for each.

G See page 186 ➡

AQA Examiner's tips

5 **What effect do environmental problems have on health?**
- Say what you do to stay healthy
- Mention how fast food affects health and the environment
- Mention how cars affect health and the environment
- Give your view on how important these things are

Here you can make use of material you learned in Chapter 1. You could explain how healthy you are by mentioning the last time your were ill or referring to your diet.

When asked to give your viewpoint, remember you can give pros as well as cons. Fast food causes litter and uses up land, but might taste nice!

Remember to keep adding to your notes, making sure you stick to the key words you really need.

AQA Examiner's tips

6 **What could be done in the future?**
- Say what could be done in your area
- Say why you think this is important
- Say what you plan to do personally
- Explain why you want to do this

You can use a variety of ways to talk about the future: the future tense with *werden*, or adverbial time phrases with the present tense.

G See page 184 ➡

When explaining why things are or should be done, you could use *um … zu …*

G See page 185 ➡

If you're feeling ambitious, you could say what you would do if you had more time, using the conditional: *Wenn ich Zeit hätte, würde ich ….* Take care when pronouncing the *ä* and the *ü*.

G See page 184 ➡

AQA Examiner's tips

7 **!** At this point you will be asked a question which you don't know in advance. However, you can try to guess what it might be and prepare various options:
- Say whether your family is environmentally friendly
- Say what your school does for the environment
- Describe how important the environment is to teenagers generally
- Say what you think the environment will be like in 20 years' time

You should now have completed your plan and prepared your answers. Give your plan to your teacher for feedback. Compare your answers to the online sample version – you might find some useful hints to make yours even better.

You could well be asked about any of these issues, so prepare answers for each of the possibilities.

If the question is totally unexpected, you can play for time by saying *Moment mal* or *Ich bin nicht sicher.* If all else fails, ask for the question to be repeated. Your teacher may rephrase it to help your understanding.

Now you should have a complete set of 40 cue words, in seven groups with either five or six words in each.

AQA Examiner's tips

3

Teste dich!

1 Give the German names for two religious festivals.

2 Give the German names for three different types of houses or dwellings.

3 Which of the following is a comparative adjective?

groß   größer   Größe   am größten

4 Provide a suitable question to prompt the following answer:

Nur ein paar Geschäfte und ein langweiliges Museum.

5 Complete the sentence with the correct prepositions:

Ich fahre _____ dem Rad _____ die Stadt, weil das besser _____ die Umwelt ist.

6 Put the words and punctuation marks below into the correct order to make a sentence.

mag / Garten / ist / obwohl / Ich / klein / er / meinen / ziemlich / . / ,

7 Provide a definition in German of an *Einwegflasche*.

8 Write a suitable ending for the sentence below:

Ich bin umweltfreundlich, weil _____.

9 Translate the sentence below into English:

Ich mache ziemlich viel für die Umwelt, obwohl ich mehr machen könnte.

10 Translate the sentence below into German:

I always try to turn the heating down.

Wusstest du schon ???

- Nur 39% der Deutschen wohnen im eigenen Haus oder in einer Eigentumswohnung. Mieten ist oft billiger. Die meisten Wohnungen sind unmöbliert – man muss das Sofa, den Tisch , den Kühlscrank usw. selber mitbringen.

- Die Deutschen sind im Vergleich zu vielen anderen Ländern sehr umweltfreundlich. Im Moment ist Deutschland ‚Windkraft-Weltmeister' – es ist der größte Markt weltweit für Windkraft.

kerboodle!

4 Work and Education

4.1 Wie ist deine Schule?

Lernziele

Describing what your school is like

Saying where you do things

Giving impressive answers to questions

■ Hermann-Friedrich-Gesamtschule

Startseite | Index | Hilfe | Kontakt | Textversion

Schule

Fachbereiche

Fotos

Personal

Schulordnung

Hallo, mein Name ist Stefan Reuter. Ich bin in der Klasse 9b und darf unsere Schule vorstellen. Sie ist eine ganz neue Gesamtschule, die 2002 eröffnet wurde. Sie liegt in der Nähe von Hannover.

In der Schule haben wir viele Klassenzimmer, wo allerlei Fächer unterrichtet werden, zum Beispiel Mathe, Erdkunde, Geschichte und Deutsch. Naturwissenschaften machen wir in den neuen Labors und für Fremdsprachen wie Englisch und Französisch gibt es ein modernes Sprachlabor. Jedes Klassenzimmer hat die neueste Technik und ich finde es gut, dass man immer das Internet benutzen kann.

Mein Lieblingsfach ist Sport. Dafür gibt es sowohl einen großen Sportplatz hinter der Schule als auch eine Turnhalle und ein Hallenbad.

In unserer Schule beginnt die erste Stunde normalerweise um halb acht. Jede Stunde dauert 45 Minuten. Wir haben sieben Stunden pro Tag und zwei große Pausen, und dürfen schon um 1.35 Uhr nach Hause gehen, weil die Schule dann aus ist.

Am Mittwoch sieht es anders aus. Da haben wir auch nachmittags Schule. Nach der siebten Stunde gehen wir zuerst einmal in die Schulkantine, wo wir zu Mittag essen können. Ich finde das Essen dort lecker und billig, aber zu Hause ist es besser! Am Nachmittag macht dann jeder eine AG. Ich bin Mitglied in der Theatergruppe, aber man kann auch Sport treiben, eine dritte Fremdsprache lernen oder einfach Hausaufgaben machen, bevor man nach Hause geht. Toll, nicht wahr?

---

1 📖 🎧 Copy and complete each sentence with one of the words below.

Beispiel: a Hermann-Friedrich ist eine Gesamtschule.

a Hermann-Friedrich ist eine _____.

b Die Schule ist ganz _____.

c In den _____ macht man Biologie, Chemie und Physik.

d Die Schule hat ein _____, wo man schwimmen kann.

e Um _____ Uhr dreißig beginnt die erste Stunde.

f Das _____ in der Schule schmeckt gut.

g Stefan findet es _____, dass er am Mittwoch Ganztagsschule hat.

> **Tipp**
> When reading the text, make a note of instances when the main verb is sent to the end of the clause. In each case, can you explain why this is?

acht	alt	Essen
Freibad	Gesamtschule	Hallenbad
Klassenzimmer	Labors	langweilig
modern	prima	sieben

2 🎧 Which subjects do these pupils do? What do they think of them? Write your answers to a–f in English.

Beispiel: a PE, favourite subject

4 Work and Education

School / college and future plans

Dieter

School subjects, places in school

Dieter beschreibt seine Schulfächer.

> Ich gehe jeden Tag zu Fuß zur Schule. Wir haben sieben Stunden pro Tag. Ich lerne Englisch, Mathe, Musik, Deutsch, Kunst, Erdkunde, Geschichte, Sport, Naturwissenschaften und Informatik. Mein Lieblingsfach ist Sport. Englisch und Musik mache ich nicht gern. Naturwissenschaften und Informatik sind in Ordnung, aber Erdkunde und Geschichte finde ich nicht gut. Ich mag Mathe. Deutsch gefällt mir nicht, aber Kunst ist toll.

1a 📖🎧 Read Dieter's description of his school subjects. Make three lists under the following headings:

- subjects he likes ■ subjects he finds okay ■ subjects he doesn't like

1b ✏️ Using Dieter's text as a model write about your own school subject likes and dislikes.

Dieter beschreibt seine Schule.

> Meine Schule ist ziemlich alt. Wir haben eine ganz normale Turnhalle, aber der Sportplatz ist sehr klein, und wir haben keine Sporthalle. In der Pause unterhalten wir uns auf dem Schulhof. Die Kantine ist auch ziemlich alt und ich mag das Essen nicht. Die Lehrer essen dort auch nicht gern. Sie bleiben immer im Lehrerzimmer während der Mittagspause. In der Bibliothek gibt es viele Bücher und auch einige Computer, wo man Informationen im Internet suchen kann.

2a 📖🎧 Read Dieter's description of his school. Match the following sentences to the locations in his school in the box on the right. One word is left over – why?

Sporthalle
Bibliothek
Sportplatz
Schulhof
Kantine
Lehrerzimmer

a   Die Schüler können hier essen.
b   Dort unterhält man sich in der Pause.
c   Hier bleiben die Lehrer in der Mittagspause.
d   Hier gibt es einige Computer.
e   Hier macht Dieter Sport.

2b ✏️ Design a plan of a new school. Label the rooms and open areas in German. Which subjects would be taught in each part of the school?

2c 💬 You are showing a German visitor around your new school. Prepare a short speech to describe the school you have designed and say what you do in each area.

Beispiel: Hier ist die Kantine. Ich esse hier. Das ist mein Klassenzimmer. Hier lerne ich Englisch …

Vokabeln

Mein Lieblingsfach ist …	My favourite subject is …
Biologie	biology
Chemie	chemistry
Deutsch	German
Englisch	English
Erdkunde	geography
Französisch	French
Geschichte	history
Informatik	IT
Kunst	art
Mathe	maths
Musik	music
Naturwissenschaften	science
Physik	physics
Religion	RS
Spanisch	Spanish
Sport	PE
Werken	D&T

Vokabeln

die Aula	hall
die Bibliothek	library
der Gang	corridor
die Kantine	canteen
das Labor	laboratory
das Lehrerzimmer	staff room
der Schulhof	playground
die Sporthalle	sports hall
der Sportplatz	playing fields
die Turnhalle	gymnasium

Word order

Remember to put the verb second.

*Hier **ist** die Kantine. Ich **esse** hier.*

*Das **ist** mein Klassenzimmer. Hier **lerne** ich Englisch.*

Grammatik *Seite 186*

Current and future jobs

Jobs and workplaces

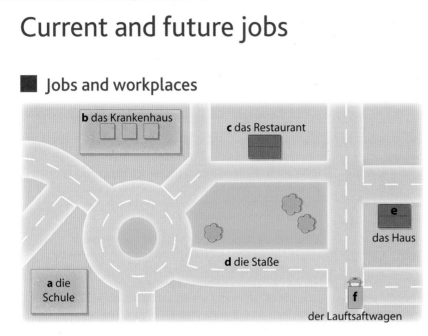

b das Krankenhaus
c das Restaurant
e
das Haus
d die Staße
a die Schule
f
der Lauftsaftwagen

Vokabeln

Arzt/Ärztin	doctor
Briefträger/in	postman/ woman
Elektriker/in	electrician
Friseur/in	hairdresser
Hausfrau/ Hausmann	housewife/ husband
Ingenieur/in	engineer
Leherer/in	teacher
Kauffrau/ Kaufmann	businesswoman/ man
Kellner/in	waiter/waitress
Klempner/in	plumber
Koch/Köchin	cook
Krankenpfleger/ Krankenschwester	nurse
LKW-Fahrer/in	lorry driver
Mechaniker/in	mechanic
Metzger/in	butcher
Polizist/in	policeman/ woman
Sekretär/in	secretary
Tierarzt/ Tierärztin	vet
Zahnarzt/Zahnärztin	dentist

1a 📖🎧 Look at the words in the vocabulary box on the right. Who would work where? Match as many people as you can to the different places on the map.

Beispiel: **a** Sekretär/in …

1b ✏️ Design a plan of a new town centre. Label the streets and buildings. Write sentences to describe who works where.

Beispiel: Der Arzt arbeitet im Krankenhaus.

1c 💬 Work in pairs. Each write down the name of five jobs in German. Take it in turns to try to guess what your partner has chosen.

Beispiel: Hast du „Kellnerin"?

Ja! Hast du „Lehrer"?…

1d 💬 Work in pairs. Now each write down the name of one job in German. Take it in turns to ask questions to try to guess what your partner has chosen.

Beispiel:

Arbeitest du in der Stadt?

Ja.

Arbeitest du in einem Krankenhaus?

Nein. …

The dative case

When saying someone works in a particular building remember to use the dative case:

*Die Kellnerin arbeitet **in dem Restaurant**.*

Remember that with the dative case, *der* and *das* become *dem* and *die* becomes *der*. *In dem* can also be shortened to *im*:

*Die Kellnerin arbeitet **im Restaurant**.*

See page 102 ➡️

Grammatik *Seite 176*

Vokabeln

das Büro	office
das Geschäft	shop
das Krankenhaus	hospital
die Fabrik	factory
das Hotel	hotel
das Restaurant	restaurant
die Schule	school

Lernziele

Describing what your school is like

Saying where you do things

Giving impressive answers to questions

■ Hermann-Friedrich-Gesamtschule

Startseite | Index | Hilfe | Kontakt | Textversion

Schule

Fachbereiche

Fotos

Personal

Schulordnung

Hallo, mein Name ist Stefan Reuter. Ich bin in der Klasse 9b und darf unsere Schule vorstellen. Sie ist eine ganz neue Gesamtschule, die 2002 eröffnet wurde. Sie liegt in der Nähe von Hannover.

In der Schule haben wir viele Klassenzimmer, wo allerlei Fächer unterrichtet werden, zum Beispiel Mathe, Erdkunde, Geschichte und Deutsch. Naturwissenschaften machen wir in den neuen Labors und für Fremdsprachen wie Englisch und Französisch gibt es ein modernes Sprachlabor. Jedes Klassenzimmer hat die neueste Technik und ich finde es gut, dass man immer das Internet benutzen kann.

Mein Lieblingsfach ist Sport. Dafür gibt es sowohl einen großen Sportplatz hinter der Schule als auch eine Turnhalle und ein Hallenbad.

In unserer Schule beginnt die erste Stunde normalerweise um halb acht. Jede Stunde dauert 45 Minuten. Wir haben sieben Stunden pro Tag und zwei große Pausen, und dürfen schon um 1.35 Uhr nach Hause gehen, weil die Schule dann aus ist.

Am Mittwoch sieht es anders aus. Da haben wir auch nachmittags Schule. Nach der siebten Stunde gehen wir zuerst einmal in die Schulkantine, wo wir zu Mittag essen können. Ich finde das Essen dort lecker und billig, aber zu Hause ist es besser! Am Nachmittag macht dann jeder eine AG. Ich bin Mitglied in der Theatergruppe, aber man kann auch Sport treiben, eine dritte Fremdsprache lernen oder einfach Hausaufgaben machen, bevor man nach Hause geht. Toll, nicht wahr?

---

1 📖 🎧 Copy and complete each sentence with one of the words below.

Beispiel: **a** Hermann-Friedrich ist eine Gesamtschule.

a Hermann-Friedrich ist eine _____.

b Die Schule ist ganz _____.

c In den _____ macht man Biologie, Chemie und Physik.

d Die Schule hat ein _____ , wo man schwimmen kann.

e Um _____ Uhr dreißig beginnt die erste Stunde.

f Das _____ in der Schule schmeckt gut.

g Stefan findet es _____ , dass er am Mittwoch Ganztagsschule hat.

> **Tipp**
>
> When reading the text, make a note of instances when the main verb is sent to the end of the clause. In each case, can you explain why this is?

acht	alt	Essen
Freibad	Gesamtschule	Hallenbad
Klassenzimmer	Labors	langweilig
modern	prima	sieben

2 🎧 Which subjects do these pupils do? What do they think of them? Write your answers to a–f in English.

Beispiel: **a** PE, favourite subject

3 **G** Join these phrases using *wo*.

a Es gibt einen Sportplatz. Wir spielen Hockey.

b Ich gehe in die Schulkantine. Ich esse zu Mittag.

c Die Schule hat viele Labors. Wir machen Experimente.

d Es gibt auch ein Sprachlabor. Ich kann Englisch sprechen.

e Neben meinem Klassenzimmer ist die Bibliothek. Ich mache meine Hausaufgaben.

4 🗨 🌐 Work with a partner. One partner asks the questions and the other answers. Then swap roles. See if you can think of some other questions to ask.

Was für eine Schule besuchst du?

Was lernst du in der Schule?

Wie findest du deine Schule?

Beschreib einen typischen Schultag.

Ich besuche _____.

Ich lerne _____.

Ich finde meine Schule _____.

Die erste Stunde beginnt um _____.

Meine Schule ist	eine Gesamtschule / ein Gymnasium / eine Realschule / ein Internat.
In der Schule lerne ich	Mathe / Englisch / Französisch.
Ich mag, … / Mein Lieblingsfach ist, …	weil / da es … ist.
… finde ich toll / langweilig / prima / gut / interessant.	
Die erste Stunde / Der Schultag beginnt um …	
Dann / Danach / Nach der Pause haben wir …	
Die Schule ist um … Uhr aus.	

Grammatik — **Seite 185**

Saying where you do things

If you use the word *wo* to join two phrases, the **verb** in the phrase after *wo* goes to the **end**.

Meine Schule hat ein Sprachlabor, wo ich Französisch lerne.

Also learn about other words which have the same effect.

See page 142 ➡

Strategie

🗨 Giving impressive answers to questions

When answering questions remember to:

Answer the question, add

Details

Opinions and

Reasons to produce

Excellent work.

If you do your teacher will ADORE you!

kerboodle!

■ Der Austausch

Paula und Tom beschreiben einen Schüleraustausch, den sie eben in Deutschland gemacht haben.

Paula

Für mich war der Austausch ganz interessant. Wir besuchten ein Gymnasium, dessen Stundenplan überhaupt nicht wie bei uns in England war. Wir mussten sehr früh aufstehen, weil die erste Stunde schon um 7:55 Uhr begonnen hat! Die Stunden dauerten auch nur 45 Minuten. Das habe ich gut gefunden, da man sich nicht so lange konzentrieren musste. Nach der dritten Stunde hatten wir eine große Pause, und wir konnten uns dann unterhalten oder auf dem Schulhof spielen. Das beste daran war, dass wir zu Mittag nach Hause gehen durften, denn die letzte Stunde endete um Viertel nach eins.

Tom

Die Schule meines Austauschpartners war völlig anders als in England. Ganz toll war natürlich, dass ich jeden Morgen meine Jeans und ein T-Shirt anziehen durfte, denn in Deutschland braucht man keine Schuluniform zu tragen. Die Pausen waren ziemlich kurz, nur 10 Minuten meistens, aber in den Pausen durften wir in den Klassenzimmern essen und trinken. Und wir waren den ganzen Tag im gleichen Klassenzimmer. Das hat mir gut gefallen, weil die Lehrer immer zu uns kommen mussten. Nur an einem Tag sind wir nachmittags in der Schule geblieben. Das war Mittwoch, glaube ich, und die deutschen Schüler mussten alle eine AG machen. Mein Austauschpartner war in der Schulmannschaft für Handball und durfte an dem Nachmittag trainieren.

1a 📖 🎧 Answer the following questions in English:

Beispiel: a   Because the first lesson started at 7:55.

a   Why did Paula have to get up so early?

b   Why did she think the shorter lessons were good?

c   What was Paula able to do in the main break?

d   What did Paula find best about the school day in Germany?

e   What is the first positive thing Tom mentions about school life in Germany?

f   What was Tom allowed to do at break time?

g   Why was Tom pleased about being in one classroom for all lessons?

h   What did the German pupils do on Wednesday afternoons?

1b 📖 🎧 🌐 Read Tom and Paula's descriptions again, picking out the key words relating to the topic of school life.

- Which words are familiar?
- Which are new but easy to work out?
- Which did you need to look up?

Make a list of new words to revise and use again in future!

2 Ⓖ Rewrite these sentences in the imperfect tense.

Beispiel: **a** Ich musste um 8 Uhr aufstehen.

a Ich muss um 8 Uhr aufstehen.

b Im Klassenzimmer darf ich nicht essen.

c In der Pause kann ich mich mit meinen Freunden treffen.

d In Deutschland müssen die Schüler eine AG machen.

e Wir können zu Mittag in der Schulkantine essen.

f In Deutschland darf man tragen, was man will.

3 🎧 These pupils are talking about their school day. Are the following statements true (T) or false (F)? Correct the false ones.

a Hans's school day begins early at half past 8.

b Paul likes not having to wear a uniform at school.

c Martina buys a sandwich from the caretaker at break.

d Bettina has every afternoon free and goes to the gym.

e Michael does drama every Wednesday afternoon.

4 🖊 Imagine you have just been to a German school on an exchange visit. Write a short report saying what was different. Use Paula and Tom's texts to help you.

📖 **Revising vocabulary**

If you are having difficulty revising vocabulary try to:

1 Find pairs of words which mean the same, e.g. *klug* & *intelligent*.

2 Find pairs of words which mean the opposite, e.g. *fleißig* & *faul*.

3 Challenge yourself to make a list of 10 words from the same category, e.g. 10 school subjects.

And remember, vocabulary revision is best done little and often. Set yourself a realistic target each week or even each day and increase your word power!

Ⓢ **Strategie**

Using the imperfect tense of modal verbs.

Ich musste 'I had to'

Ich konnte 'I was able to'

Ich durfte 'I was allowed to'

Ich wollte 'I wanted to'

Ich sollte 'I was supposed to'

Ich mochte 'I liked to'

Look for other forms of these verbs (e.g. *wir mussten*) in Paula and Tom's texts. The endings are the same as for regular verbs. Remember that the second verb still needs to go to the end of the clause.

Also learn different ways of denoting possession.

See page 142 ➡

Ⓖ **Grammatik** Seite 183

Remember that you can join sentences with *obwohl* ('although') or *während* ('whereas'). Both these words send the verb to the end.

Tipp

In Deutschland / In der Schule meines Austauschpartners / meiner Austauschpartnerin	musste ich / man konnte ich / man durfte ich / man	früh aufstehen. keine Uniform tragen. im Klassenzimmer ... am Nachmittag ...
Die Schulstunden in Deutschland	dauerten	fünfzig Minuten / anderthalb Stunden ...
	waren	lustig / langweilig / amüsant / einfach / schwierig
Ich finde das Schulwesen in	Deutschland / England	besser, weil ...

Lernziele

Talking about pressures and problems at school

Saying what you could or ought to do

Matching people to information

■ Hilfe!

1

Ich bin nicht so gut in der Schule wie meine Schulfreunde und bekomme immer schlechte Noten. Letzte Woche hatte ich mich sehr gut vorbereitet, aber ich bekam trotzdem nur eine Drei. Ich habe Angst, dass ich vielleicht nächstes Jahr sitzen bleibe. Ich werde nervös, wenn ich eine Klassenarbeit oder eine Prüfung habe. Was soll ich machen?

Klaus

2

Ich möchte auf die Uni gehen und brauche dafür einen guten Abschluss. Ich muss viel arbeiten, wenn ich gute Noten im Abitur will. Aber deswegen habe ich keine Freizeit mehr, und meine Freunde meinen, dass ich langweilig bin. Sie lachen mich auch immer aus, wenn ich meine alten Klamotten anziehe oder mein altes Handy benutze. Ich glaube, sie verstehen nicht, wie traurig ich dann bin.

Gabi

3

Es ist alles zu viel für mich. Ich treibe viel Sport, spiele ein Instrument im Schulorchester und muss dann auch nach der Schule Zeit für Hausaufgaben usw finden. Kein Wunder, dass ich manchmal vergesse, sie zu machen und deshalb nachsitzen muss. Das ist mir immer peinlich.

Wilhelm

1a 📖 🎧 🌐 Read the problem page letters. Which of the teenagers …

- a … wants to get good marks in order to go to university?
- b … gets nervous about exams?
- c … sometimes has to stay behind after school?
- d … is worried about having to repeat a year?
- e … has lots of hobbies?
- f … uses an old mobile phone?

1b 📖 🎧 🌐 Now read the responses and match each to the correct letter.

a

Du solltest deine Zeit besser organisieren. Du könntest alles in einen Terminkalender eintragen.

b

Du solltest dir keine Sorgen machen. Du könntest die Situation mit deinen Lehrern besprechen. Sie werden dich bestimmt verstehen und dir helfen.

c

Freizeit und Freunde sind immer wichtig. Du solltest versuchen, mehr Spaß zu haben und mehr Zeit mit deinen Freunden zu verbringen. Vielleicht könntest du das Wochenende dafür frei lassen. Du solltest ihnen auch sagen, dass du traurig wirst, wenn sie dich immer auslachen. Gute Freunde werden dann damit aufhören.

📖 **Matching people to information**

Read the questions carefully and decide what information you are looking for.

Find a phrase which matches the information you are looking for. (In a listening task you should listen for a phrase which might show the answer is coming.)

Watch out for red herrings and the effect of negatives. Sometimes the most obvious answer is not the correct one!

Strategie

2 **G** Complete these sentences with either 'could' or 'should'.

> *Beispiel:*   **a** *Ich brauche Geld für meinen Urlaub. Ich könnte vielleicht mein Taschengeld sparen.*

a Ich brauche Geld für meinen Urlaub. Ich _____ vielleicht mein Taschengeld sparen. (können)

b Mein Rad ist kaputt. Ich _____ ein neues Rad kaufen. (sollen)

c Wenn es regnet, _____ du mit dem Bus zur Schule fahren. (können)

d Wenn du die Schule nicht verlassen willst, _____ du nächstes Jahr weiterstudieren. (können)

e Ich _____ fleißig sein und hart arbeiten, aber ich habe keine Lust dazu. (sollen)

f Was _____ wir machen, um bessere Noten zu bekommen? (sollen)

Grammatik   Seite 184

Saying what you could or ought to do

You have already seen one form of the imperfect subjunctive: *ich möchte …* to say that you 'would like' something (see page 75). To talk about things you 'could' or 'should' do, you need to use the imperfect subjunctive of the modal verbs *können* and *sollen*.

sollen – *ich sollte, du solltest* etc ('ought to')

e.g. *Ich sollte meine Hausaufgaben machen.*

können – *ich könnte, du könntest* etc ('could')

e.g. *Du könntest alles in einen Terminkalender eintragen.*

Also learn about the pluperfect tense.

See page 143 ➡️

3a 🎧 Clara is spending the school year in England. What problems does she have? Listen to the recording and complete the sentences.

a Clara is studying at a _____ school.

b She finds the _____ too long.

c She has little time for her _____.

Probleme

Freunde   *nachsitzen*

Prüfungen

Eltern   **Schulstress**

keine Freizeit

Hausaufgaben   *Noten*

3b 🎧 Now listen carefully to the next part and complete the sentences.

a Clara does not understand her fellow pupils when _____.

b She find the teachers hard to understand because they _____.

c She cannot always do her work because _____.

4 🗨️ What problems do you have at school? Work out how to tell your partner about your problems. When you are both ready take it in turns to get things off your chest! Your partner should try to offer some advice.

In der Schule habe ich Probleme mit	Hausaufgaben. / Lehrern. / schlechten Noten.	
Ich bin	nervös / altmodisch / nicht so gut wie …	
Ich finde	Französisch / Mathe / Prüfungen	schwer / schwierig / kompliziert / stressig …
	meine Lehrer	streng / nett / freundlich …
Ich habe	wenig Zeit / viel Angst.	

Du könntest	fleißiger sein / mit … sprechen /
Du solltest	Hilfe von … bekommen.

Tipp

Vary your conversation by not always starting your sentences with *ich*. Remember that the verb still needs to be the second idea!

Du solltest vielleicht …
Vielleicht solltest du …

kerboodle!

4.4 Eine bessere Schule

Lernziele
Describing the ideal school
Saying what you would do
Knowing which tense to use

■ Als Direktor(in) meiner Traumschule würde ich ...

Thomas

Die neue Schule muss modern sein. Ich würde die neueste Technologie einführen. Die Schüler würden in jedem Klassenzimmer Computer benutzen, um ihre Aufgaben zu schreiben. Wir würden Experimente in den nagelneuen Labors machen und in allen Fächern Kameras, Handys und Video benutzen.

Martha

Ich würde Versammlungen organisieren, und die erste Stunde würde erst um halb zehn anfangen. Die Stunden müssten kürzer sein. Nach jeder Stunde müssten wir eine Pause haben. Wir würden anderthalb Stunden für das Mittagessen brauchen. Dann würden wir nicht nur essen sondern auch auf dem Sportplatz spielen oder Zeit für den Chor und das Schulorchester haben. Das Essen in der Kantine müsste auch billig und gesund sein. Keine fettigen Pommes mehr!

Jens

Ich würde eine Schuluniform tragen. Ich würde Prüfungen, Klassenarbeiten usw. verbieten. Kein Stress mehr! Sitzenbleiben ist auch unfair. Wir würden alle unsere Hausaufgaben in der Bibliothek oder in der Klasse machen und die Lehrer würden uns dabei helfen. Außerdem hätten wir mehr Zeit für Projekte, Sport und Drama.

1 📖 🎧 Who would these people most like as a head teacher?

Beispiel: **a** Martha

a Für mich ist das Essen in der Schule ganz wichtig.

b Ich möchte meine Hausaufgaben in der Schule machen.

c Ich arbeite gern mit Computern.

d Ich singe gern und möchte in der Schule Geige spielen.

e Ich ziehe zwar gern meine eigenen Kleider an, aber ich finde, eine Uniform ist keine schlechte Idee.

f Ich würde gerne jeden Morgen in die Aula gehen.

> **Tipp**
> When reading the text, also think about who you would most like as a head teacher. Can you explain why in German?

2 🎧 Michaela is asking her fellow pupils what they would like in their new school. Listen to the recording and write details in English about each feature mentioned.

- ■ Buildings ■ Equipment ■ Sport ■ Lesson times
- ■ Uniform ■ Food ■ Homework

3 **G** What would these people say? Make up sentences to describe their thoughts using the conditional mood. The box below will help you.

Beispiel: **a** Ich würde einen neuen Tennisplatz bauen.

Grammatik Seite 184

Saying what you would do

To say what someone 'would do' in German you use the imperfect subjunctive of *werden* (*ich würde, du würdest* etc.) followed by an infinitive. This is called the **conditional mood**.

'School would begin at half past nine.' – *Die Schule würde um halb zehn anfangen.*

Also practise how to say 'would have' (*hätte*), 'would be' (*wäre*) and 'there would be', (*es gäbe*).

See page 143 ➡

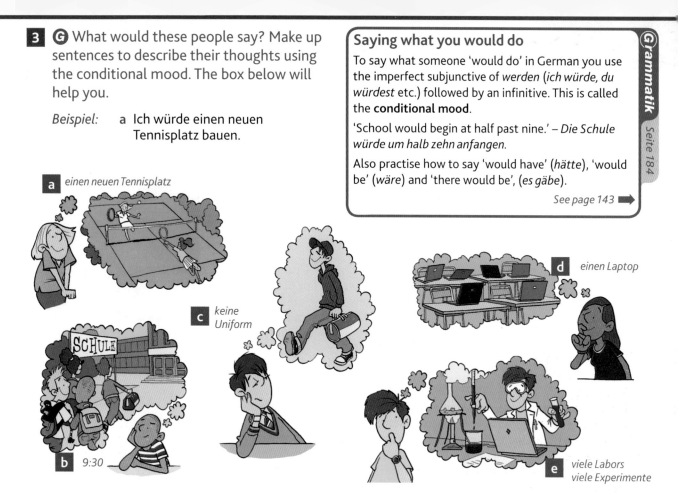

a einen neuen Tennisplatz

c keine Uniform

d einen Laptop

b 9:30

e viele Labors viele Experimente

Ich würde	viele Labors / neue Sportplätze bauen.	
Man würde	Prüfungen verbieten.	
Die Schüle würde	Laptops kaufen.	
Wir würden	keine Hausaufgaben machen.	
	um 11 Uhr anfangen.	
Meine (ideale) Schule	hätte	einen Laptop./
Jeder Schüler		gesundes Essen. /
Jede Schülerin		viele Labors.
In der idealen Schule gäbe es		
Eine lange Pause / ein neuen tennisplatz		... wäre eine gute Idee.

🗨 Knowing which tense to use

Look for clues in the questions to help you with the tense of your answer. Present tense questions need a present tense answer. If the question starts with *Wie wäre …?* or *Was würdest du …?* your answer should be in the conditional mood (using the imperfect subjunctive).

Strategie

4 🗨 ⚫ Practise a conversation with a partner about your school and how it could be improved. Include the following questions:

- Wie ist deine Schule?
- Wie wäre deine ideale Schule?
- Was macht man in deiner Schule?
- Was würde man in deiner idealen Schule machen?

kerboodle!

School / college and future plans

13 Jahre Schule!

Johann Gerber ist 19 Jahre alt und hat eben die Schule verlassen. Er beschreibt seine Schulkarriere.

Grundschule

Als ich sechs Jahre alt war, bin ich zum ersten Mal in die Grundschule gegangen. Ich habe gehört, dass man in England schon mit 5 Jahren in die Schule geht. Das wäre für mich zu früh gewesen. An meinem ersten Schultag habe ich geweint, als ich ohne Mutti in dem großen Klassenzimmer war. In der Grundschule habe ich mich gut amüsiert, weil ich durch Spielen lernen konnte.

Johanns erster Schultag

Gesamtschule

Als ich die Grundschule verlassen habe, bin ich in eine Gesamtschule gegangen, wo alles ganz anders war. In der Grundschule hatten wir meistens nur einen Lehrer für alle Fächer gehabt. In der Gesamtschule musste ich viele neue Lehrer und Lehrerinnen kennen lernen. Mein Lieblingslehrer war Herr Weber, der Englisch und Französisch unterrichtet hat. Er war sympathisch. Aber einige Lehrer waren ziemlich streng und wir mussten in fast jeder Stunde sehr viel schreiben. Dazu gab es auch Hausaufgaben, was natürlich ganz fürchterlich war.

Viele Schüler und Schülerinnen haben in der Schule geraucht, und in unserer Schule gab es eine Raucherecke hinter der Bibliothek, wo die älteren Schüler rauchen durften. Das habe ich schrecklich gefunden, weil Rauchen stinkt, und man konnte den Gestank in der Bibliothek selbst riechen.

In der Oberstufe habe ich nur 5 Prüfungsfächer gemacht. Da ich mich für Fremdsprachen interessierte, habe ich natürlich Englisch und Französisch gewählt. Ich durfte auch andere Fächer wie Sport machen, aber sie waren nicht so wichtig. Als ich mein letztes Zeugnis gelesen habe, war ich sehr glücklich. In der zwölften Klasse hatte ich eine Drei für Englisch bekommen, aber diesmal hatte ich eine Eins.

Nachdem ich meine Noten bekommen hatte, wurde mir klar, dass ich auf die Uni gehen würde. Die Schulzeit war zu Ende. Ich habe viele gute Freunde in meinem Schulleben gemacht und nächstes Jahr werde ich meine alten Schulfreunde alle vermissen, wenn ich an der Uni bin.

Johannes Kepler Gesamtschule

Zeugnis

Jahrgang 13

Prüfungsfächer

Englisch	1
Deutsch	2
Mathe	1
Geschichte	3
Französisch	1

1a 📖🎧 Are the following statements true, false or not mentioned in the text. Write T, F or N.

a   Johann was 5 when he first went to school.
b   At the primary school he wore a uniform.
c   After primary school Johann went to a grammar school.
d   The pupils were allowed to smoke at school.
e   In the sixth form Johann's worst subject was history.
f   At university Johann will study languages.

1b 📖🎧 Answer the following questions in English.

a   What happened on Johann's first day at school?
b   What did Johann particularly like about primary school?
c   What was the first difference Johann noticed when he went to secondary school?
d   Why did Johann not like the smokers' corner?
e   Why was Johann particularly pleased about his last report?

2a 🎧 Nicola Gerber, Johann's sister, is talking about her school. Which pictures best match what she says?

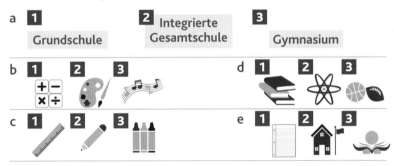

a   **1** Grundschule   **2** Integrierte Gesamtschule   **3** Gymnasium

2b 🎧 Nicola and Johann discuss their teachers. Choose the correct answers.

a   Nicola thinks Herr Franz was
    1 serious   2 strong   3 funny
b   She found he would
    1 talk a lot   2 explain things well   3 always set easy homework
c   Johann found Herr Franz
    1 quite good   2 quite bad   3 okay
d   Johann thinks Herr Meier is a good teacher because
    1 he is friendly   2 he is easy to understand   3 he can be strict but fair
e   Nicola thinks Herr Meier is
    1 a good teacher   2 hard to understand   3 one of the best teachers
f   Nicola thinks calling teachers "du" instead of "Sie" in the sixth form is
    1 disrespectful   2 childish   3 sensible

Grammatik **Seite 183**

How many of these features can you find in the text?
a   Pluperfect tenses
    page 143 ➡
b   Subordinating conjunctions
    page 133 ➡
c   Modal verbs in the imperfect
    page 135 ➡

AQA *Examiner's tip*

Gain confidence in your knowledge of grammar and grammatical terms. This will not only impress your teacher, but help you to take apart and understand new phrases when it comes to the exam.

❝ *I think you'll find I've used one or two excellent subordinating conjunctions to go with my imperfect modals, miss.* ❞

AQA *Examiner's tip*

Don't always go for the obvious answer. If you are doing a reading task make sure you read both the question and the text carefully.

Vokabeln

die Raucherecke	smokers' corner
das Zeugnis	school report
School marks	
1 = *sehr gut*	Very good
2 = *gut*	Good
3 = *befriedigend*	Satisfactory
4 = *ausreichend*	Fair
5 = *mangelhaft*	Poor
6 = *ungenügend*	Insufficient

kerboodle!

School / college and future plans

1a ✏ Join the phrases below using the conjunctions indicated.

Beispiel: **a** Ich gehe ins Bett, nachdem ich Musik gehört habe.

a Ich gehe ins Bett. Ich habe Musik gehört. (nachdem)

b Ich mag meine Schule. Ich habe viele Freunde hier. (weil)

c Ich finde Englisch in Ordnung. Der Lehrer ist streng. (obwohl)

d Ich frühstücke. Ich gehe in die Schule. (bevor)

e Ich finde es doof. Ich muss jeden Abend Hausaufgaben machen. (dass)

1b ✏ Once your teacher has checked your answers, rewrite the sentences from activity 1a, starting each with the subordinate conjunction.

2 📖 Read the passage below. Make a list of the things described and who they belong to. How many different ways of showing possession can you find?

In Deutschland war das Klassenzimmer meines Austauschpartners prima. Ich habe ein Foto davon gemacht. Das Arbeitsheft meines Partners liegt auf dem Tisch. Die Jacke auf dem Stuhl gehört mir. Neben dem Fenster sieht man den Lehrer, dessen Butterbrote neben seinem Computer liegen.

Grammatik — Seite 186

Subordinate clauses

When two phrases are joined using a subordinating conjunction, the verb in the phrase which starts with the conjunction goes to the end of the clause:

*Ich gehe sofort ins Bett, **nachdem** ich ferngesehen **habe**.*

Remember that if you start a sentence with a subordinating conjunction you will have 'verb, verb' in the middle of your sentence:

***Nachdem** ich ferngesehen **habe**, **gehe** ich sofort ins Bett.*

(*Nachdem* is often used with the pluperfect, e.g. *Nachdem ich gegessen **hatte**, habe ich meine Hausaufgaben gemacht* (see activity 3). Show your expertise by using a variety of tenses.

Grammatik — Seite 181

Ways of denoting possession

There is more than one way of showing possession in German. You could use the genitive case:

*Hier ist **das Lineal meines Freundes**.*
                              see page 176 ➡

von + the dative:

*Hier ist **das Lineal von meinem Freund**.*   see page 176 ➡

add an –s, like in English (note that there is no apostrophe used in German):

*Hier ist **Peters Lineal**.*

use possessive adjectives:

*Hier ist **sein Lineal**.*   see page 35 ➡

You can also use *dessen* (for masculine and neuter nouns) or *deren* (for feminine nouns), meaning 'whose':

*Hier ist Peter, **dessen Lineal** auf dem Tisch liegt.*

Note that *dessen* and *deren* send the verb to the end.

3a 🖊 Join the following pairs of phrases with *nachdem*, putting the second phrase into the pluperfect tense (if wished, you could start the sentences with the *nachdem* clause).

Beispiel: **a** Ich bin ins Klassenzimmer gegangen, nachdem ich meine Schulfreunde getroffen hatte.

a Ich bin ins Klassenzimmer gegangen. Ich habe meine Schulfreunde getroffen.

b Peter hat seine Hausaufgaben gemacht. Er hat zu Abend gegessen.

c Ich habe mit meiner Freundin geplaudert. Ich bin in der Schule angekommen.

d Renate durfte nicht ins Kino gehen. Sie hat eine schlechte Note in Mathe bekommen.

> ### The pluperfect tense
>
> The pluperfect tense refers to something that **had happened** before something else happened, e.g.
>
> *Ich bin in die Schule gegangen, nachdem ich gefrühstückt **hatte**.* – I went to school after I **had** eaten my breakfast.
>
> For the pluperfect the auxiliary is the appropriate form of the imperfect of *sein* or *haben* e.g.
> *Ich **hatte** meine Arbeit gemacht.* – I **had** done my work.
>
> *Ich **war** ins Kino gegangen.* – I **had** been to the cinema.
>
> The past participle remains the same.
>
> For the imperfect forms of *sein* and *haben*,
> *see page 65* ➡

Grammatik Seite 183

3b 🖊 Translate the following sentences into German.

a After I did my homework I went to the cinema.

b I got good marks in German because I had been to Germany.

c Yesterday I was ill because I had eaten in the canteen.

d My friend got bad marks in English because he hadn't read the book.

4 🖊 Use the conditional forms of the verbs *sein* and *haben* and/or the phrase *es gäbe …* to describe an ideal school as indicated by the pictures. The phrases in the box may also help you.

Beispiel: Meine ideale Schule wäre auf dem Land. Mein Klassenzimmer hätte die neueste Technologie.

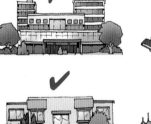

> ### The conditional forms of *haben*, *sein* and *geben*
>
> The conditional (imperfect subjunctive) forms of *haben* and *sein* are the German equivalents of the English 'would have' and 'would be':
>
> | | |
> |---|---|
> | ich hätte | ich wäre |
> | du hättest | du wärst |
> | er/sie/es hätte | er/sie/es wäre |
> | wir hätten | wir wären |
> | ihr hättet | ihr wärt |
> | sie hätten | sie wären |
> | Sie hätten | Sie wären |
>
> To say 'there would be' you need to use the imperfect subjunctive form of *es gibt*: *es gäbe*.

Grammatik Seite 184

eine moderne Sporthalle	einen Sportplatz
ein großes Zimmer, wo …	die neueste Technologie
eine kleine Schule	nicht streng
ich könnte	freundliche Lehrer und Lehrerinnen
ein modernes Labor	Musik hören
fernsehen	plaudern

School / college and future plans

Wie ist deine Schule? ➡ *Seite 132–133*

die	AG	extra-curricular group activity chosen by students
	allerlei	all sorts of
	benutzen	to use
die	Bibliothek	library
	danach	afterwards
	dann	then
	dauern	to last (time)
	Deutsch	German
	dreckig	dirty
	Englisch	English
	Erdkunde	geography
das	Experiment	experiment
das	Fach	school subject
	Französisch	French
	Fremdsprachen (pl)	foreign languages
	ganz	completely
die	Gesamtschule	comprehensive school
	Geschichte	history
	gründen	to found, to set up
die	Grundschule	primary school
das	Gymnasium	grammar school
	hassen	to hate
die	Hauptschule	secondary modern school (up to age 15)
	Hausaufgaben (pl)	homework
	in Ordnung	fine, okay
das	Internat	boarding school
das	Internet	internet
die	Kantine	canteen
die	Klasse	class
das	Klassenzimmer	classroom
	Kunst	art

das	Labor	laboratory, lab
das	Lehrerzimmer	staff room
	lesen	to read
	malen	to paint
	Mathe(matik)	maths
	Musik	music
	Naturwissenschaften (pl)	science
die	Note	mark
die	Pause	break
das	Pflichtfach	compulsory subject
	pro	per
die	Realschule	secondary modern school
	schon	already
	schreiben	to write
die	Schule	school
die	Schulordnung	school rules
das	Sekretariat	school office
der	Sport	sport, PE
der	Sportplatz	playing field
das	Sprachlabor	language laboratory
die	Stunde	hour, lesson
die	Technologie	technology
	treiben	to drive, to do
die	Turnhalle	gymnasium
der	Umkleideraum	changing room
	vorstellen	to introduce
das	Wahlfach	optional subject
	zeichnen	to draw

Das Schulwesen anderswo ➡ *Seite 134–135*

	anders	different
	anziehen	to put on (clothes)
	aufstehen	to get up

der	Austausch	exchange	
	beginnen	to begin	
	beschreiben	to describe	
	enden	to end, to finish	
	früh	early	
die	Ganztagsschule	school that lasts all day	
	gleich	same	
der	Hausmeister	caretaker	
	konzentrieren	to concentrate	
die	Mannschaft	team	
	plaudern	to chat	
der	Schulhof	playground	
die	Schuluniform	school uniform	
der	Stundenplan	timetable	
	überhaupt nicht	not at all	
	völlig	completely	

Schulstress ➡ *Seite 136–137*

das	Abitur	exams taken at 18 (A-level equivalent)
der	Abiturient	Abitur candidate
der	Abschluss	final examination
das	Abschlusszeugnis	school leaving certificate
	abwesend	absent
	„blau" machen	to skip work
	brauchen	to need
	deswegen	because of this / that
die	Fachhochschule	university of applied sciences
	fleißig	hard-working
die	Freizeit	free time
	hart	hard
das	Heimweh	homesickness
das	Instrument	instrument
die	Klassenarbeit	class test
	klug	clever
	lachen	to laugh
der	Lehrer	male teacher
die	Lehrerin	female teacher
der	Leistungsdruck	pressure to achieve

	meinen	to think
die	Mittlere Reife	intermediate school certificate
	nachsitzen	to have detention
	nervös	nervous
der	Notendruck	exam pressure
das	Orchester	orchestra
	peinlich	painful, embarrassing
die	Prüfung	exam
	sitzen bleiben	to repeat a school year
	streng	strict
	studieren	to study (at university level)
die	Uni(versität)	university
	verbringen	to spend (time)
	verstehen	to understand
	weiterstudieren	to do further study

Eine bessere Schule ➡ *Seite 138–139*

die	Aula	school hall
die	Auswahl	choice, selection
	bauen	to build
der	Chor	choir
der	Direktor	headmaster
die	Direktorin	headmistress
das	Freibad	open-air swimming pool
der	Fußballplatz	football pitch
das	Gebäude	building
die	Kamera	camera
die	Leichtathletik	athletics
die	Meinung	opinion
	mindestens	at least
	nagelneu	brand new
die	Speise	dish, food
die	Sporthalle	sportshall
der	Traum	dream
	übrig bleiben	to be left
der	Unterricht	lessons, classes
	verbieten	to forbid, to ban
die	Versammlung	assembly
	vorschlagen	to suggest

4.5 Nebenjobs und Arbeitspraktikum

Lernziele

Discussing part time jobs and work experience

Remembering when not to use the indefinite article

Planning a piece of writing

1 Ⓥ Unjumble the following anagrams to make the names of some job titles in German.

a her Liner   b niche Maker   c tzAr   d hocK   e Fur rise

Mein Nebenjob

Karin

Ich habe viele Nebenjobs. Jeden Morgen muss ich früh aufstehen, um Zeitungen auszutragen, und abends gehe ich oft babysitten. Manchmal arbeite ich auch in einem Café, wo ich die Teller abwasche. Ab und zu bin ich auch Kellnerin im Café, aber nur wenn jemand krank ist. Ich habe fast so gut wie keine Freizeit, aber ich kann eine Menge Geld verdienen.

Georg

Ich arbeite samstags in einer Bäckerei. Ich möchte nämlich Bäcker werden, wenn ich mit der Schule fertig bin. Ich bekomme nicht viel Geld dafür, aber ich lerne viel. Der Nachteil an der Arbeit ist, dass es durch die Backöfen sehr heiß werden kann.

Monika

Am Wochenende helfe ich meinem Vater. Er ist Gärtner. Wir arbeiten natürlich im Freien und ich muss Rasen mähen usw. Er gibt mir nur €10 pro Tag und ich spare es für meinen Urlaub. Es macht Spaß, wenn die Sonne scheint, aber es ist auch anstrengend.

2 📖📖 🎧 Read the texts about part-time jobs. Who does what? Match the pictures to the people.

Beispiel: **a** Karin

> **Tipp**
>
> Remember German job titles are usually different according to gender.
>
> *Lehrer / Lehrerin,
> Kellner / Kellnerin*

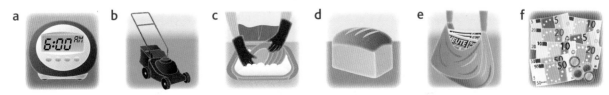

a   b   c   d   e   f

3 🎧 What did these young people do on work experience? Fill in the gaps in the diaries.

1 **Florian**
sorted mail.....
....
....
LUNCH..............
....
....
....

2 **Brigitte**
....
....
....
LUNCH..............
....
....
....

4 **G** Complete the following sentences. Sometimes you will need an article and sometimes you will not.

Beispiel: **a** Er ist Mechaniker.

a Er ist _____ .

b Sie ist _____ .

c In unserer Schule haben wir _____ .

d Sie ist _____ .

e In meinem Dorf gibt es nur _____ .

f Er ist _____ .

5 ✏️ 🌐 Write a report about your work experience (real or imaginary). Include the following information:

- ■ Where you worked
- ■ When you were there and for how long
- ■ What you did
- ■ What you thought of it
- ■ What you would like to do in the future

Remembering when not to use the indefinite article

Grammatik Seite 174

In German the indefinite article is not used if you want to express what someone's job is.

Er ist Koch – 'He is **a** chef'

Sie ist Krankenschwester – 'She is **a** nurse'

You do use the indefinite article if you are talking about a job without identifying a particular person, e.g.

Sie ist Kellnerin – 'She is **a** waitress

BUT

Wir suchen eine Kellnerin – 'We are looking for **a** waitress'

Note also other occasions when the indefinite article is not used in German where it would be used in English.

See page 158 ➡️

✏️ Planning a piece of writing

Strategie

- ● Make sure you know what you have to include in your work.
- ● Write one paragraph per bullet point.
- ● Make a checklist of the structures you want to use, e.g. tenses, subordinate clauses.
- ● Remember ADORE. See page 133.

Ich war Praktikant / Praktikantin	in	einem Büro / einer Schule.
	bei	der Firma.
Dort habe ich	als ... gearbeitet / das Telefon beantwortet / meinen Kollegen beim ... geholfen / Tee und Kaffee gemacht.	
Dort musste ich	als ... arbeiten / das Telefon beantworten / meinen Kollegen beim ... helfen / Tee und Kaffee machen.	
Ich habe die Arbeit	langweilig / interessant / besser als in der Schule	gefunden.
In der Zukunft möchte ich als	Lehrer(in) / Koch / Köchin	arbeiten.

kerboodle!

4.6 Ich suche einen Job

Lernziele

Understanding job adverts and letters of application

Revising how to say 'when'

Using previously learned material

Ich will diesen Job

Wollen Sie als Fleischer arbeiten?

Wir bieten Schichtarbeit an

Schicken Sie Ihren Lebenslauf

möller@t-online.de

☎ 01729 287501

Kleines Gasthaus sucht Arbeitskräfte.

Tellerwäscher/in, Kellner/in

guter Lohn

adele@gasthauskrone.t-online.de

☎ **01945 436472**

Qualifiziert und arbeitslos?

Geschäftsmann sucht Sekretär/in

Vollzeit/Teilzeit

bauer@t-online.de

☎ **0147 915453**

Kiel den 14. April

Sehr geehrte Damen und Herren,

ich möchte mich um die Stelle als Metzger in Ihrem Geschäft bewerben. Ich habe letzten Juni ein Arbeitspraktikum in einer Metzgerei gemacht und will jetzt Metzger werden. Ich habe zwar keine weitere Arbeitserfahrung, aber ich bin fleißig und ehrlich und habe einen guten Schulabschluss.

Beiliegend sende ich Ihnen meinen Lebenslauf.

Ich könnte sofort anfangen, wenn Sie wollen.

Mit freundlichen Grüßen

Robert Mann

Robert Mann

---

1 📖 🎧 Complete the sentences in English.

a möller@t-online.de is offering _____ work.

b bauer@t-online.de is looking for a _____.

c The job is aimed at people with qualifications who are currently _____.

d adele@gasthauskrone.t-online.de is offering a good _____.

e Robert Mann is applying to work as _____.

f Robert Mann is sending a _____ attached to his email.

2 🎥 Fräulein Kassel has applied for a job in IT. Watch the job interview and make notes in English. Use the following headings and include as many details as you can:

■ Geld? ■ Arbeitszeit? ■ Erfahrung? ■ Arbeitspraktikum? ■ Charakter? ■ Sonstiges?

3 Ⓖ Complete the sentences by using the correct word for 'when'.

Beispiel: **a** Wann

a _____ können Sie anfangen?

b _____ ich 15 war, habe ich in einem Restaurant gearbeitet.

c _____ ich arbeite, bin ich immer fleißig.

d _____ ich die Schule verlasse, werde ich einen Job suchen.

e Ich habe oft Tee gemacht, _____ ich im Büro gearbeitet habe.

f _____ hast du dort gearbeitet?

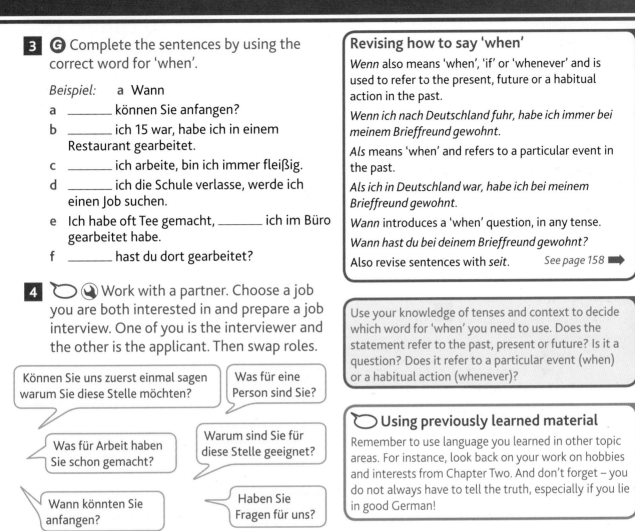

Revising how to say 'when'

Wenn also means 'when', 'if' or 'whenever' and is used to refer to the present, future or a habitual action in the past.

Wenn ich nach Deutschland fuhr, habe ich immer bei meinem Brieffreund gewohnt.

Als means 'when' and refers to a particular event in the past.

Als ich in Deutschland war, habe ich bei meinem Brieffreund gewohnt.

Wann introduces a 'when' question, in any tense.

Wann hast du bei deinem Brieffreund gewohnt?

Also revise sentences with *seit*.   *See page 158* ➡

Grammatik Seite 180

4 🗪 🔊 Work with a partner. Choose a job you are both interested in and prepare a job interview. One of you is the interviewer and the other is the applicant. Then swap roles.

Können Sie uns zuerst einmal sagen warum Sie diese Stelle möchten?

Was für eine Person sind Sie?

Was für Arbeit haben Sie schon gemacht?

Warum sind Sie für diese Stelle geeignet?

Wann könnten Sie anfangen?

Haben Sie Fragen für uns?

Tipp

Use your knowledge of tenses and context to decide which word for 'when' you need to use. Does the statement refer to the past, present or future? Is it a question? Does it refer to a particular event (when) or a habitual action (whenever)?

Strategie

🗪 **Using previously learned material**

Remember to use language you learned in other topic areas. For instance, look back on your work on hobbies and interests from Chapter Two. And don't forget – you do not always have to tell the truth, especially if you lie in good German!

5 ✍ Write a letter of application for a job. Use the letter on the previous page as a model, changing as many details as you can.

Sehr geehrte Damen und Herren,

ich habe Ihre Anzeige in ... gelesen und möchte mich um die Stelle als .... bewerben.

....
....
....
....
....
....

Mit freundlichen Grüßen

Ihr

....

kerboodle!

Lernziele

Communicating in the work place

Using dative pronouns

Taking notes effectively when listening

■ Nachricht für Herrn Schmidt

1

Fräulein Meier hat angerufen. Sie wollte etwas mit Ihnen besprechen, aber sie wird Ihnen jetzt eine E-Mail schicken. Sie müssen sie nicht zurückrufen.

2

Startseite | Index | Hilfe | Kontakt | Textversion

Sehr geehrter Herr Schmidt,

vielen Dank für Ihre Bewerbung. Bitte schicken Sie mir sobald wie möglich Ihren Lebenslauf.

Mit freundlichen Grüßen

Markus Haller

3

Hans,

Renate ist vorbeigekommen. Du solltest diese Unterlagen zuerst lesen, unterschreiben und dann kopieren, damit sie sie heute Nachmittag zurückhaben kann.

Gisela

4

Frau Kohl musste nach Hause gehen. Sie hat Magenschmerzen und Durchfall. Sie wird morgen mit Ihnen telefonieren.

1 📖 🎧 To which of Herr Schmidt's messages do the following statements refer?

Beispiel: **a** 2

a Herr Schmidt muss etwas über sein Leben und seine Laufbahn schreiben.

b Eine Kollegin ist krank.

c Jemand hat telefoniert.

d Herr Schmidt sucht einen neuen Job.

e Herr Schmidt hat einige Dokumente bekommen.

f Herr Schmidt wird eine E-Mail bekommen.

> **Tipp**
> Don't forget the effect of *nicht* or *kein*. Listen carefully to what you hear.

2 🎧 🔄 Listen to the voicemails. Make notes and fill in the missing details.

Beispiel: **a** You need to ring back on telephone number 453 …

a You need to ring back on telephone number _____.

b Frau Ballack will meet Herr Bauer at _____ in _____.

c Frank is going to _____.

d The _____ looks good. Andrea should now _____.

e Next week's meeting will be at the _____.

f To get to the office Herr Müller should take the _____. The office is _____.

g Stefanie would like to see Julia _____. Julia needs to contact her by _____.

> 🎧 **Taking notes effectively when listening**
> **Strategie**
> ● If you need to make notes of what you hear try this three step recipe for success:
> ● Write only key words.
> ● Just write the first few letters of a word to save time.
> ● Write your notes out in greater detail during pauses.

3 **G** Complete the sentences by filling the gap with an appropriate dative pronoun (for the last two, you decide whom the pronoun refers to and then translate what it means!).

Beispiel: a ihm

a Johann ist im Büro. Du sollst mit _____ telefonieren.

b Serena kommt morgen. Du sollst _____ sagen, wo das Hotel liegt.

c Ich habe kein Geld. Kannst du _____ €20 geben?

d Ich gehe mit _____ dorthin.

e Frau Gens hat _____ eine Postkarte geschickt.

4a Prepare a message to leave on an answerphone.

- ■ Say who you are
- ■ Say you can't come tomorrow
- ■ Give a reason
- ■ Suggest an alternative time and place

4b Now make up your own message to record.

5 Write an e-mail about a forthcoming visit.

> Hier spricht _____
> _____
> _____
> _____
> Auf Wiederhören!

Sehr geehrter Herr _____ / Sehr geehrte Frau _____			
Ich komme gern	morgen am _____	zu einem Vorstellungsgespräch zu einem Seminar	bei Ihnen. in Ihr Büro. im Hotel Regent.
Ich will	um _____ Uhr gegen Mittag	eintreffen.	

Mit freundlichen Grüßen

[Name]

Grammatik Seite 179

Using dative pronouns

After some prepositions and some verbs the dative case is used.

*Ich gehe mit **ihm**.*
'I'm going with **him**.'

*Schicke **mir** eine Postkarte.*
'Send **me** a postcard.'

ich	→	mir
*du	→	dir
er/es	→	ihm
sie	→	ihr
wir	→	uns
*ihr	→	euch
sie (pl)	→	ihnen
*Sie	→	Ihnen

*NB Remember to check which form of the word for 'you' to use.

See page 159 ➡

kerboodle!

4.8 Was mache ich nach meinem Schulabschluss?

Lernziele

Describing your plans

Talking about the future

Varying your language

▪ Meine Zukunft

Felix

Im Juni mache ich das Abitur. Wenn ich gute Noten bekomme, will ich auf die Uni gehen. Ich muss im Durchschnitt mindestens eine Drei haben. Ich werde wahrscheinlich Informatik studieren, weil ich mich für Computer interessiere. Danach werde ich bestimmt einen gut bezahlten Job bekommen.

Lena

Ich werde eine Lehre machen. Mein Vater ist Mechaniker und ich werde mit ihm arbeiten. Ich glaube, dass wird sehr interessant sein. Es ist harte Arbeit, das weiß ich, aber das macht mir gar nichts aus. In der Zukunft will ich mein eigenes Geschäft gründen und er kann dann für mich arbeiten. Das wäre toll!

Martina

Ich bin mir überhaupt nicht sicher, was ich beruflich machen werde. Es gibt so viele Möglichkeiten. Ich bin nicht intelligent genug, um auf die Uni zu gehen, aber ich will auch nicht sofort einen Job haben. Ich will doch zuerst ein bisschen leben. Ich werde also nächstes Jahr eine Weltreise machen, bevor ich anfange zu arbeiten. Nachher werde ich keine Zeit mehr dafür haben.

1 📖 🎧 Read about Felix, Lena and Martina's plans and complete the sentences below.

a   Felix wants to _____ providing he gets good marks.

b   After that he hopes to _____.

c   Lena wants to be a _____.

d   In the future she wants to have _____.

e   Martina is not going to university because _____.

f   Next year she is going to _____.

2 🎧 What are each of these young people going to do? Listen to the recording and make notes, including as many details as you can.

3 **G** Change these sentences into the future tense using the correct part of *werden* and an infinitive.

Beispiel: **a** Ich werde auf die Uni gehen.

a   Ich gehe auf die Uni.
b   Ich mache eine Lehre.
c   Er arbeitet in einer Fabrik.
d   Sie verlässt die Schule.
e   Ralf und Karin suchen einen Job.
f   Was machst du?

4 ✏️ 👁️ Write a short description of your future plans. Mention:

- details of what you want to do next year
- details of what job you would like
- reasons for your choices

Nach der Schule	werde ich	die Schule verlassen,	weil …	
Nächstes Jahr	möchte ich	auf die Uni gehen,	da …	
In der Zukunft	will ich	eine Lehre machen,	denn …	
Wenn ich … bin,		in einer Fabrik / einem Büro arbeiten,		
	möchte ich	Elektriker(in) / Lehrer(in)	werden.	
		als …	arbeiten.	

Talking about the future

Remember that when talking about what is going to happen you usually use the appropriate part of *werden* followed by an infinitive (see page 77).

Ich werde in Deutschland arbeiten.

You could also use the present tense and a future time reference like we sometimes do in English (see page 37).

Nächstes Jahr arbeite ich in Deutschland.

Practise more ways to talk about the future.
See page 159 ➡

Grammatik *Seite 184*

✏️ Varying your language

Try to vary the way you express your future plans. As well as the ways suggested in the grammar box you could also use *ich möchte* or *ich will* plus an infinitive to say what you want to do.

meine Zukunft

Strategie

Tipp

If you don't know what your future plans are, don't worry. Say you are not sure (*Ich bin nicht sicher*), that you don't know yet (*Ich weiß noch nicht*) or that you might possibly do something (*Ich werde vielleicht …*). If you add a reason this can be just as good an answer.

■ Mein Job

Jasmin

Ich bin LKW-Fahrerin. Es gibt nicht viele Frauen in meinem Beruf und man fragt mich immer, „Warum hast du diesen Job gewählt?". Ich mag einfach fahren! Ich musste natürlich meinen LKW-Führerschein machen, bevor ich den Job machen konnte. Das war für mich ganz schwierig, aber ich habe es geschafft und jetzt habe ich meinen Traumjob. Ich muss jeden Tag sehr früh aufstehen, denn der Arbeitstag beginnt schon um 6 Uhr! Dann bin ich den ganzen Tag unterwegs und ich bin froh, dass ich alleine arbeite.

Horst

Ich bin Friseur. Nach der Schulzeit habe ich zuerst eine Lehre gemacht. Dann habe ich drei Jahre lang für einen Freund gearbeitet aber das fand ich langweilig und frustrierend. Deswegen habe ich mein eigenes Geschäft gekauft und ich kann jetzt viel mehr Geld verdienen. Mein Arbeitstag beginnt um halb neun und endet um 5 Uhr. Ich arbeite auch am Samstag aber Montag habe ich frei. Ich finde meine Arbeit interessant, weil ich mit meinen Kunden sprechen kann, während ich arbeite.

Kai

Ich arbeite in einem Büro. Ich habe vier Jahre lang auf der Uni studiert und seitdem arbeite ich. Mein Arbeitstag ist fast immer langweilig. Ein Tag ist wie der andere. Ich fahre mit dem Auto zum Büro, sitze am Computer, mache meine Arbeit und habe nie Kontakt mit anderen Leuten, nur per E-Mail. Ich hätte gern einen anderen Beruf. Ab und zu kann ich von zu Hause arbeiten. Das gefällt mir besser, weil ich dann wenigstens mit meiner Frau zu Mittag essen kann.

1 📖 🎧 Read the texts above and complete the table.

	Job	Training	Routine	Opinion
Jasmin	HGV Driver	HGV Licence		
Horst				
Kai				

2 🎧 Listen to the recording. These people are answering questions about their jobs, but what were they asked? Match the questions below with the answers you hear.

Beispiel: **a**   **4** Wann beginnst du morgens?

1 Wo arbeitest du?   **2** Was für Qualifikationen hast du?   **3** Wie viel verdienst du pro Stunde?

4 Wann beginnst du morgens?   **5** Warum magst du deine Arbeit?   **6** Wie findest du deinen Job?

3 Ⓖ Complete these questions with an appropriate interrogative.

Beispiel: **a** Wie

a _____ findest du deinen Arbeitstag?

b _____ Geld bekommst du pro Tag?

c _____ kannst du nach Hause gehen?

d _____ findest du deinen Job so super?

e _____ ist dein Büro?

f _____ ist dein Arbeitgeber?

g Von _____ hast du Informationen über deinen Job bekommen?

h Mit _____ hast du im Büro gearbeitet und gesprochen?

4 🗨 🌐 Work with a partner. You should each imagine you have one of the following jobs. Take it in turns to interview one another about the job. Use the questions suggested, then make up some of your own.

> Klempner / Klempnerin

> Verkäufer / Verkäuferin

> Metzger / Metzgerin

> Zahnarzt / Zahnärztin

> Bauer / Bäuerin

> Kellner / Kellnerin

Revising interrogatives

These are some of the words that introduce questions. Can you remember what the following words mean?

> *wohin?*
>
> *wie?*
>
> *warum?*
>
> *wie viel(e)?*
>
> *welche(r/s)?*

The interrogative *wer?* ('who') is often used with prepositions and changes its form. For example:

> *Mit wem?* 'With whom?'
>
> *Von wem?* 'From whom?'

Also revise using the conditional.

See page 159 ➡

Grammatik Seite 187

🗨 Finding out information

Don't limit yourself to answering questions when speaking. Find out information by asking questions. Use as many of the interrogatives you have learnt as possible.

Strategie

■ Wo arbeitest du?

■ Was machst du an einem normalen Tag?

■ Wie findest du deinen Job? Warum?

Ich arbeite in .... / bei ...

An einem normalen Tag	muss ich	Briefe tippen.	
		am Computer arbeiten.	
		das Telefon beantworten.	
	mache ich den Tee.		
	spreche ich mit Kunden.		
Ich finde meinen Job / meinen Beruf	gut,	weil es	Spaß macht.
	schlecht,		langweilig ist.
	in Ordnung,	weil ich	alleine arbeite.

Tipp

Use *in* to say where you work (*ich arbeite in einer Fabrik*) or *bei* to say whom you work for (*ich arbeite bei McDonalds*). You need to use the dative after *in* or *bei* (see page 176).

Current and future jobs

■ Wir arbeiten

Ralf

Seit Oktober 2005 arbeite ich als Rechtsanwalt bei der Firma Bauer u. Bauer. Die Arbeit ist manchmal langweilig, aber ab und zu darf ich etwas besonders Interessantes machen. Ich musste sieben Jahre lang studieren, bevor ich meinen ersten Job als Assistent bei einer Rechtsanwaltspraxis bekommen konnte. Zwei Jahre später habe ich mich um diese neue Stelle beworben.

Wenn ich genug Geld und auch mehr Erfahrung habe, möchte ich in der Zukunft beruflich selbstständig sein. Wann wird das sein? Wer weiß?

Anika

Ich bin Fabrikarbeiterin. Die Arbeitsstunden sind lang und ich muss leider auch Schichtarbeit machen. Das heißt, ich muss jede dritte Woche nachts arbeiten. Ich arbeite meistens am Fließband, aber wenn eine Sekretärin krank ist, dann darf ich im Büro helfen, was mir am besten gefällt.

Als ich 21 Jahre alt war, war ich arbeitslos und dann gab es einen Streik in der Fabrik. Der Fabrikbesitzer war natürlich sehr verärgert, aber der Streik hat nur ein paar Tage gedauert. Danach ist die Situation im Unternehmen besser geworden und ich habe einen Job in der Fabrik bekommen.

Kirsten

Ich bin Landwirtin. Mein Bauernhof liegt in einem schönen Dorf auf dem Land in der Nähe von Bremen. Auf dem Bauernhof haben wir Kühe, Schafe und Schweine. Es gibt auch einige Hühner, die ich früh

am Morgen füttern muss. Ich stehe immer sehr früh auf und nach zwei Stunden Arbeit oder so frühstücke ich. Normalerweise essen wir frische Eier.

Mein Mann sagt mir immer, dass der Job zu hart ist. Ich mag aber die frische Luft und auch wenn ich bis spät in die Nacht arbeiten muss, gefällt es mir hier auf dem Bauernhof. Die langen Arbeitstage stören mich überhaupt nicht.

Eckhard

Ich interessiere mich sehr für andere Kulturen und kann gut Englisch und Italienisch sprechen. In der Zukunft möchte ich Dolmetscher werden, aber zur Zeit habe ich einen Job in einem Reisebüro. Wenn ich im Büro bin, habe ich viel Kontakt mit Leuten, die reisen mögen, genau wie ich.

Wenn ich Dolmetscher werde, werde ich wahrscheinlich in England oder Italien wohnen. Hoffentlich werde ich auch die Gelegenheit haben, Spanisch oder Französisch zu lernen. Dann könnte ich vielleicht eine noch bessere Stelle finden. Das wäre toll!

1a 📖🎧 Read about each person's job, then fill in the gaps below with the correct names.

a _____ works in the countryside.
b _____ works in a factory.
c _____ sometimes works at night.
d _____ has lots of animals.
e _____ likes speaking foreign languages.
f _____ studied law.

1b 📖🎧 Read about the jobs again and answer the following questions in English.

a What are Ralf's plans for the future?
b What will he need before he can achieve his aim?
c What does Anika like best about her job?
d What happened just before she got her current job?
e What is Kirsten's attitude to her hours of work?
f What does Eckhard want to do to improve his job prospects?

2a 🎧 Listen to the recordings. Each speaker needs someone to get a job done. Can you choose the correct picture for each?

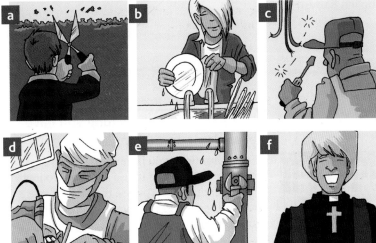

2b 🎧 Whilst working in a hotel you receive a message on the answerphone about a forthcoming conference. Your boss wants to know what it is about. Listen to the recording and write down as many details as you can in English.

Vokabeln

die Rechtsanwaltspraxis lawyer's practice
die Schichtarbeit shift work
das Fließband conveyor belt, production line
das Unternehmen business
der Dolmetscher interpreter

Grammatik

Look and listen for the following features in the texts and recordings. Note down the examples you find.

a Avoiding the definite article when saying what jobs people do
   Ich bin Fabrikarbeiterin
   See page 158 ➡

b Using the future tense
   Wir werden am Mittwoch ankommen.
   See page 159 ➡

AQA Examiner's tip

Before listening to the recording for activity 2a, prepare for what you might hear. What is the German for these professions? What other key words might you hear which you would associate with them?

AQA Examiner's tip

What details might you need to listen out for in Activity 2b? Make a list of possible headings before you hear the recording.

Vokabeln

tagen to meet
der Drucker printer

(G) Current and future jobs

1 ✏ Complete the sentences below to describe each picture.

a Ich habe _____ .

b Mein Vater ist _____ .

c Heinrich ist _____ .

d Meine Mutter ist _____ .

e Sarah ist _____ .

> ### Knowing when not to use the indefinite article
>
> Remember that, unlike in English, you will not use the indefinite article when describing someone's profession or nationality, or when talking about an ailment.
>
> *Ich bin Elektriker.* – I am **an** electrician.
>
> *Er ist Engländer.* – He's **an** Englishman.
>
> *Ich habe Halsschmerzen.* – I've got **a** sore throat.

Grammatik Seite 174

2a 🗩 Work in pairs. Using *seit* with the present tense, say how long you have been doing each of the activities pictured (you decide how long in each case). Use the phrases in the box to help you if you need to.

Beispiel: **a** Seit einem Jahr mache ich Babysitten.

> Babysitten   Deutsch lernen
>
> in einem Geschäft arbeiten
>
> Klavier spielen
>
> Zeitungen austragen

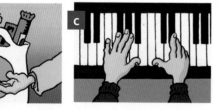

> ### Using *seit* to say how long you have been doing something
>
> To say how long you have been doing something you need to use *seit* ('for') followed by the dative case. You use the present tense rather than the past (as you would in English):
>
> *Ich **besuche seit vier Jahren** diese Schule.* – I've **been going** to this school **for four years.**
>
> ***Seit einem Monat** arbeite ich bei Aldi.* – I've **been working** at Aldi **for a month.**
>
> Remember to use the correct dative endings after *seit*:
>
> | masc. | fem. | neut. | pl. |
> |-------|------|-------|-----|
> | *einem* | *einer* | *einem* | |
> | *dem* | *der* | *dem* | *den* |
>
> Plural nouns in the dative add an *–n* at the end:
>
> *Er arbeitet seit drei Monaten dort.* – He's been working there for three months.

Grammatik Seite 185

2b ✏ Now write up your answers from activity 2a and add two more *seit* sentences of your own.

3a ✍ Write down which word for 'you' you would use in each of the following scenarios:

a talking to a best friend
b talking to your teacher
c talking to a group of classmates
d talking to your grandma
e talking to your boss on work experience
f talking to your penfriend's mother or father

3b ✍ Prepare a series of questions to ask in the following situations. Remember to decide first which word for 'you' to use.

- a discussion about work experience with a group of fellow students
- talking about life at work with a group of adults
- discussing future job prospects with a friend
- a job interview (as interviewer and/or interviewee)

Grammatik · Seite 179

Using the correct word for 'you' (revision)

If you talk to someone you know well enough to use their first name, a child, a friend or a member of your family, use *du*.

If you are talking to more than one friend or family member, use *ihr* (*du* + *du* = *ihr*).

In other situations, when talking to an adult whom you do not know well or in a professional context, use *Sie* for both singular and plural (unless the person gives you permission to *duzen* – to call someone 'du').

Grammatik · Seite 184

Talking about the future (revision)

Remember that there are different ways to talk about the future in German:

Future tense with *werden*   See page 77 ➡

Present tense (with future time indicators)   See page 37 ➡

People may also use *ich möchte* to say what they would like to do in the future (page 184).

Mein Traumjob wäre in der Filmindustrie. Ich möchte Schauspielerin werden. Ich bin schon Mitglied in einer Theatergruppe und arbeite am Wochenende im Kino in der Stadtmitte. Ich verdiene zwar nicht viel, aber es macht Spaß, und ich kann die neuesten Filme umsonst sehen. Nächste Woche läuft der neue James Bond Film.

Ich habe vor, in fünf Jahren Millionärin zu sein, und wenn ich berühmt bin, werde ich nur einen oder zwei Filme in einem Jahr machen. Bis dann muss ich hart arbeiten. Nächstes Jahr gehe ich auf die Uni, wo ich Medienwissenschaft studieren werde. Ich freue mich schon darauf.

4 📖 How many different references to the future can you find in the text above? Make a list.

5 ✍ Write five (or more) sentences describing what your ideal workplace would be like, using different conditional forms. If wished, use the phrases below as prompts, but try to include your own ideas.

um … Uhr anfangen

früh nach Hause gehen

Pause machen

wenig Arbeit

bequem

freundliche Kollegen

viel Geld verdienen

Grammatik · Seite 184

Conditional sentences (revision)

Remember that there are various ways of expressing a conditional in German:

To say 'I would' use *Ich würde* plus an infinitive (page 139).

To say what something 'would be' or 'would have' use *wäre* and *hätte* (page 143).

To say that 'there would be' something use *es gäbe* (page 143).

Current and future jobs

Nebenjobs und Arbeitspraktikum
➡ *Seite 146–147*

	abwaschen	to wash up
	arbeiten	to work
das	Arbeitspraktikum	work experience
der	Arbeitstag	working day
die	Aufgabe	task, job
	babysitten	to babysit
der(die)	Bäcker(in)	baker
die	Bäckerei	bakery
	beantworten	to answer
	bekommen	to receive
	beschäftigt	busy
der	Brief	letter
die	Briefmarke	stamp
der	Briefumschlag	envelope
das	Büro	office
	entweder ... oder ...	either ... or ...
die	Firma	company
die	Freizeit	free time
der(die)	Gärtner(in)	gardener
	helfen	to help
	im Freien	out in the open
der	Kellner	waiter
die	Kellnerin	waitress
	kleben	to stick, to glue
der	Koch/die Köchin	cook
der	Kollege	male colleague
die	Kollegin	female colleague
	kopieren	to copy, to photocopy
	mit etwas fertig sein	to be finished with something
der	Nebenjob	second or extra job, job outside school
	Rasen mähen	to mow lawns
der(die)	Sekretär(in)	secretary

	sparen	to save
das	Telefon	telephone
	verdienen	to earn
	Zeitungen austragen	to deliver newspapers

Ich suche einen Job ➡ *Seite 148–149*

die	Anzeige	advertisement
der(die)	Arbeitgeber(in)	employer
	arbeitslos	unemployed
	beiliegend	enclosed
	bewerben sich um etw.	to apply for sth.
der(die)	Bewerber(in)	applicant
	ehrlich	honest
die	Erfahrung	experience
der(die)	Fleischer(in)	butcher
die	Gelegenheitsarbeit	casual work
das	Geschäft	shop, business
der	Job	job
der(die)	Kandidat(in)	candidate
die	Karriere	career
	kündigen	to hand notice in for
der	Lebenslauf	CV
der	Lohn	wage
der(die)	Metzger(in)	butcher
	mit freundlichen Grüßen	yours sincerely, best wishes
die	Person	person
die	Qualifikation	qualification
	qualifiziert	qualified
die	Schichtarbeit	shift work
	schicken	to send
	Sehr geehrte Dame	Dear madam
	Sehr geehrter Herr	Dear sir
	sofort	straight away
die	Stelle	post, position
	Teilzeit-	part-time

der(die)	Tellerwäscher(in)	dish washer (person)
	Überstunden (pl)	overtime
	verabschieden (sich)	to say goodbye
die	Verantwortung	responsibility
	verbringen	to spend (time)
	verlassen	to leave
	Vollzeit-	full-time
das	Vorstellungsgespräch	job interview
	werden	to become

Am Arbeitsplatz ➡ *Seite 150–151*

	absagen	to cancel, to call off
	am Apparat	speaking (when on the phone)
	anrufen	to telephone, to ring up
	Auf Wiederhören	goodbye (when using the telephone)
	besprechen	to discuss
die	Besprechung	discussion, meeting
die	Bewerbung	application
die	E-Mail	e-mail
die	Entscheidung	decision
	möglich	possible
	morgen	tomorrow
die	Nachricht	message, piece of news
	schade	it is a shame
	telefonieren	to telephone
die	Telefonnummer	telephone number
	übermorgen	the day after tomorrow
	unterschreiben	to sign
	vorbei	past, by
	zurückrufen	to call back

Was mache ich nach meinem Schulabschluss?
➡ *Seite 152–153*

	ankommen auf etw.	to depend on sth.
	auf die Uni gehen	to go to university
	ausgeben	to spend (money)

	beruflich	career-wise, in terms of a job
	bestimmt	definitely
	brauchen	to need, to use
das	macht nichts aus	it does not matter
der(die)	Elektriker(in)	electrician
	gut bezahlt	well paid
	im Durchschnitt	on average
die	Informatik	IT
	Jura	law
die	Lehre	apprenticeship
der(die)	Mechaniker(in)	mechanic
die	Medizin	medicine
die	Möglichkeit	possibility
der	Profi	professional
die	Weltreise	tour of the world

Jobs und Berufe ➡ *Seite 154–155*

der	Bauer/die Bäuerin	farmer
der	Beruf	job, profession
	erfolgreich	successful
der(die)	Friseur(in)	hairdresser
der	Führerschein	driver's licence
der(die)	Klempner(in)	plumber
der	Kontakt	contact
der(die)	Kunde/Kundin	customer
	Leute (pl)	people
der(die)	LKW-Fahrer(in)	lorry driver
	nur	only
	schaffen	to manage, to pass
	suchen	to look for
	tippen	to type
	unterwegs	on the move
der(die)	Verkäufer(in)	shop assistant, salesperson
	wählen	to choose
	während	while
der(die)	Zahnarzt/Zahnärztin	dentist

4  Geld verdienen

You are talking to a German friend about what you do to earn money, any paid work you have done and your career plans for the future.

Your teacher will play the role of the friend. He or she could ask you the following:

1 do you get money from your parents or family?
2 do you have a part-time job?
3 where did you do your work experience?
4 what were your colleagues like?
5 what are your career plans for the future?
6 would you like to work abroad?
7 **!**

Remember you will have to respond to something that you have not yet prepared.

AQA Examiner's tips

Remember that the main aim of this conversation is to show how good you are at German. You can make up details if the truth is not very interesting.

Start off by making a plan, listing your key words. Write five or six words for each of the seven sections that make up the task (you are allowed a total of 40 words).

1 **Do you get money from your parents or family?**
   - Say whether you get pocket money and if the answer is yes, say how much you get and from whom
   - Say what you do to help at home and whether you get paid for it
   - Give your view on whether you should get paid for helping at home
   - Mention something you do with the money you get

AQA Examiner's tips

Now start your notes. Here are some suggested words for the first section:

1 *Taschengeld, verdienen, bekommen, Pfund, sparen, kaufen*

You can use *zu Hause* to say 'at home'.

Remember to give reasons for your opinions. ADORE applies to speaking as well as writing.

🔊 See page 133 ➡

Remember to add variety to what you say. You might not just spend, spend, spend!

2 **Do you have a part-time job?**
   - Say whether you have a part-time job
   - Describe what you do
   - Give your opinion of your job
   - Mention how you get to work

AQA Examiner's tips

Remember to use the dative case after *in* or *bei* to say where you work: *ich arbeite in einem Geschäft, ich arbeite bei Topshop*

🅖 See page 176 ➡

If you don't have a part-time job, you could say why not e.g. no time, pressures of schoolwork. You could also say whether you would like one.

Give a reason for your choice of how you get to work. Are you *umweltfreundlich*?

3 **Where did you do your work experience?**
   - Say where you did your work experience
   - Describe what you did
   - Say what the advantages of work experience are
   - Mention any disadvantages

AQA Examiner's tips

If you have not yet been on work experience remember that you can make things up!

You will need to use the perfect and imperfect tenses to talk about what you did and describe it.

Perfect tense: 🅖 See page 182 ➡

Imperfect tense: 🅖 See page 182 ➡

If you want to say what you had to do, use the imperfect tense of *müssen*: *ich musste um halb sieben aufstehen.*

🅖 See page 183 ➡

Vorteile and *Nachteile* may be words for your notes here.

4 What were your colleagues like?
- Describe your work colleagues
- Say how you got on with them
- Mention whether you did things together after work
- Say what you think makes a good colleague and/or boss

AQA Examiner's tips

Again you will need to use the past tense. You can use *Ich bin gut / schlecht mit … ausgekommen* to say 'I got on well / badly with …', or you could say how you found a particular colleague by using *Ich habe … freundlich / sympathisch gefunden*.

G See page 59 ➡

Remember to pronounce the *sy* in *sympathisch* like a *z* followed by a *u* in English.

Your words for your list will probably be adjectives this time but be selective. Only write words you might forget or that prompt the next thing you want to say.

5 What are your career plans for the future?
- Say what sort of job you would like
- Mention what sort of qualifications / training you will need
- Say what your dream job would be
- Explain why you would like it

AQA Examiner's tips

You are now being asked to talk about the future, so you will need to use the future tense with *werden* or the present tense with future indicators.

G See page 184 ➡

If you are uncertain about what you will do, you could say *ich weiß noch nicht* or, better still, suggest something but say *vielleicht*.

If you want to be really impressive, you might try the future tense with a modal verb: *ich werde an der Uni studieren müssen; ich werde gute Noten bekommen müssen*.

6 Would you like to work abroad?
- Say whether you would like to work abroad
- Say where you would like to work
- Give reasons for your choices
- Mention what you think of job opportunities for young people in Europe

AQA Examiner's tips

If you don't yet know where you want to work, you could say *ich habe mich noch nicht entschieden* or *ich weiß noch nicht, wo ich arbeiten werde*.

To say 'I would like', use *Ich möchte*. Make sure you pronounce it correctly – *ich mochte* means 'I used to like'!

G See page 184 ➡

Arbeitsmöglichkeiten is the German word for 'job opportunities' and may make a good addition to your notes.

7 **!** At this point you will be asked a question which you don't know in advance. However, you can try to guess what it might be and prepare various options:
- Say whether earning lots of money is important to you, giving justifications
- Say whether you think foreign language skills are important for work
- Talk about a friend's work experience
- Say whether you think it's a good idea to do the same job as your parents

AQA Examiner's tips

Prepare answers for all the possibilities suggested. For each possibility, make three different points e.g. good wages? = buying power, independence, job satisfaction. Now choose the two most likely questions, in your opinion.

In your plan, write three words that illustrate each of the two most likely options.

Remember to check the total number of words you have used. It should be 40 or fewer.

You should now have completed your plan and prepared your answers. Give your plan to your teacher for feedback. Compare your answers to the online sample version – you might find some useful hints to make yours even better.

4 ✏ Das britische Schulwesen

Your local council has asked you to write an article in German for a brochure they are producing to celebrate a twinning relationship with a village in Germany. The article is to be entitled *Das britische Schulwesen*. You could include:

1 a description of your school
2 your school routine
3 your subjects
4 school trips and exchanges
5 your school uniform
6 extra-curricular activities
7 post-16 options

1 A description of your school
- ■ Introduce your school, giving its name and location
- ■ Say what type of school it is, e.g. comprehensive, boarding, grammar etc. Also mention the age range.
- ■ Mention the size of the school and how old it is
- ■ Say what classrooms and facilities there are

2 Your school routine
- ■ Say how you get to school and what time you arrive
- ■ Say how many lessons you have each day and when they begin
- ■ Mention what you do at break and lunchtime
- ■ Say when school finishes

3 Your subjects
- ■ Mention compulsory subjects (*Pflichtfächer*) and options (*Wahlfächer*)
- ■ Say which subject is your favourite and why
- ■ Say which subject is your least favourite and why
- ■ Give your view on homework and exam pressures

AQA Examiner's tips

Start off by giving the name of your school. Use the *–t* ending on the verb, as you are referring to something in the third person: *Meine Schule heißt …*

G See page 180 ➡

Use the *Tipp* and *Strategie* boxes from this unit to help with your preparation for this task.

AQA Examiner's tips

Now start your notes. Write five or six words.
1 *Gesamtschule, Schüler, Gebäude, Bibliothek, Umkleideraum*
2 …
Only choose words you might otherwise forget or that are difficult to spell.

Use *es gibt* (there is, there are) and *wir haben* (we have) to describe what there is in the school. Remember that the items that follow will be direct objects and need to take the accusative case.

G See page 175 ➡

AQA Examiner's tips

Use the present tense to refer to what you normally do. Make sure to put the verb second if you start with a time phrase e.g. *Normalerweise komme ich …*

G See page 186 ➡

Add five or six more words to your notes. If you use a verb check that it is in the infinitive form. Remember that you only have 40 words to play with.

AQA Examiner's tips

You can use the perfect tense to say which subjects you have chosen: *Ich habe … gewählt.*

G See page 182 ➡

For compulsory subjects, you could say *Als Pflichtfächer mache ich …*

Link your sentences using words like *weil* and *obwohl*. Check your word order in subordinate clauses.

G See page 186 ➡

Your list words here may contain school subjects, adjectives and ways to express your opinion. Again, make sure verbs are in the infinitive form.

4 School trips and exchanges
- Give some information about trips your school organises
- Mention any links your school has with schools abroad
- Mention a trip or exchange you went on recently
- Describe what you did and give your opinion on it

AQA Examiner's tips

Be creative in this section and show off the grammar you have learnt. Try to use phrases and structures you haven't yet used.

Use different ways to compare your school and schools abroad e.g. *besser als ...*, *genauso groß wie ...*

G See page 108 ➡

You can invent an exchange or school trip to describe if you haven't been on one recently.

5 Your school uniform
- Describe your school uniform
- Give and justify your opinion on it
- Mention any changes you would make to the uniform
- Give your view on German students not having to wear school uniform

AQA Examiner's tips

You can use adjectives other than colours in your uniform description e.g. *gestreift*, *altmodisch*. Add them to your list if you need to.

Remember that if an adjective appears in front of a noun, you will need to use the correct ending.

G See page 177 ➡

Use the conditional to describe what your ideal uniform would be like.

G See page 184 ➡

If you would like to abolish (*abschaffen*) uniform, make sure you give a justification.

6 Extra-curricular activities
- Mention some extra-curricular activities on offer in your school
- Mention an activity in which you are involved
- Say what you think of it
- Mention any other activities you would like to take part in in the future

AQA Examiner's tips

You can use *man kann ...* to say what kind of things you can do. Remember to put the infinitive at the end of the sentence or clause when using a modal verb.

G See page 181 ➡

Do not worry if you are not involved in any extra-curricular activities. You do not have to always tell the truth!

To say what you would like to do you could use *ich möchte ...*

G See page 184 ➡

7 Post-16 options
- Say what sixth form opportunities there are where you live
- Mention the courses of study available and give your opinions on them
- Say what employment or training prospects there are for 16-year-olds
- Finish your article by giving an overall opinion of *das britische Schulwesen*

AQA Examiner's tips

Useful words to add to your list could be *Oberstufe, Lehre, Ergebnis.*

Future plans may depend on exam results. *Es kommt auf ... an* is a useful idiom to use (here you need to use the accusative case after *auf*).

G See page 177 ➡

Now you should have a complete set of 40 cue words, in seven groups with either five or six words in each.

When you have written your article, compare it and your cue card with the online sample version – you might find some useful hints to make yours even better.

kerboodle!

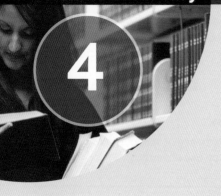

1 Give the correct German name for the school being described:

Die Schule, die man besucht, bevor man in die Gesamtschule geht.

2 Give the correct German name for the place being described:

Das Zimmer, wo die Lehrer die Pause verbringen.

3 Complete the following statement with a suitable conjunction:

Ich lerne gern Mathe, _____ ich immer gute Noten bekomme.

4 Which tense is being used in the following sentence?

Ich musste meine Hausaufgaben machen.

5 Translate the following sentence into English:

In meiner Traumschule würde die erste Stunde um halb elf anfangen.

6 Complete the following:

Er repariert Autos. Er ist _____.

7 If you saw the following in a job advert, what would you have to supply?

Schicken Sie Ihren Lebenslauf.

8 How would you ask someone in German when their working day begins?

9 Complete the following sentence, using your own ideas:

Nächstes Jahr werde ich _____.

10 What is the German word for this job?

Wusstest du schon ???

■ Hast du den Film "Kindergarten Cop" gesehen? Kindergarten ist kein englisches Wort. In Deutschland und in Österreich dürfen junge Kinder einen Kindergarten besuchen, bevor sie alt genug sind, in die Grundschule zu gehen. In der Schweiz ist der Besuch eines Kindergartens für Kinder ab vier Jahren sogar obligatorisch.

■ Wenn sie in die Grundschule gehen, bekommen deutsche Kinder am ersten Schultag eine Tüte Bonbons.

■ Großbritannien ist Mitglied der EU. Deswegen hat man das Recht in Deutschland, Österreich und den anderen Mitgliedsländern zu arbeiten, wenn man in Großbritannien geboren ist.

kerboodle!

Frequently asked questions

This general guidance is in the form of answers to 'Frequently asked questions' (FAQs).

1 How many tasks do I have to complete for the speaking part of my GCSE German?

There are two tasks, both of a similar kind. Your teacher will ask you the questions and listen to your answers. One of your tasks will be recorded as it may have to be submitted to the AQA Examination Board. Each task lasts between four and six minutes. The Speaking test counts for 30% of the whole GCSE German – so, each of the two speaking tasks is worth 15%.

2 When do the tasks have to be done?

There is no specified time for the completion of the tasks. When your teacher thinks that you have been taught the language you need and feels that you are ready, you will be given the task to prepare. It could be a task designed by the AQA Examination Board or a task designed by German teachers in your school. Your teacher will decide how long you are allowed to prepare for the task (it cannot be more than six hours).

3 Who will mark my work?

Your teacher will mark your work. A Moderator (i.e. an examiner) will sample the work of your school and check that it has been marked correctly. A Team Leader will check the work of the Moderator. The Principal Moderator will check the work of the Team Leader. The Chief Examiner will check the work of the Principal Moderator. This complicated but secure system ensures that candidates are given the correct mark.

4 What am I allowed to write on my plan?

You are allowed to write a maximum of 40 words on your plan. Those words can be in German or English. Choose them carefully so that your plan works well as a memory aid. Remember that you are not allowed to use conjugated verbs (i.e. verbs with an ending other than the infinitive or the past participle) on your plan. Codes, letters or initialled words, e.g. *i … b … g …* as being *ich bin gegangen*, are not allowed. There is no limit to the number of visuals you can use, and you can mix visuals and words if you wish.

5 What help is allowed from the moment I am given the task to prepare?

Your teacher is allowed to discuss the task in English with you, including the kind of language you may need and how to use your preparatory work. You can have access to a dictionary, your German books and Internet resources. This is the stage when you will prepare your plan using the Task Planning Form. You will then give this form to your teacher who will give you feedback on how you have met the requirements of the task. When you actually perform the task, you will only have access to your plan and your teacher's comments (i.e. the Task Planning Form).

6 How can I prepare for the unpredictable element (the exclamation mark)?

Ask yourself: What question would logically follow the questions I have already answered? Practise guessing what the unpredictable bullet point might be about. You are likely to come up with 2 or 3 possibilities. Prepare answers to cover those possibilities. Practise your possible responses. When you are asked the question, focus on the meaning of the question itself to make sure you understand it and then give it your full answer.

7 How best can I practise for the test?

Treat each bullet point as a mini task. Practise your answer to one bullet point at a time. Say your answer aloud for what is illustrated by one word on your plan. Repeat the process for each word on your plan. Next, try to account for 2 words, then for 3 words, etc … Time your answer for one whole bullet point. Repeat the process for each bullet point. Practise saying things aloud. Record yourself if possible.

8 Does it matter that my verbs are wrong as long as I can get myself understood?

Communication can break down because of poor grammatical accuracy. If that happens, you will lose marks in Communication and also in Accuracy. If you give the correct message but grammatical accuracy is poor, you will only lose marks in Accuracy. Communication is of primary importance, of course, but the quality of that communication matters too and is enhanced by grammatical accuracy.

9 How do I make sure I get the best possible marks for my answers?

You will score well in the Speaking test if:

- you say a lot that is relevant to the question.
- you have a good range of vocabulary.
- you can include complex structures.
- you can refer to present, past and future events.
- your German accent is good.
- you can speak fluently.
- you can show initiative.
- you can speak with grammatical accuracy.

10 How will my mark be affected if my German accent is not very good?

You will receive a mark for Pronunciation. However, as long as your spoken German is understandable, your Communication mark will not suffer.

11 What will I gain by giving long answers?

Consider the task as an opportunity for you to show off what you can do in German. Offer long answers whenever possible, develop the points you are trying to make, give your opinion and justify that opinion as appropriate, etc.. As a general rule, the more German you speak, the more credit you will be given (provided that what you say is relevant and understandable).

12 What does speaking with fluency mean?

Fluency is your ability to speak without hesitation. Try and speak with fluency but not too fast. If you are likely to be nervous when performing the task, practise it and practise it again. Time your whole response. Make a point of slowing down if you feel that you are speaking too fast. Practise with your plan in front of you so that you know what you are going to say next and therefore do not hesitate when delivering your contribution to the dialogue.

13 What does showing initiative mean?

Showing initiative does not mean that you suddenly ask your teacher 'What about you, where did you go on holiday?' (although you could do that!). You are generally expected to answer questions. For instance, a question like *Spielst du gern Fußball?*, you would first answer it directly then try to develop your answer e.g. *Ja, ich spiele sehr gern Fußball. Ich bin in einer Mannschaft mit meinen Freunden und wir spielen jeden Samstag.*

Showing initiative means that you take the conversation elsewhere in a way that is connected to your answer and still relevant to the original question e.g. *Ich spiele auch gern Tennis. Tennis ist mein Lieblingssport.* You were not asked about tennis. You decided to add it to your response. It is relevant, linked to what you were asked and follows your developed answer quite naturally. That is showing initiative. Use it to extend your answers and therefore show off extra knowledge of German.

14 Why is it important to refer to present, past and future events?

If you are aiming at a grade C, you will need to use a variety of structures, and you may include different time frames and make reference to past and future events in your spoken language. To achieve grade A, you will be expected to use a variety of verb tenses.

15 How many bullet points are there in each task?

There are typically between 5 and 8 bullet points. One of the bullet points will be the unpredictable element and will appear on your task as an exclamation mark. All bullet points will be written in English.

16 Will I be asked questions which are not written in the task?

That is possible. Although you will have prepared the task thoroughly and will have a lot to say, your teacher may want you to expand or give further details on particular points you have made. You must listen to your teacher's questions attentively as you will have to understand his/her questions in the first place.

Frequently asked questions

This general guidance is in the form of answers to 'Frequently asked questions' (FAQs).

1 How many writing tasks do I have to complete and what proportion of my German GCSE is the writing test?

You have to complete two writing tasks. The tasks can be those provided by the AQA Examination Board, although your German teachers have the option of devising their own tasks if they so wish. As in the speaking, the two tasks count for 30% of your grade (15% for each writing task).

2 How much time do I have to complete the final version of a task?

You will be given sixty minutes to complete the final version of a task. It will be done under the direct supervision of your teacher. You will not be allowed to interact with others.

3 What resources will I be able to use on the day?

You can have access to a dictionary. You will also have the task itself, your plan and your teacher's feedback on your plan. These will be on the AQA Task Planning Form. That is all. You cannot use your exercise book, textbook or any drafts you may have written to help you practise.

4 What am I allowed to write on my plan?

Much the same as you are allowed in your plan for Speaking i.e. a maximum of 40 words and no conjugated verbs or codes. You also have the option of using visuals instead of or as well as words in your Task Planning Form. Your teacher will comment on your plan, using the AQA Task Planning Form. Make sure you take that information on board before you write the final version.

5 How many words am I expected to write for each task?

Students aiming at grades G – D should produce 200 – 350 words across the two tasks, i.e. 100 – 175 words per task.

Students aiming at grades C – A* should produce 400 – 600 words across the two tasks, i.e. 200 – 300 words per task.

6 Can I write a draft?

You may produce a draft but this is for your use only. You teacher cannot comment on it and you cannot have access to any draft when you write the final version.

7 What do I have to do to gain the best possible mark?

You will score well if:

- you communicate a lot of relevant information clearly.
- you can explain ideas and points of view.
- you have a good range of vocabulary.
- you can include complex structures.
- you can write long sentences.
- you can refer to past, present and future events.
- you can write with grammatical accuracy.
- you organise your ideas well.

You will have noticed that there are similarities between the ways writing and speaking are assessed. As most of the points above are discussed in the FAQs for Speaking, you are advised to read the answers again, before you embark on your first task.

8 When will I do the tasks?

When your teacher has taught you the necessary language for you to complete a task, you will be given the task to prepare. You may be asked to do a plan, using the Task Planning Form. You will get some feedback from your teacher at that point on how you have met the requirements of the task. The final version will be done after that, under the direct supervision of your teacher.

9 Who will mark my work?

AQA Examiners will mark your work. A Team Leader will check the work of the Examiner. The Principal Examiner will check the work of the Team Leader. The Chief Examiner will check the work of the Principal Examiner – a complicated but secure system to ensure that candidates are given the correct mark for their work.

Mein Geburtstag

You have agreed to take part in a survey about how people celebrate birthdays.

Your teacher will play the role of the person carrying out the survey. He or she could ask you the following:

1 how old are you and when is your birthday?
2 how do you usually celebrate your birthday?
3 which family members and friends do you celebrate with?
4 what sort of presents did you get on your last birthday?
5 how did you spend your last birthday?
6 what would you like to do on your next birthday?
7 !

Remember you will have to respond to something that you have not yet prepared.

1 How old are you and when is your birthday?
- Say how old you are
- Say when your birthday is
- Mention the year in which you were born
- You could also mention your star sign (*Sternzeichen*)

2 How do you usually celebrate your birthday?
- Say what you usually do at home
- Say what you usually do outside of the home
- Give your opinion of these activities
- Mention what you eat and drink

3 Which family members and friends do you celebrate with?
- Say which family members and/or friends you celebrate with
- Give a brief description of each person
- Say why you like celebrating with them
- Mention any other people (e.g. famous people) you would like to invite to your birthday

4 What sort of presents did you get on your last birthday?
- Mention several different sorts of presents you got
- Say which was your favourite and who it was from
- Describe your favourite present and say why you like it best
- Say what you spent your birthday money on

5 How did you spend your last birthday?
- Say what activities you did during the day
- Say what activities you did during the evening
- Compare this with what you usually do
- Say what you thought of the day

6 What would you like to do on your next birthday?
- Give details of the activities you would like to do
- Say why you would like to do these things
- Say what you would like to receive as a present
- Say who you hope to be celebrating with

7 ! At this point you will be asked a question which you don't know in advance. However, you can try to guess what it might be and prepare various options:
- Say how other family members celebrate their birthdays
- Say how important family celebrations are to you
- Say what other festivals you celebrate
- Give your view on the amount of money people spend on celebrations

kerboodle! You should now have completed your plan and prepared your answers. Give your plan to your teacher for feedback. Compare your answers to the online sample version – you might find some useful hints to make yours even better.

Controlled assessment

Kommen Sie nach ... !

You have entered a competition aimed at attracting more people to move to your area and join your school. You could include:

1 An introduction to the local area
2 What facilities are available in the area
3 Where the school is, a brief description of its size etc.
4 A description of the timetable, teachers, sports etc., giving your opinions
5 Details of a recent event at the school that you were involved with
6 Why people should choose the school
7 Your plans for when you leave school and how the school has helped you

1 An introduction to the local area
- Say the name of the town/village and give its geographical location
- Say how big it is
- Say what the weather is like
- Say what types of house there are

2 What facilities are available in the area
- Say what young people can do in the area
- Give details of shopping
- Say what transport is like
- Give some comments from recent arrivals/ visitors and say why people should move to the area

3 Where the school is and describe it
- Say where the school is and what type of school it is
- Say when the school opened and how old it is
- Describe the school – size, number of classrooms etc.
- Give your opinion – remember you are trying to attract people!

4 A description of the timetable, teachers etc., giving your opinions
- Describe the timetable – subjects on offer, length of the day etc.
- Give details of the teachers in general and describe your favourite teacher
- Describe the sports on offer, including school teams
- Give your overall opinion of these, comparing them with another school in your area

5 Details of a recent event at the school that you were involved with
- Give details of a recent event such as a play or concert at the school
- Say what you did and who else was involved
- Say what you thought of it
- Say why it was successful

6 Why people should choose the school – remember you want people to choose it!
- Give details of the food on offer
- Say what you wear to school and give your opinion
- Explain plans for modernisation e.g. new classrooms, different subjects
- Explain why people should choose the school

7 Your plans for when you leave school and how the school has helped you
- Say what you plan to do in the holidays after you leave school
- Say what your future plans are
- Explain how the school has helped you
- Say what you would like to do as a career and why

 When you have written your article, compare it and your cue card with the online sample version – you might find some useful hints to make yours even better.

Grammatik

Contents

■ Glossary of terms

Adjectives   *die Adjektive*
... are words that describe somebody or something:
groß big   *blau* blue

Adverbs   *die Adverbien*
... are words that describe an action:
Ich laufe schnell. I run fast.

**Articles (definite   *die Artikel*
and indefinite)**
... are the words 'the' and 'a':
der, die, das   the
ein, eine, ein   a

Cases
... tell you what words are doing in the sentence.
The nominative case is used for the subject:
Der Junge spielt Klavier.
The accusative case is used for the object and after some prepositions:
Amelie kauft einen Kuli.
Ich fahre durch die Stadt.
The dative case is used for the indirect object and after some prepositions:
Ich gebe dem Kind einen Apfel.
Die Katze ist neben der Lampe.
The genitive case is used to indicate possession:
Hier ist das Auto meiner Mutter.

Infinitive   *der Infinitiv*
... is the name of the verb as listed in the dictionary and always ends in *–en* :
spielen   to play
gehen   to go
haben   to have
sein   to be

Nouns   *die Nomen*
... are words for somebody or something:
das Haus   *die Tür*
der Bruder   *Susanne*

Object   *das Objekt*
... is a person or thing affected by the verb:
Ich esse einen Apfel.
Ich spiele Tennis.

Prepositions   *die Präpositionen*
... are words used with nouns to give information about where, when, how, with whom:
mit, aus, nach, zu, in, ...

Pronouns   *die Pronomen*
... are short words used instead of a noun or name, e.g.:
ich   I
du   you
er   he / it
sie   she / it
es   it

Singular and plural
Singular refers to just one thing or person:
Hund   *Bruder*
Plural refers to more than one thing or person:
Hunde   *Brüder*

Subject   *das Subjekt*
A person or thing 'doing' the verb:
Martina lernt Deutsch.
Ich gehe ins Kino.
Mein Haus hat zwei Schlafzimmer.

Verbs   *die Verben*
... express an action or state:
ich wohne   I live
ich habe   I have
ich bin   I am
ich mag   I like

A Number and gender

Number

Many words in German change according to whether they are **singular** or **plural**. You use the singular when there is only one of something or someone. You use the plural when there is more than one of something or someone:

das Auto	the car	*die Autos*	the cars
ich wohne	I live	*wir wohnen*	we live

Gender

Many words in German also change according to whether they are **masculine**, **feminine** or **neuter**. This is called grammatical gender. It does not exist in English, but it does in most other languages.

The grammatical gender of something has nothing to do with its sex or gender in real life. For instance, in German, 'table' is masculine but 'girl' is neuter!

Articles

Articles are words like 'the' and 'a', and are usually used with nouns. There are three kinds of article in German: **definite** ('the'), **indefinite** ('a') and **negative** ('not a').

The **gender** of an article must match the gender of the word(s) it is with. Its **number** must match the number of the word(s) it is with. In the plural, all genders have the same article.

The definite article: *der, die, das, die*

The definite article means 'the':

masculine	feminine	neuter	plural
der	*die*	*das*	*die*

*Das ist **der** Tisch.* That is the table.

The indefinite article: *ein, eine, ein*

The indefinite article means 'a' or 'an'. There is no plural because 'a' has no plural!

masculine	feminine	neuter
ein	*eine*	*ein*

*Das ist **ein** Tisch.* That is a table.

You do not use the indefinite article in German if you are talking about what job someone does or what nationality they are, or for ailments:

Ich bin Lehrerin.	I'm **a** teacher.
Er ist Deutscher.	He's **a** German.
Sie hat Halsschmerzen.	She has **a** sore throat.

The negative article: *kein, keine, kein, keine*

The negative article means 'not a' or 'not any' or 'no'.

masculine	feminine	neuter	plural
kein	*keine*	*kein*	*keine*

*Das ist **kein** Tisch.* That is not a table / That isn't a table.

Nouns

A noun is a word used to name something. Nouns are objects or things, but not all nouns are things that can be touched (e.g. 'laughter'). A good test of a noun is whether or not you can put 'the' in front of it (e.g. the book ✓; the have ✗).

All German nouns are either **masculine**, **feminine** or **neuter**, and either **singular** or **plural**. When you see a noun, you can often work out its **gender** or **number** from its **article**:

masculine	feminine	neuter	plural
der Tisch	*die Tasche*	*das Heft*	*die Hefte*

Plurals of nouns

There are different ways of making nouns plural in German, just as in English. Unfortunately, there isn't really a quick rule – you just have to get the feel of them!

- Feminine nouns which end in *–e* usually just add *–n*: *eine Katze – zwei Katzen*
- Some nouns stay the same in the plural: *ein Hamster – drei Hamster*
- Some nouns (mainly those borrowed from English) just add *–s*, as in English: *ein Auto – zwei Autos*
- Some nouns add *–e*: *ein Hund – drei Hunde*
- Some nouns add *–e*, but also take an umlaut (¨) on the first vowel: *eine Maus – hundert Mäuse*
- A few nouns add *–er*: *ein Ei – sechs Eier*
- Some nouns add *–er* and take an umlaut on the first vowel: *ein Mann – zwei Männer*

Weak nouns

There is a small group of nouns that are called weak nouns. They add an *–(e)n* ending in the accusative, dative and genitive singular and all plural forms. (For cases, see Section B.)

	singular	plural
nominative	*der Junge*	*die Jungen*
accusative	*den Jungen*	*die Jungen*
dative	*dem Jungen*	*den Jungen*
genitive	*des Jungen*	*der Jungen*

Possessive adjectives

Possessive adjectives are words like 'my', 'your', 'his' and 'her'. Their gender and number must match (or 'agree with') the noun they refer to and their endings change (just like *der*, *ein*, etc.).

Their endings follow the same pattern as *kein* (see page 174):

	masculine	feminine	neuter	plural
my	*mein*	*meine*	*mein*	*meine*
your	*dein*	*deine*	*dein*	*deine*
his	*sein*	*seine*	*sein*	*seine*
her	*ihr*	*ihre*	*ihr*	*ihre*
our	*unser*	*unsere*	*unser*	*unsere*
your	*euer*	*eure*	*euer*	*eure*
their	*ihr*	*ihre*	*ihr*	*ihre*

mein Bruder	my brother
deine Schwester	your sister
sein Vater	his father
ihre Schwestern	her sisters

Demonstrative adjectives and quantifiers

Demonstrative adjectives are words like 'this' or 'that' and quantifiers are words like 'each' or 'every'. You use them in sentences such as these:

Diese Hose ist schön.   These trousers are beautiful.

Jedes Kind darf mitmachen.   Each child may join in.

masculine	feminine	neuter	plural
dieser Mann	*diese Frau*	*dieses Kleid*	*diese Röcke*
jeder Mann	*jede Frau*	*jedes Kleid*	–

Interrogative adjectives

The interrogative adjective 'which' is used in questions (see also Interrogatives, page 187):

Welcher Pullover ist zu klein?   Which pullover is too small?

masculine	feminine	neuter	plural
welcher Mann	welche Frau	welches Kleid	welche Röcke

B Case

Besides number and gender, German nouns and the words that go with them have a **case**. The way cases work is quite complex, but they tell you certain simple things about the noun.

The nominative

A word is in the nominative if it is the **subject** or 'doer' of an action (and actions include words like 'is').

Der Tisch ist braun.   The table is brown.

Mein Bruder wohnt in London.   My brother lives in London.

Diese Katze ist launisch.   This cat is moody.

	masculine	feminine	neuter	plural
the	*der*	*die*	*das*	*die*
a	*ein*	*eine*	*ein*	–
not a	*kein*	*keine*	*kein*	*keine*
my	*mein*	*meine*	*mein*	*meine*
this	*dieser*	*diese*	*dieses*	*diese*
each	*jeder*	*jede*	*jedes*	–
which	*welcher*	*welche*	*welches*	*welche*

The accusative

For the **object** of most verbs (like *haben* or *es gibt*), and after some **prepositions**, you use the accusative.

Der, *ein*, *mein*, etc. are different in the accusative – but only in the masculine form:

*Ich habe **einen** Bruder.*   I have a brother.

*Er hat **keinen** Stuhl.*   He hasn't got a chair.

*Es gibt **einen** Supermarkt.*   There's a supermarket.

*Er geht in **den** Park.*   He goes into the park.

	masculine	feminine	neuter	plural
the	*den*	*die*	*das*	*die*
a	*einen*	*eine*	*ein*	–
not a	*keinen*	*keine*	*kein*	*keine*
my	*meinen*	*meine*	*mein*	*meine*
this	*diesen*	*diese*	*dieses*	*diese*
each	*jeden*	*jede*	*jedes*	–
which	*welchen*	*welche*	*welches*	*welche*

The dative

After some **prepositions** (e.g. *zu*, *mit*) you use the dative.

Words like *ein*, *mein*, etc. are different in the dative. You will have to learn them.

*mit **dem** Mann*   with the man

*mit **meinem** Bruder*   with my brother

	masculine	feminine	neuter	plural
the	*dem*	*der*	*dem*	*den*
a	*einem*	*einer*	*einem*	–
not a	*keinem*	*keiner*	*keinem*	*keinen*
my	*meinem*	*meiner*	*meinem*	*meinen*
this	*diesem*	*dieser*	*diesem*	*diesen*
each	*jedem*	*jeder*	*jedem*	–
which	*welchem*	*welcher*	*welchem*	*welchen*

In the plural, an extra *–(e)n* is added to the end of the noun:

*Ich komme mit meinen Brüder**n**.*   I am coming with my brothers.

Some prepositions combine with *dem*, *der*, *dem* to make shortened forms: see section C.

The genitive

You use the genitive to indicate **possession** (and with certain **prepositions**). Words like *ein* and *mein* are different in the genitive. You will have to learn them.

In English, we say 'my brother's room' but in German you have to say 'the room of my brother'. The 'of my' part is incorporated into one word – *meines*:

Das Zimmer meines Bruders

Das Zimmer meiner Schwester

Das Zimmer meines Kindes

Note the extra *–(e)s* on the end of masculine and neuter nouns.

	masculine	feminine	neuter	plural
the	*des Bruders*	*der Schwester*	*des Kindes*	*der Kinder*
a	*eines Bruders*	*einer Schwester*	*eines Kindes*	–
not a	*keines Bruders*	*keiner Schwester*	*keines Kindes*	*keiner Kinder*
my	*meines Bruders*	*meiner Schwester*	*meines Kindes*	*meiner Kinder*
this	*dieses Bruders*	*dieser Schwester*	*dieses Kindes*	*dieser Kinder*
each	*jedes Bruders*	*jeder Schwester*	*jedes Kindes*	–
which	*welches Bruders*	*welcher Schwester*	*welches Kindes*	*welcher Kinder*

C Other parts of a German sentence

Prepositions

Prepositions are words that tell you **where** things are (or their 'position'), for example 'on', 'under', 'by', 'at', 'with'.

Prepositions + dative

These prepositions are always followed by the dative:

aus	from, out of	*bei*	at the house of, with
gegenüber	opposite	*mit*	with
nach	after, to	*seit*	since
von	from, of	*zu*	to

Shortened forms:

zu dem ➡ *zum*   *zu der* ➡ *zur*

bei dem ➡ *beim*   *von dem* ➡ *vom*

zur Schule   to school

gegenüber dem Haus   opposite the house

bei ihnen   at their house

Prepositions + accusative

These prepositions are always followed by the accusative:

bis	until	*durch*	through
für	for	*gegen*	against
ohne	without	*um*	around
für meine Freundin		for my friend	

um die Ecke	around the corner
ohne Geschenke	without gifts
durch den Tunnel	through the tunnel

Prepositions + dative or accusative

Most of the prepositions you have met are sometimes followed by the dative and sometimes (but not as often) by the accusative. Here is a list of them with their meaning when followed by the dative:

an	at, on (vertical things)	über	over, above
auf	on (horizontal things)	unter	under, underneath
hinter	behind	vor	in front of
in	in	zwischen	between
neben			near, next to
an *der* Wand			on the wall
auf *einem* Tisch			on a table
in *seiner* Tasche			in his pocket
unter *dem* Bett			under the bed

Usually when there is movement involved (e.g. 'into' rather than 'in'), these same prepositions are followed by the accusative.

an	up to, over to	über	(go) over, across
auf	onto	unter	(go) under
hinter	(go) behind	vor	(go) in front of
in	into	zwischen	(go) between
neben			(go) next to, beside
in *die* Schule			into school
ins Schwimmbad			into the swimming pool
auf *den* Tisch			on to the table
Die Katze geht unter *den* Stuhl.			The cat goes under the chair.
Der Hund springt über *die* CDs.			The dog jumps over the CDs.

Shortened forms:

| in das ➡ ins | in dem ➡ im |
| an das ➡ ans | an dem ➡ am |

Prepositions + genitive

These prepositions are always followed by the genitive:

(an)statt	instead of	wegen	because of
außerhalb	outside of, excluding	trotz	in spite of
innerhalb	inside of, within	während	during
wegen des Wetters		because of the weather
außerhalb der Stadt		outside of the town
während der Reise		during the journey

Adjectives

Adjectives are words that describe nouns. When adjectives come **after** the noun, they work just like English adjectives:

| Die Blume ist **schön**. | The flower is pretty. |
| Das Haus ist **rot**. | The house is red. |

However, when adjectives come **before** the noun, you have to give them an ending.

Here are the adjective endings for nominative, accusative, dative, genitive and plural nouns after *der / die / das / die*.

	masculine	feminine	neuter	plural
nominative	der schöne Park	die schöne Stadt	das schöne Haus	die schönen Blumen
accusative	den schönen Park	die schöne Stadt	das schöne Haus	die schönen Blumen
dative	dem schönen Park	der schönen Stadt	dem schönen Haus	den schönen Blumen
genitive	des schönen Parkes	der schönen Stadt	des schönen Hauses	der schönen Blumen

Here are the adjective endings for nominative, accusative, dative and genitive nouns after *ein / eine / ein*. Note that the genitive and dative adjective endings are all *–en*.

	masculine	feminine	neuter	plural
nominative	ein schöner Park	eine schöne Stadt	ein schönes Haus	schöne Blumen
accusative	einen schönen Park	eine schöne Stadt	ein schönes Haus	schöne Blumen
dative	einem schönen Park	einer schönen Stadt	einem schönen Haus	schönen Blumen
genitive	eines schönen Parkes	einer schönen Stadt	eines schönen Hauses	schönen Blumen

Adjectives as nouns

Adjectives can be used as nouns by giving them a capital letter and adding the correct adjective ending. This is most common when using an adjective of nationality to talk about a person:

deutsch   German

der Deutsche / ein Deutscher   the / a German (male)

die Deutsche / eine Deutsche   the / a German (female)

The noun behaves like an adjective, as if another noun were to follow it.

Adjectives after *etwas / nichts*, etc.

After the following words, an adjective changes its form:

etwas (something), *nichts* (nothing), *viel* (much), *wenig* (little).

If you want to say 'something interesting' or 'nothing new', for example, the adjective gains a capital letter (becomes a noun) and you add *–es* to the end of it:

etwas Interessantes

nichts Neues

After *alles* (everything), you just add *–e* to the adjective. You may already be familiar with the form *Alles Gute* (all the best) at the end of informal cards or letters.

Comparative and superlative

Comparative

When comparing two things in English, we usually add *–er*, for example 'quick – quicker'. This applies in German as well:

schnell ➡ *schneller*

There are some exceptions, however, where an umlaut (") is added to the vowel. Some common ones are:

alt ➡ *älter*

groß ➡ *größer*

jung ➡ *jünger*

kalt ➡ *kälter*

In English, we stop adding '–er' to longer adjectives and use 'more', e.g. 'more interesting'. In German, though, *–er* is added to all adjectives:

interessant ➡ *interessanter*

To say 'than' when making a comparison, use *als*:

*Mein Haus ist größer **als** deine Wohnung.* My house is bigger than your flat.

Superlative

When talking about 'the quickest', you use the word *am* and add *–sten* to the adjective.

*Ich bin schnell, er ist schneller, aber sie ist **am** schnell**sten**.*

To form the noun for 'the quickest', you add the relevant adjective ending:

der Schnellste   *die Schnellste*

das Schnellste   *die Schnellsten*

Adverbs

Adverbs are used to qualify the action of the verb.

*Der Bus ist **langsam**.*   The bus is slow. (adjective)

*Ich gehe **langsam** in die Schule.*   I walk to school slowly. (adverb)

In English we add '–ly' to the adverb, but in German the adjective and adverb forms are the same.

Adverbs of frequency and place

immer	always
manchmal	sometimes
selten	rarely
nie	never
normalerweise	normally
draußen	outside
dort	there
hier	here

Adverbs of degree (quantifiers / intensifiers)

Adverbs of degree qualify other adverbs and adjectives:

sehr	very
ziemlich	fairly
zu	too
fast	almost
ein bisschen	a little, a bit
Du isst zu schnell.	You eat too quickly.

Interrogative adverbs

Interrogative adverbs are used when asking questions and need to be learnt (see also, Interrogatives page 187):

Wann?	When?
Warum?	Why?
Wo?	Where?
Wie?	How?

Adverbial phrases

Adverbial phrases give additional information about when, where or how an action takes place. Examples are:

nach dem Essen, vor der Schule, jeden Tag

Words for 'you'

There are **three** German words for 'you', depending on the number of people and your relationship to them:

du Informal singular – for talking to one young person or friend: *Kommst du mit?*

ihr Informal plural – for talking to more than one young person or friend: *Kommt ihr mit?*

Sie Formal singular or plural – for talking to one or more than one older person or stranger: *Kommen Sie mit?*

Words for 'it'

The German word for 'it' is not always *es*! It depends on the gender of the noun 'it' refers to. For the nominative case, you use *er* (masc.), *sie* (fem.) and *es* (neut.). So *das Buch* is *es*, but *die Banane* is *sie*. Don't be put off by the fact that *er* and *sie* also mean 'he' and 'she' – it should be clear from the context what the particular meaning is.

Ich habe einen Apfel. Er ist lecker.
I have an apple. It is delicious.

Subject pronouns

Subject pronouns are words like 'I', 'you', 'he', etc. They are usually used with a verb.

ich	I
du	you (informal singular)
er	he
sie	she
es	it
man	one, people, you (non-specific)
wir	we
ihr	you (informal plural)
Sie	you (formal singular or plural)
sie	they

The subject pronoun *man* is used when you are not talking about anyone in particular. It is used to say 'one', 'people', 'you', 'they' or 'we', see page 29:

Man *darf nicht rauchen.*
You're not allowed to smoke.

Man *muss eine Uniform tragen.*
We have to wear a uniform.

Object pronouns

Object pronouns are used to replace the object in a sentence. **Direct objects** are in the **accusative** and **indirect objects** in the **dative**:

	accusative	dative
me	*mich*	*mir*
you (inf. sing.)	*dich*	*dir*
him/her/it	*ihn/sie/es*	*ihm/ihr/ihm*
us	*uns*	*uns*
you (inf. pl.)	*euch*	*euch*
you (form.)/them	*sie/Sie*	*Ihnen/ihnen*

Nimmst du Toby mit nach Köln? Ja, ich nehme **ihn** *mit nach Köln.* (direct object)

Gibst du mir bitte ein Eis? Ja, ich gebe **dir** *ein Eis.* (indirect object)

Reflexive pronouns

Reflexive pronouns are used with reflexive verbs, which are listed in the infinitive with *sich*, e.g. *sich fühlen, sich waschen, sich treffen*. The reflexive pronoun usually changes as follows:

ich fühle **mich**	*wir fühlen* **uns**
du fühlst **dich**	*ihr fühlt* **euch**
er/sie/es/man fühlt **sich**	*sie/Sie fühlen* **sich**

Some reflexive verbs use *mir* and *dir* (dative reflexive pronouns) instead of *mich* and *dich* (accusative reflexive pronouns):

*Ich wasche **mich**.*	I wash (lit. I wash myself). (accusative reflexive pronoun)
*Ich putze **mir** die Zähne.*	I brush my teeth (lit. I clean the teeth to me). (dative reflexive pronoun)

Relative pronouns and clauses

Relative pronouns ('who', 'whom', 'which', 'that') are used to introduce a relative clause. In German, they vary according to the **gender** and **number** of the word they refer back to, and their **case** depends on their function in the relative clause. The verb in the relative clause goes to the end.

These examples show the nominative form:

*Das ist mein Bruder, **der** Jürgen heißt.*
This is my brother, who is called Jürgen.

*Ingrid, **die** sehr schön ist, kommt heute.*
Ingrid, who is very beautiful, is coming today.

*Das Meerschweinchen, **das** sehr klein ist, ist schwarz.*
The hamster, which is very small, is black.

Relative clauses can also be introduced by question words like 'where' and 'why':

*Meine Schule hat ein Sprachlabor, **wo** ich Französisch lerne.*
My school has a language lab where I learn French.

Words for 'when'

Wenn means 'when', 'if' or 'whenever' and is used to refer to the present, future or a habitual action in the past.

***Wenn** ich nach Deutschland fuhr, habe ich immer bei meinem Brieffreund gewohnt.*
When I used to go to Germany, I always stayed with my penfriend.

Als means 'when' and refers to a particular event in the past.

***Als** ich in Deutschland war, habe ich bei meinem Brieffreund gewohnt.*
When I was in Germany (one occasion) I stayed with my penfriend.

Wann introduces a 'when' question, in any tense.

***Wann** hast du bei deinem Brieffreund gewohnt?*
When did you stay with your penfriend?

D Verbs

The present tense

Verbs are 'doing words' – they describe actions. You use a **noun** (e.g. *mein Bruder*) or a **pronoun** (*ich, du*, etc.) as the **subject** or doer of the action. For each different person or pronoun you need to use the correct verb ending.

Regular verbs

In the present tense, regular (or weak) verbs (verbs which follow the usual pattern) have the following endings:

*ich spiel**e***	I play, I'm playing
*du spiel**st****	you play, you're playing
*er spiel**t***	he plays, he's playing
*sie spiel**t***	she plays, she's playing
*es spiel**t***	it plays, it's playing
*man spiel**t***	one plays, one's playing
*wir spiel**en***	we play, we're playing
*ihr spiel**t****	you play, you're playing
*sie spiel**en***	they play, they're playing
*Sie spiel**en****	you play, you're playing

* For *du/ihr/Sie* ('you') see section C, page 179.

***Ich** spiele Tennis.*	I play tennis.

***Mein Onkel** spielt gern Fußball.*
My uncle likes playing football.

***Sie** spielen Schach.*	They're playing chess.

Other verbs that work like this are:

machen	to do	*wohnen*	to live (location)
kaufen	to buy	*kochen*	to cook

Regular verbs which end in *–ten* (e.g. *antworten* to answer) add *–est* in the *du* form and *–et* in the *er/sie/es/man* form.

*Warum antwort**est** du nicht?*	Why don't you answer?

Irregular verbs

Irregular (or strong) verbs use the same endings as regular verbs, but there is a difference: the first vowel usually changes in the *du* and *er/sie/es* forms:

laufen to run, to walk

ich laufe	*wir laufen*
*du l**ä**ufst*	*ihr lauft*
*er/sie/es/man l**ä**uft*	*sie/Sie laufen*

essen to eat

ich esse	wir essen
du isst	ihr esst
er/sie/es isst	sie/Sie essen

Other common verbs in this category are: *fallen, fahren, helfen, schlafen, geben, tragen* and *treffen*.

Some irregular verbs change their vowel sound more radically, such as *lesen* and *sehen*:

lesen to read

ich lese	wir lesen
du liest	ihr lest
er/sie/es/man liest	sie/Sie lesen

Haben

Another important irregular verb is *haben* (to have) which drops the **b** in the *du* and *er/sie/es* forms:

haben to have

ich habe	wir haben
du **hast**	ihr habt
er/sie/es/man **hat**	sie/Sie haben

Sein

The verb *sein* (to be) is totally different and must be learnt!

sein to be

ich **bin**	wir **sind**
du **bist**	ihr **seid**
er/sie/es/man **ist**	sie/Sie **sind**

Modal verbs

These are verbs like 'will', 'must', 'can' and 'could', and they usually have to be used with another verb, which is in the **infinitive** and goes to the **end** of the sentence.

Usually, the singular forms of modal verbs are different from others because the vowel changes. An exception to this is *sollen* (should, to ought to). For all modal verbs there is no *–e* ending for the first person singular.

müssen must, to have to	**mögen** to like
ich **muss**	ich **mag**
du **musst**	du **magst**
er/sie/es/man **muss**	er/sie/es/man **mag**
wir **müssen**	wir **mögen**
ihr **müsst**	ihr **mögt**
sie/Sie **müssen**	sie/Sie **mögen**

wollen to want to	**können** can, to be able to
ich **will**	ich **kann**
du **willst**	du **kannst**
er/sie/es/man **will**	er/sie/es/man **kann**
wir **wollen**	wir **können**
ihr **wollt**	ihr **könnt**
sie/Sie **wollen**	sie/Sie **können**

dürfen may, to be allowed to	**sollen** should, ought to
ich **darf**	ich **soll**
du **darfst**	du **sollst**
er/sie/es/man **darf**	er/sie/es/man **soll**
wir **dürfen**	wir **sollen**
ihr **dürft**	ihr **sollt**
sie/Sie **dürfen**	sie/Sie **sollen**

*Ich **will** mein Geld nicht verschwenden.*
I don't want to waste my money.

*Sie **soll** das Rauchen aufgeben.*
She should give up smoking.

Separable verbs

Some verbs are in **two parts**. They consist of the **normal verb** and a **separable prefix**.

The normal verb goes in the usual place (second idea), but the prefix goes at the end of the sentence. When listed in a dictionary or glossary, the separable prefix is always listed first.

Here is a separable verb, *einkaufen* (to shop), in full:

ich **kaufe ein**	wir **kaufen ein**
du **kaufst ein**	ihr **kauft ein**
er/sie/es/man **kauft ein**	sie/Sie **kaufen ein**

*Ich **kaufe** am Montag **ein**.* I go shopping on Monday.

*Er **kauft** mit seiner Mutter **ein**.*
He goes shopping with his mother.

*Sie **kaufen** in Berlin **ein**.*
They go shopping in Berlin.

These are some other separable verbs you have met:

abwaschen (ich **wasche ab**)	to wash up
aufräumen (ich **räume auf**)	to tidy up
aufstehen (ich **stehe auf**)	to get up
ausgeben (ich **gebe aus**)	to spend (money)
aufmachen (ich **mache auf**)	to open
ansehen (ich **sehe an**)	to look at
fernsehen (ich **sehe fern**)	to watch TV

The perfect tense

The perfect tense is used to talk about things that happened in the past.

It is made up of two parts: the **auxiliary** (or 'helping') **verb** and the **past participle**. The auxiliary verb goes in the usual place (second): it is usually *haben*. The past participle goes at the end of the sentence.

The perfect tense with *haben*

To form the past participle, you take the *–en* off the infinitive of the verb. Then you (usually) add *ge–* to the beginning of the word and *–t* to the end.

ich **habe gespielt**	I played, I have played
du **hast gemacht**	you did, you have done
er/sie/es/man **hat gekauft**	he/she/it bought, has bought
wir **haben gespielt**	we played, we have played
ihr **habt gemacht**	you did, you have done
sie/Sie **haben gekauft**	they/you bought, have bought

Verbs which begin with *ver–* and *be–* and verbs which end in *–ieren* do not add the *ge–* to the beginning:

Ich **habe versucht**.	I tried.
Ich **habe** Gabi **besucht**.	I visited Gabi.
Hast du dich **amüsiert**?	Did you enjoy yourself?

With separable verbs, the *ge–* goes after the separable prefix:

Ich **habe** in der Stadt **eingekauft**.
I went shopping in town.

Irregular past participles

Some verbs are irregular in the perfect tense. They still make their perfect tense with *haben*, but the past participle is formed differently. You (usually) change the **vowel** in the participle and keep the *–en* from the infinitive on the end. Here are some you have learnt so far:

essen (to eat)	gegessen
lesen (to read)	gelesen
sehen (to see)	gesehen
finden (to find)	gefunden
trinken (to drink)	getrunken
nehmen (to take)	genommen
schreiben (to write)	geschrieben
treffen (to meet)	getroffen

Again, verbs which begin with *ver–* and *be–* do not add the *ge–* to the beginning of the verb:

Ich habe begonnen.	I began.
Ich habe vergessen.	I forgot.

The perfect tense with *sein*

Another group of verbs form their perfect tense with *sein* (to be). These are usually **verbs of movement**. As with the other verbs, the auxiliary (*sein*) is in second place and the participle at the end of the sentence.

Here are the ones you have learnt so far:

fahren ➡ ich **bin gefahren**	I went / drove, I have gone / driven
gehen ➡ ich **bin gegangen**	I went / walked, I have gone / walked
kommen ➡ ich **bin gekommen**	I came, I have come
fliegen ➡ ich **bin geflogen**	I flew, I have flown
fallen ➡ ich **bin gefallen**	I fell, I have fallen
laufen ➡ ich **bin gelaufen**	I ran, I have run

ich **bin gefahren**
du **bist gegangen**
er/sie/es/man **ist gekommen**
wir **sind geflogen**
ihr **seid gefahren**
sie/Sie **sind gekommen**

With separable verbs, the *ge–* goes after the separable prefix:

Ich **bin** um 7 Uhr **aufgestanden**.

The imperfect tense

Regular verbs

The imperfect tense is another way of talking about the past but is not usually used in speech.

To form the imperfect tense, take the infinitive of the verb, remove the *–en* and add the endings as follows:

ich spiel**te**
du spiel**test**
er/sie/es/man spiel**t**
wir spiel**ten**
ihr spiel**tet**
sie/Sie spiel**ten**

Irregular verbs

Irregular (strong) verbs have set stems to which the following endings are added. Note that nothing is added in the *ich* and *er/sie/es/man* forms. This example shows the endings for *fahren* (to travel, to drive):

ich fuhr

*du fuhr**st***

er/sie/es/man fuhr

*wir fuhr**en***

*ihr fuhr**t***

*sie/Sie fuhr**en***

Some common stems are as follows:

beginnen (to begin)	*begann*
essen (to eat)	*aß*
gehen (to go)	*ging*
lesen (to read)	*las*
sehen (to see)	*sah*
trinken (to drink)	*trank*

Some verbs are mixed verbs and have set stems but add regular endings, e.g. *bringen*:

*ich brach**te***

*du brach**test***

*er/sie/es/man brach**te***

*wir brach**ten***

*ihr brach**tet***

*sie/Sie brach**ten***

Other examples are:

denken (to think)	*dachte*
kennen (to know)	*kannte*

The most common irregular forms used, and ones to learn, are:

sein to be	*haben* to have
ich war	*ich hatte*
du warst	*du hattest*
er/sie/es/man war	*er/sie/es/man hatte*
wir waren	*wir hatten*
ihr wart	*ihr hattet*
sie/Sie waren	*sie/Sie hattet*

It's also useful to remember the imperfect tense for *es gibt* (there is / are) – *es gab* (there was / were).

Modal verbs

These are the imperfect tense forms for the modal verbs you have encountered.

müssen must, to have to	*mögen* to like
ich musste	*ich mochte*
du musstest	*du mochtest*
er/sie/es/man musste	*er/sie/es/man mochte*
wir mussten	*wir mochten*
ihr musstet	*ihr mochtet*
sie/Sie mussten	*sie/Sie mochten*

wollen to want to	*können* can, to be able to
ich wollte	*ich konnte*
du wolltest	*du konntest*
er/sie/es/man wollte	*er/sie/es/man konnte*
wir wollten	*wir konnten*
ihr wolltet	*ihr konntet*
sie/Sie wollten	*sie/Sie konnten*

dürfen may, to be allowed to	*sollen* should, to ought to
ich durfte	*ich sollte*
du durftest	*du solltest*
er/sie/es/man durfte	*er/sie/es/man sollte*
wir durften	*wir sollten*
ihr durftet	*ihr solltet*
sie/Sie durften	*sie/Sie sollten*

The pluperfect tense

The pluperfect tense conveys a moment **further back** in time than the perfect tense and is formed with 'had' in English, e.g. 'By the time I was 16, I had moved house three times.' For verbs which form their perfect tense with *haben*, use the correct form of *haben* in the imperfect tense (*hatte*, etc.) plus the past participle.

ich hatte gekauft (I had bought)

du hattest gekauft

er/sie/es/man hatte gekauft

wir hatten gekauft

ihr hattet gekauft

sie/Sie hatten gekauft

For verbs which form their perfect tense with *sein*, use the correct form of *sein* in the imperfect tense (*war*, etc.) plus the past participle.

ich war gegangen (I had gone)

du warst gegangen

er/sie/es/man war gegangen

wir waren gegangen

ihr wart gegangen

sie/Sie waren gegangen

The future tense

Present tense with future meaning

As in English, the present tense can be used to convey a future meaning if a **future time indicator** is used:

Nächstes Jahr gehe ich auf die Uni.
I'm going to university next year.

Future tense with *werden*

To form the future tense, use the correct present tense form of the verb *werden* plus the infinitive:

*Ich **werde** nach Berlin **fahren**.* I will travel to Berlin.*

*ich **werde***

*du **wirst***

*er/sie/es/man **wird***

*wir **werden***

*ihr **werdet***

*sie/Sie **werden***

* Remember that *ich will* doesn't mean 'I will', but 'I want to'.

The conditional tense

The conditional tense (strictly speaking, the conditional 'mood') uses 'would' and is used to talk about actions that are dependent on certain conditions being fulfilled.

Use *ich würde, du würdest, er/sie/es/man würde, wir würden* etc. plus the infinitive:

*Was **würdest** du mit einem Lottogewinn **machen**?*
What would you do with a lottery win?

*Ich **würde** um die Welt **fahren**.*
I would travel around the world.

The conditional tense of three modal verbs is also commonly used. The forms of *mögen* are *möchte/möchtest/möchten* (would like):

*Ich **möchte heiraten** und Kinder **haben**.*
I'd like to get married and have children.

The forms of *sollen* are *sollte/solltest/sollten* ('should' in the conditional):

*Ich **sollte** meine Hausaufgaben **machen**.*
I should do my homework.

(This form is the same as the imperfect of *sollen*.)

The forms of *können* are *könnte/könntest/könnten* ('could' in the conditional):

*Ich **könnte** um die Welt **fahren**.*
I could travel around the world.

(Do not confuse this form with *konnte* – 'could' in the past.)

It's also useful to know the forms for 'would have' (*ich hätte, du hättest* etc.) and 'would be' (*wäre, wär(e)st* etc.):

*Wenn ich reich **wäre**, **hätte** ich mein eigenes Flugzeug.*
If I were rich, I would have my own plane.

All of these forms (*würde, möchte, könnte, wäre* etc.) are known as the **imperfect subjunctive** of the verbs. You do not need to learn about subjunctive forms in detail at this stage, but you may want to find out more about it as you progress in your studies.

The passive

The passive is used to describe what is **being done to** someone or something. It is formed by using the verb *werden* ('to become') with a past participle:

*Das Auto **wird gewaschen**.*
The car is being washed.

*Der Film **wird** heute noch einmal **gezeigt**.*
The film is being shown once more today.

You will not have to recognise passive forms in your reading or listening exams at GCSE, but you may wish to use them in your spoken and written work.

Impersonal verbs

Some verbs are 'impersonal', which means they do not have a subject like *ich* or *du*. They are used with the impersonal subject *es* (it).

If you want to say 'there is' or 'there are', you use *es gibt* with the accusative case:

Es gibt einen Supermarkt. There is a supermarket.

If you want to say 'there is no' or 'there are no', use *es gibt + kein(e)(n)* + accusative case:

Es gibt kein Schwimmbad.
There is no swimming pool.

Other examples of impersonal verbs are:

Es tut mir Leid.	I'm sorry.
Es geht.	It's OK.
Wie geht es dir?	How are you?
Mir geht's gut.	I'm well.

Infinitive constructions

Um ... zu, ohne ... zu, anstatt ... zu

To say 'in order to', you use the construction *um ... zu* plus the infinitive at the end of the clause. Note the comma before the *um*:

Ich treibe Sport, **um** *gesund* **zu** *bleiben.*
I do sport in order to stay healthy.

Ohne ... zu ('without doing something') and *anstatt ... zu* ('instead of doing something') work in a similar way. You need to put the object after *um* and the verb in the infinitive after *zu*:

Ich werde nach Amerika fliegen, **ohne** *viel Geld* **aus**zu**geben.**
I will fly to America without spending a lot of money.*

Ich werde in den Osterferien Skifahren, **anstatt** *auf meine Prüfungen* **zu** *lernen.*
I will go skiing in the Easter holidays instead of studying for my exams.

* Note that with separable verbs such as *ausgeben*, *zu* goes after the prefix.

Zu + infinitive

After modal verbs, you do not need *zu* (*Ich* **will** *mit dem Bus* **fahren**), but after the following verbs, the use of *zu* is required:

beginnen	to begin
beschließen	to decide
helfen	to help
hoffen	to hope
vergessen	to forget
versuchen	to try
vorhaben	to intend

Ich **versuche***, Energie* **zu** *sparen.*
I'm trying to save energy.

Lassen + infinitive

Lassen with an infinitive is used to say 'get/have something done':

Ich **lasse** *meine Waschmaschine* **reparieren***.*
I'm having my washing machine repaired.

Ich **lasse** *meine Bluse* **reinigen***.*
I'm having my blouse cleaned.

Imperfect tense: *ich* **ließ**

Perfect tense: *ich* **habe** *...* **lassen**

Nicht

Nicht means 'not' and it usually comes after the verb:

Ich bin **nicht** *doof.*   I am not stupid.

However, when there is an object in the sentence, *nicht* comes after the object:

Lena mag Englisch **nicht***.*   Lena doesn't like English.

(Don't forget that you use *kein* to say 'not a', see page 29.)

Gern

When you want to say that you 'like doing' something, you use *gern*. It comes after the verb.

Ich gehe **gern** *einkaufen.*   I like going shopping.

When you want to say that you 'don't like' doing something, you use *nicht gern*:

Ich gehe **nicht gern** *einkaufen.*
I don't like going shopping.

Giving instructions (the imperative)

When you give someone instructions (e.g. 'Turn right!') you use a particular form of the verb called the imperative.

■ With teachers or adults you don't know very well, use the *Sie* form. The verb goes first, with *Sie* after:

  Sie machen das Licht aus. ➡ ***Machen Sie** das Licht aus!*
  Turn the light out!

■ With one friend or family member, use the *du* form without the *–st* ending. Put the verb first and omit *du*:

  Du **mach***st das Licht aus.* ➡ ***Mach** das Licht aus!*
  Turn the light out!

■ With more than one one friend or family member, use the *ihr* form without the pronoun *ihr*:

  Ihr **macht** *das Licht aus.* ➡ ***Macht** das Licht aus!*
  Turn the light out!

Seit

Seit means 'since' and is usually used with the present tense in German:

Ich **bin** *seit 9 Uhr hier.*   I've been here since 9 o'clock.

It is also used to mean 'for', again with the present tense:

Ich **lerne** *seit vier Jahren Deutsch.*
I have been learning German for four years.

(Note that *seit* takes the dative, which is why *Jahren* has an *–n* at the end.)

1st *erste*	11th *elfte*	
2nd *zweite*	12th *zwölfte*	
3rd *dritte*	13th *dreizehnte*	
4th *vierte*	14th *vierzehnte*	
5th *fünfte*	15th *fünfzehnte*	
6th *sechste*	16th *sechzehnte*	
7th *siebte*	17th *siebzehnte*	
8th *achte*	18th *achtzehnte*	
9th *neunte*	19th *neunzehnte*	
10th *zehnte*	20th *zwanzigste*	

To make the ordinal numbers from 20th upwards you add **–ste** to the cardinal number.

*Nimm **die dritte** Straße rechts.*
Take the third street on the right.

When giving dates, use *am* before the number and add **–n** (because *am* takes the dative case):

*Ich habe **am zwölften** Dezember Geburtstag.*
My birthday is on the twelfth of December.

The time

To tell the time, you say *es ist* followed by:

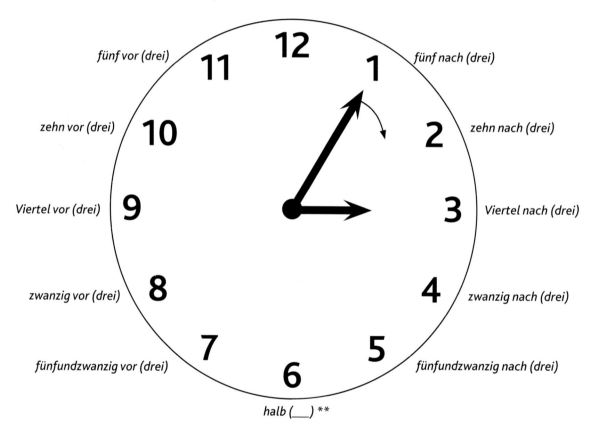

fünf vor (drei) — 11
zehn vor (drei) — 10
Viertel vor (drei) — 9
zwanzig vor (drei) — 8
fünfundzwanzig vor (drei) — 7
halb (___) ** — 6
fünf nach (drei) — 1
zehn nach (drei) — 2
Viertel nach (drei) — 3
zwanzig nach (drei) — 4
fünfundzwanzig nach (drei) — 5

** *Es ist **halb drei*** means 'It's half two', not 'It's half three' – the *halb* indicates **half to the hour**, not half past.

To say at what time something happens, you use *um* followed by the above:

Um *halb neun gehe ich in die Schule.*
I go to school at half past eight.*

Infinitive constructions

Um ... zu, ohne ... zu, anstatt ... zu

To say 'in order to', you use the construction *um ... zu* plus the infinitive at the end of the clause. Note the comma before the *um*:

*Ich treibe Sport, **um** gesund **zu** bleiben.*
I do sport in order to stay healthy.

Ohne ... zu ('without doing something') and *anstatt ... zu* ('instead of doing something') work in a similar way. You need to put the object after *um* and the verb in the infinitive after *zu*:

*Ich werde nach Amerika fliegen, **ohne** viel Geld aus**zu**geben.*
I will fly to America without spending a lot of money.*

*Ich werde in den Osterferien Skifahren, **anstatt** auf meine Prüfungen **zu** lernen.*
I will go skiing in the Easter holidays instead of studying for my exams.

* Note that with separable verbs such as *ausgeben*, *zu* goes after the prefix.

Zu + infinitive

After modal verbs, you do not need *zu* (*Ich **will** mit dem Bus **fahren***), but after the following verbs, the use of *zu* is required:

beginnen	to begin
beschließen	to decide
helfen	to help
hoffen	to hope
vergessen	to forget
versuchen	to try
vorhaben	to intend

*Ich **versuche**, Energie **zu** sparen.*
I'm trying to save energy.

Lassen + infinitive

Lassen with an infinitive is used to say 'get/have something done':

*Ich **lasse** meine Waschmaschine **reparieren**.*
I'm having my washing machine repaired.

*Ich **lasse** meine Bluse **reinigen**.*
I'm having my blouse cleaned.

Imperfect tense: *ich **ließ***

Perfect tense: *ich **habe** ... **lassen***

Nicht

Nicht means 'not' and it usually comes after the verb:

*Ich bin **nicht** doof.*   I am not stupid.

However, when there is an object in the sentence, *nicht* comes after the object:

*Lena mag Englisch **nicht**.*   Lena doesn't like English.

(Don't forget that you use *kein* to say 'not a', see page 29.)

Gern

When you want to say that you 'like doing' something, you use *gern*. It comes after the verb.

*Ich gehe **gern** einkaufen.*   I like going shopping.

When you want to say that you 'don't like' doing something, you use *nicht gern*:

*Ich gehe **nicht gern** einkaufen.*
I don't like going shopping.

Giving instructions (the imperative)

When you give someone instructions (e.g. 'Turn right!') you use a particular form of the verb called the imperative.

- With teachers or adults you don't know very well, use the *Sie* form. The verb goes first, with *Sie* after:

  Sie machen das Licht aus. ➡ ***Machen Sie** das Licht aus!*
  Turn the light out!

- With one friend or family member, use the *du* form without the *–st* ending. Put the verb first and omit *du*:

  *Du **mach**st das Licht aus.* ➡ ***Mach** das Licht aus!*
  Turn the light out!

- With more than one one friend or family member, use the *ihr* form without the pronoun *ihr*:

  *Ihr **macht** das Licht aus.* ➡ ***Macht** das Licht aus!*
  Turn the light out!

Seit

Seit means 'since' and is usually used with the present tense in German:

*Ich **bin** seit 9 Uhr hier.*   I've been here since 9 o'clock.

It is also used to mean 'for', again with the present tense:

*Ich **lerne** seit vier Jahren Deutsch.*
I have been learning German for four years.

(Note that *seit* takes the dative, which is why *Jahren* has an *–n* at the end.)

E Word order

Basic word order

Here is the basic word order in a German sentence:

subject	verb	rest of the sentence
Ich	spiele	Gitarre.
Lukas	geht	in die Stadt.

Verb as second idea

In German, the verb is always in second place in a sentence or clause. It's not always the second word, because you can't separate a phrase like *in meinem Zimmer*, but the verb must be the **second idea** or concept in the sentence:

1	2	3	4
[Ich]	[**treibe**]	[manchmal]	[Sport] .

1	2	3	4
[Manchmal]	[**treibe**]	[ich]	[Sport].

Changing a sentence so that the first idea is no longer the subject is called using **inversion**.

Subordinate clauses

A subordinate clause is dependent on a main clause and does not make sense on its own, e.g. *weil es 11 Uhr ist*.

▪ The conjunctions *weil, dass, da, obwohl* and *wenn* send the verb to the end of the subordinate clause which they introduce:

*Ich kann nicht gut schlafen, **weil** ich Angst **habe**.*
I can't sleep well because I'm afraid.

*Ich weiß, **dass** er obdachlos **ist**.*
I know that he's homeless.

*Er ist dick, **da** er viel **isst**.* He is fat, as he eats a lot.

*Ich will eine Karriere haben, **obwohl** meine Eltern reich sind.*
I want to have a career even though my parents are rich.

*Ich gehe zum Strand, **wenn** die Sonne **scheint**.*
I go to the beach when the sun shines.

▪ If two verbs appear in a subordinate clause, the **finite verb** (not the infinitive or past participle) is sent to the end of the clause. The finite verb is often an auxiliary verb (*haben, sein*) or a modal verb (*können, müssen*):

Ich kann im Meer schwimmen. ➡ *Ich gehe gern zum Strand, **weil** ich im Meer schwimmen **kann**.*

Ich bin im Meer geschwommen. ➡ *Der Urlaub war toll, **weil** ich im Meer geschwommen **bin**.*

▪ If a sentence begins with the subordinate clause, the verbs meet in the middle, separated by a comma.

***Wenn** die Sonne **scheint**, **gehe** ich zum Strand.*
When the sun shines, I go to the beach.

▪ Other subordinate clauses are introduced by *damit, so dass, ob* and *als*.

*Ich schreibe schnell, **damit** ich bald fertig **bin**.*
I'm writing fast, so that (in order that) I finish quickly.

*Ich esse viel Obst, **so dass** ich gesund **bleibe**.*
I eat lots of fruit, so that (as a result) I stay healthy.

*Ich weiß nicht, **ob** er **kommt**.*
I don't know whether he is coming.

***Als** das Wetter gut **war**, **bin** ich zum Strand gegangen.*
When the weather was good, I went to the beach.

Time – manner – place

When you mention when (time), how (manner) and where (place) you do something, you give the time first, then the manner and then the place.

	Time	Manner	Place
Ich fahre	[**am Wochenende**]	[**mit dem Auto**]	[**nach Paris**].

	Time	Place
Er fährt	[**mit dem Zug**]	[**nach Berlin**].

Conjunctions

Conjunctions are words that join sentences (or clauses, which are parts of sentences) together.

Coordinating conjunctions

Common conjunctions are *und* (and) and *aber* (but). *Und* and *aber* do not affect the word order in a sentence:

Er hat kein Geld. Er kann die Sprache nicht verstehen.
➡ *Er hat kein Geld **und** er kann die Sprache nicht verstehen.*

He has no money. He can't understand the language.
➡ He has no money and he can't understand the language.

Ich kenne ein paar Leute. Wir sind keine richtigen Freunde. ➡ *Ich kenne ein paar Leute, **aber** wir sind keine richtigen Freunde.**

I know a few people. We aren't really friends. ➡ I know a few people but we aren't really friends.

* When using *aber* and *denn*, put a comma before them.

Subordinating conjunctions

Some conjunctions including *weil* (because) send the verb in the clause they introduce right to the end (see E3 Subordinate clauses, page 186).

F Asking questions

Verb first

You can ask questions by putting the verb first in the sentence:

Du hörst Musik. ➡ **Hörst du** Musik?

You are listening to music. ➡ Are you listening to music?

Birgit ist sportlich. ➡ **Ist Birgit** sportlich?

Birgit is sporty. ➡ Is Birgit sporty?

Interrogatives (question words)

You can ask a question by starting with a question word or interrogative. Most German question words start with **w**:

Wer?	Who?
Wann?	When?
Was?	What?
Welche(r/s)?	Which?
Wie?	How?
Warum?	Why?
Wie viel(e)?	How much/many?
Wie lange?	How long?
Wo?	Where?
Wohin?	Where to?
Woher?	Where from?
Womit?	What with?

Most of these are pronouns or adverbs (see Interrogative adverbs, page 179) and are immediately followed by a verb:

Wer kommt mit?	Who's coming with us?
Wann kommt sie?	When is she coming?
Wohin fahren wir?	Where are we going (to)?

Welche(r/s) and *wie viel(e)* can be used as adjectives and followed by a noun (see Interrogative adjectives, page 175):

Wie viel Taschengeld bekommst du?
How much pocket money do you get?

G Numbers and time

Numbers

Cardinal numbers

1 *eins*		25 *fünfundzwanzig*	
2 *zwei*		10 *zehn*	
3 *drei*		20 *zwanzig*	
4 *vier*		30 *dreißig*	
5 *fünf*		40 *vierzig*	
6 *sechs*		50 *fünfzig*	
7 *sieben*		60 *sechzig*	
8 *acht*		70 *siebzig*	
9 *neun*		80 *achtzig*	
10 *zehn*		90 *neunzig*	
11 *elf*		100 *hundert*	
12 *zwölf*		15 *fünfzehn*	
13 *dreizehn*		25 *fünfundzwanzig*	
14 *vierzehn*		35 *fünfunddreißig*	
15 *fünfzehn*		45 *fünfundvierzig*	
16 *sechzehn*		55 *fünfundfünfzig*	
17 *siebzehn*		65 *fünfundsechzig*	
18 *achtzehn*		75 *fünfundsiebzig*	
19 *neunzehn*		85 *fünfundachtzig*	
20 *zwanzig*		95 *fünfundneunzig*	
21 *einundzwanzig*		200 *zweihundert*	
22 *zweiundzwanzig*		305 *dreihundertfünf*	
23 *dreiundzwanzig*		411 *vierhundertelf*	
24 *vierundzwanzig*			

525 *fünfhundertfünfundzwanzig*

1000 *tausend*

2500 *zweitausendfünfhundert*

1984 *neunzehnhundertvierundachtzig* (in dates)

Ordinal numbers

To make the ordinal numbers (first, second, etc.) up to 19th you add *–te* to the cardinal number. There are a few exceptions: first (*erste*), third (*dritte*), seventh (*siebte*) and eighth (*achte*).

1st *erste*	11th *elfte*	
2nd *zweite*	12th *zwölfte*	
3rd *dritte*	13th *dreizehnte*	
4th *vierte*	14th *vierzehnte*	
5th *fünfte*	15th *fünfzehnte*	
6th *sechste*	16th *sechzehnte*	
7th *siebte*	17th *siebzehnte*	
8th *achte*	18th *achtzehnte*	
9th *neunte*	19th *neunzehnte*	
10th *zehnte*	20th *zwanzigste*	

To make the ordinal numbers from 20th upwards you add **–ste** to the cardinal number.

Nimm **die dritte** *Straße rechts.*
Take the third street on the right.

When giving dates, use *am* before the number and add **–n** (because *am* takes the dative case):

Ich habe **am zwölften** *Dezember Geburtstag.*
My birthday is on the twelfth of December.

The time

To tell the time, you say *es ist* followed by:

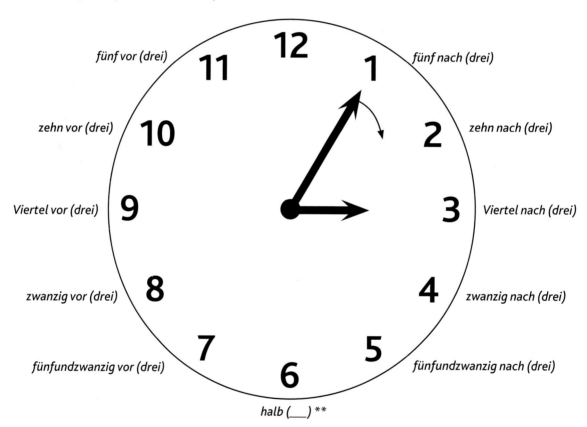

fünf vor (drei) — *fünf nach (drei)*
zehn vor (drei) — *zehn nach (drei)*
Viertel vor (drei) — *Viertel nach (drei)*
zwanzig vor (drei) — *zwanzig nach (drei)*
fünfundzwanzig vor (drei) — *fünfundzwanzig nach (drei)*
halb (___) **

** *Es ist* **halb drei** means 'It's half two', not 'It's half three' – the *halb* indicates **half to the hour**, not half past.

To say at what time something happens, you use *um* followed by the above:

Um *halb neun gehe ich in die Schule.*
I go to school at half past eight.*

Verb tables

Verbs which take *sein* in the perfect and pluperfect tenses.

infinitive	present	imperfect	perfect	English
beginnen	beginnt	begann	begonnen	to begin
beißen	beißt	biss	gebissen	to bite
bewegen	bewegt	bewog	bewogen	to move
biegen	biegt	bog	gebogen	to bend
bieten	bietet	bot	geboten	to offer
binden	bindet	band	gebunden	to tie
bitten	bittet	bat	gebeten	to ask
blasen	bläst	blies	geblasen	to blow
bleiben	bleibt	blieb	geblieben*	to stay
brechen	bricht	brach	gebrochen	to break
brennen	brennt	brannte	gebrannt	to burn
bringen	bringt	brachte	gebracht	to bring
denken	denkt	dachte	gedacht	to think
dürfen	darf	durfte	gedurft	to be allowed to
empfehlen	empfiehlt	empfahl	empfohlen	to recommend
essen	isst	aß	gegessen	to eat
fahren	fährt	fuhr	gefahren*	to go, travel
fallen	fällt	fiel	gefallen*	to fall
fangen	fängt	fing	gefangen	to catch
finden	findet	fand	gefunden	to find
fliegen	fliegt	flog	geflogen*	to fly
fliehen	flieht	floh	geflohen*	to flee
fließen	fließt	floss	geflossen*	to flow
frieren	friert	fror	gefroren	to freeze

infinitive	present	imperfect	perfect	English
geben	gibt	gab	gegeben	to give
gehen	geht	ging	gegangen*	to go
gelingen	gelingt	gelang	gelungen*	to succeed
genießen	genießt	genoss	genossen	to enjoy
geschehen	geschieht	geschah	geschehen*	to happen
gewinnen	gewinnt	gewann	gewonnen	to win
graben	gräbt	grub	gegraben	to dig
greifen	greift	griff	gegriffen	to grasp
haben	hat	hatte	gehabt	to have
halten	hält	hielt	gehalten	to stop
hängen	hängt	hing	gehangen	to hang
heben	hebt	hob	gehoben	to lift
heißen	heißt	hieß	geheißen	to be called
helfen	hilft	half	geholfen	to help
kennen	kennt	kannte	gekannt	to know
kommen	kommt	kam	gekommen*	to come
können	kann	konnte	gekonnt	to be able to
laden	lädt	lud	geladen	to load
lassen	lässt	ließ	gelassen	to allow
laufen	läuft	lief	gelaufen*	to run
leiden	leidet	litt	gelitten	to suffer
leihen	leiht	lieh	geliehen	to lend
lesen	liest	las	gelesen	to read
liegen	liegt	lag	gelegen	to lie
lügen	lügt	log	gelogen	to tell a lie
meiden	meidet	mied	gemieden	to avoid
misslingen	misslingt	misslang	misslungen*	to fail

infinitive	present	imperfect	perfect	English
mögen	mag	mochte	gemocht	to like
müssen	muss	musste	gemusst	to have to
nehmen	nimmt	nahm	genommen	to take
nennen	nennt	nannte	genannt	to name
raten	rät	riet	geraten	to guess
reißen	reißt	riss	gerissen	to rip
reiten	reitet	ritt	geritten	to ride
rennen	rennt	rannte	gerannt*	to run
riechen	riecht	roch	gerochen	to smell
rufen	ruft	rief	gerufen	to call
schaffen	schafft	schuf	geschaffen	to manage
scheiden	scheidet	schied	geschieden*	to separate
scheinen	scheint	schien	geschienen	to shine
schlafen	schläft	schlief	geschlafen	to sleep
schlagen	schlägt	schlug	geschlagen	to hit
schließen	schließt	schloss	geschlossen	to shut
schneiden	schneidet	schnitt	geschnitten	to cut
schreiben	schreibt	schrieb	geschrieben	to write
schreien	schreit	schrie	geschrien	to cry
sehen	sieht	sah	gesehen	to see
sein	ist	war	gewesen*	to be
senden	sendet	sandte	gesandt	to send
singen	singt	sang	gesungen	to sing
sitzen	sitzt	saß	gesessen	to sit
sollen	soll	sollte	gesollt	ought to
sprechen	spricht	sprach	gesprochen	to speak
stehen	steht	stand	gestanden*	to stand

infinitive	present	imperfect	perfect	English
stehlen	stiehlt	stahl	gestohlen	to steal
steigen	steigt	stieg	gestiegen*	to climb
sterben	stirbt	starb	gestorben*	to die
stoßen	stößt	stieß	gestoßen	to push
streichen	streicht	strich	gestrichen	to paint
tragen	trägt	trug	getragen	to carry
treffen	trifft	traf	getroffen	to meet
treiben	treibt	trieb	getrieben	to do
treten	tritt	trat	getreten	to step
trinken	trinkt	trank	getrunken	to drink
tun	tut	tat	getan	to do
überwinden	überwindet	überwand	überwunden	to overcome
vergessen	vergisst	vergaß	vergessen	to forget
verlieren	verliert	verlor	verloren	to lose
verschwinden	verschwindet	verschwand	verschwunden*	to disappear
verzeihen	verzeiht	verzieh	verziehen	to pardon
wachsen	wächst	wuchs	gewachsen*	to grow
waschen	wäscht	wusch	gewaschen	to wash
weisen	weist	wies	gewiesen	to show
wenden	wendet	wandte	gewendet	to turn
werben	wirbt	warb	geworben	to advertise
werden	wird	wurde	geworden*	to become
werfen	wirft	warf	geworfen	to throw
wiegen	wiegt	wog	gewogen	to weigh
wissen	weiß	wusste	gewusst	to know
wollen	will	wollte	gewollt	to want to
ziehen	zieht	zog	gezogen	to pull

German pronunciation

🎧 The alphabet sounds

A	ah	B	bay
C	tsay	D	day
E	ay	F	ef
G	gay	H	hah
I	ee	J	yot
K	kah	L	el
M	em	N	en
O	oh	P	pay
Q	koo	R	air
S	ess	T	tay
U	oo	V	fow
W	vay	X	iks
Y	oopsilon	Z	tset

🎧 German pronunciation

Many consonants are pronounced the same as in English. The ones you need to extra care over are:

j	ja, jung
qu	quälen, Quantität
v	viel, Vater
w	wie, Wasser
z	zu, Zeitung

Some consonants are the same as in English except when they appear at the end of a word. Then you need to pronounce them differently:

b	ab, Dieb
d	Kind, Hund
g	Tag, sag

Pay attention to the following consonant combinations:

ch	machen, Tochter
sp	Spanien, spannend
st	ständig, Strand

The ess-tset (ß) is used in place of *ss* after a long vowel or diphthong, and has the same sound; *ss* is used after a short vowel.

Er heißt Felix. Er isst gern Pommes.

Umlauts on *a*, *o* and *u* change the sound of these vowels.

A	lachen	Ä	lächeln
O	mochte	Ö	möchte
U	unter	Ü	über

With vowel combinations, make sure you don't confuse the following:

ie	viel	ei	weil

Typing German accents

Use the following PC shortcuts:

Ctrl + :, then a	ä	Ctrl + :, then Shift + a	Ä
Ctrl + :, then o	ö	Ctrl + :, then Shift + o	Ö
Ctrl + :, then u	ü	Ctrl + :, then Shift + u	Ü
Ctrl + &, then s	ß		

Use the following Mac shortcuts:

Option + U, then a	ä	Option + U, then A	Ä
Option + U, then o	ö	Option + U, then O	Ö
Option + U, then u	ü	Option + U, then U	Ü
Option + S	ß		

You can also set your computer to work like a German keyboard. You will need to remember what the characters on your keys now correspond to:

' ➡ ä		@ ➡ Ä	
; ➡ ö		: ➡ Ö	
[➡ ü		{ ➡ Ü	
- ➡ ß			

Also note:

z ➡ y		y ➡ z	

If you really can't find the accents you want, use *ae* for *ä*, *oe* for *ö*, *ue* for *ü* and *ss* for *ß*.

Using a dictionary

When looking up new meanings, it's useful to know what type of word (noun, verb etc.) you want to find. Re-read the Glossary of terms (page 173) if you're unsure about these.

Nouns

Your dictionary should tell you the **gender** of the noun you look up (whether it is masculine, feminine or neuter). It will do so either by giving the nominative definite article (**der Mann; die Frau; das Kind**) or by giving the initial of the noun's particular gender (*Mann* **m**; *Frau* **f**; *Kind* **n**).

The dictionary should also give you the **genitive ending** of the noun and show you how the **plural** is formed. The genitive form is given first, then the plural:

Kind n (–(e)s, –er)

From the above example you should be able to work out that the genitive form of *Kind* is *Kinds* or *Kindes*, and the plural of *Kind* is *Kinder*.

Verbs

When looking up a verb, you should be able to find out whether or not it is irregular. This may be indicated by an abbreviation e.g. *essen* **irreg** or *essen* **unreg**, or by the fact that the dictionary also gives you the imperfect second person form and the past participle e.g. *essen* pret. *aß* ptp. *gegessen*.

The abbreviation **sep** tells you that a verb is separable e.g. *mitkommen* **sep**. Remember, not all prefixes added to verbs make them separable – for instance, *ankommen* is separable, but *bekommen* is not.

The letters **vt** and **vi** tell you whether a verb is transitive (it takes a direct object) or intransitive (it doesn't take a direct object). Often a verb is both and will have **vti.** Sometimes you will find separate sections on the transitive and intransitive forms of the verb, as these can offer different meanings.

Adjectives and adverbs

Remember that in German, an adjective (e.g. slow) and an adverb (e.g. slowly) are usually translated by the same word (e.g. *langsam*). Sometimes a dictionary will only give the translation from German to English as an adjective, but you can usually work out from context if you need to make this into an adverb. The dictionary abbreviations for adjectives and adverbs are *adj.* and *adv.*

Cases

If you look up a preposition, the dictionary should tell you what case needs to follow it e.g. *mit* **prep + dat**. If you are looking up a preposition which can take both the dative and the accusative, the dictionary should indicate the differences in meaning e.g. *in* prep.**(+ dat) in, inside, (+ acc.) into.**

The abbreviations *jdn* and *jdm* both mean 'somebody (sb)' – *jdn* is accusative, *jdm* is dative. If you find these after a verb, it shows you whether it needs to be followed by a direct (accusative) or indirect (dative) object pronoun:

helfen to help (***jdm*** sb) ➡ Er hilft **mir**.

bitten to ask (***jdn*** *um etw* sb for sth) ➡ *Ich bitte* **dich**!

Glossar

Following each noun, its plural form is indicated in brackets. If the form given is already plural, it is followed by (pl). Following each verb, its past participle is given in brackets.

A

ab off, away, from

ab und zu now and again

der *Abend (-e)* evening

das *Abendessen(-)* dinner

abends in the evenings

aber but

die *Abfahrt (-en)* departure

der *Abfall (¨e)* waste, litter

der *Abfalleimer (-)* waste bin

die *Abgase (pl)* gas emissions

abgesehen davon apart from this

abhängig dependent

das *Abitur* exams taken at 18 (A-level equivalent)

der *Abiturient (-en)* Abitur candidate

absagen (abgesagt) to cancel, to call off

der *Abschluss* final examination

das *Abschlusszeugnis (-se)* school leaving certificate

der *Abstellraum (-räume)* storeroom

die *Abstinenz* abstinence

abtrocknen (abgetrocknet) to dry the dishes

abwaschen (abgewaschen) to wash up

abwechslungsreich varied

abwesend absent

die *Achterbahn (-en)* rollercoaster

adoptiert adopted

die *AG* extra-curricular group activity chosen by students

ähnlich similar

die *Ahnung (-en)* idea, suspicion

keine Ahnung haben to have no idea

akzeptieren (akzeptiert) to accept

der *Alkohol* alcohol

der *Alkoholiker (-)* alcoholic (noun)

alkoholisch alcoholic (adj.)

der *Alkoholismus* alcoholism

alle/er/es all

alle sein to be all gone, to have run out

allein alone

der/die *Alleinerziehende (-n)* single parent

alleinstehend single, living alone

die *Allergie (-n)* allergy

allerlei all sorts of

alles everything

Alles Gute! All the best!

die *Alpen (pl)* the Alps

als ob as though, as if

also so, therefore

das *Alter (-)* age

älter older

altmodisch old-fashioned

das *Altpapier* recycled paper

amüsant fun

(sich) *amüsieren (amüsiert)* to enjoy (oneself)

an at, to, close by

die *Ananas (-)* pineapple

anderer/e/es other

ändern (geändert) to change

anders different(ly)

anderswo somewhere else

anderthalb one and a half

der *Anfang (¨e)* beginning

anfangen (angefangen) to begin

die *Anfänger (pl)* beginners

angeberisch boastful, pretentious

das *Angebot (-e)* offer

angenehm pleasant

angenommen dass assuming that

der/die *Angestellte (-n)* employee, office worker

Angst haben to be afraid

ängstlich fearful

ankommen auf etw. (angekommen) to depend on sth.

es kommt darauf an, ob … it depends on whether …

die *Anprobe (-n)* changing room

anprobieren (anprobiert) to try on (e.g. clothes)

anrufen (angerufen) to telephone, to ring up

ansehen (sich etwas) (angesehen) to see, to watch

der *Anstieg (-e)* rise

der *Anstreicher / die Anstreicherin* house painter

anstrengend exhausting

die *Anzeige (-n)* advertisement

(etwas) *anziehen (angezogen)* to put on (clothes)

(sich) *anziehen (angezogen)* to get dressed

der *Apfel (¨)* apple

am *Apparat* speaking (when on the phone)

April April

arbeiten (gearbeitet) to work

der *Arbeitgeber / die Arbeitgeberin* employer

arbeitslos unemployed

die *Arbeitslosigkeit* unemployment

das *Arbeitspraktikum (-ka)* work experience

die *Arbeitsstelle (-n)* job, post

der *Arbeitstag (-e)* working day

das *Arbeitszimmer (-)* study (room)

ärgern (geärgert) to annoy, to irritate

arm poor

der *Arm (-e)* arm

die *Armut* poverty

die *Art (-en)* species

der *Arzt / die Ärztin* doctor

der *Atem* breath

atmen (geatmet) to breathe

das *Atomkraftwerk (-e)* nuclear power station

ätzend lousy

auch also, too

auf on, onto, on top of

auf *Achse* on the road, out and about

auf dem Lande in the countryside

auf den Wecker gehen   to get on someone's nerves

auf die Nerven gehen   to get on someone's nerves

auf die Uni gehen   to go to university

Auf Wiederhören!   goodbye (when using the telephone)

Auf Wiedersehen!   goodbye (when in someone's presence)

aufdrehen (aufgedreht) to turn up

der *Aufenthalt (-e)*   stay

die *Aufgabe (-n)*   task, job

aufgeben (aufgegeben) to give up

aufhören (aufgehört)   to stop

aufmachen (aufgemacht) to open

aufpassen (auf + accusative) (aufgepasst)   to look after

aufräumen (aufgeräumt) to tidy up

aufstehen (aufgestanden) to get up

aufstellen (aufgestellt) to establish

auftreten (aufgetreten) to perfom

aufwachen (aufgewacht) to wake up

die *Augen (pl)*   eyes

der *Augenblick (-e)*   moment, instant

August   August

die *Aula (-len)*   school hall

aus   out, made of

der *Ausgang (-̈e)*   exit

ausgeben (ausgegeben) to spend (money)

ausgeglichen   balanced, equal

ausgehen (ausgegangen) to go out

ausgezeichnet   excellent(ly)

die *Auskunft (-̈e)*   information

der *Ausländer (-)*   foreigner

ausmachen¹ (ausgemacht)   to turn off

ausmachen² (ausgemacht)   to matter

das macht nichts aus   it doesn't matter

aussehen (ausgesehen) to look (appearance)

außen   outside

der *Außenseiter (-)*   outsider

außer   besides, apart from

außerdem   besides

außerhalb   outside of

aussetzen (ausgesetzt) to abandon

die *Aussicht (-en)*   view

(keine) Aussicht auf Arbeit   (no) prospect of work

aussterben (ausgestorben)   to die out

der *Austausch (-e)*   exchange

ausverkauft   sold out

die *Auswahl*   choice, selection

ausziehen (sich) (ausgezogen)   to get undressed

das *Auto (-s)*   car

B

babysitten (babygesittet) to babysit

der *Bäcker / die Bäckerin*   baker

die *Bäckerei (-en)*   bakery

baden (gebadet)   to bathe

die *Badewanne (-n)*   bathtub

das *Badezimmer (-)*   bathroom

der *Bahnhof (-̈e)*   train station

der *Bahnsteig (-e)*   platform

bald   soon

der *Balkon (-e)*   balcony

die *Banane (-n)*   banana

das *Bargeld*   cash

bauen (gebaut)   to build

der/die *Bauer/Bäuerin*   farmer

der *Baum (-̈e)*   tree

die *Baumwolle*   cotton

beantworten (beantwortet)   to answer

der *Becher (-)*   cup

bedeckt   covered

bedrohen (bedroht)   to threaten

bedürftig   needy

der/die *Bedürftige*   person in need

der *Beginn*   beginning

beginnen (begonnen)   to begin

begleiten (begleitet)   to accompany

bei   at the house of, with

beide   both

beiliegend   enclosed

bekommen (bekommen) to receive

Belgien   Belgium

benachteiligen (benachteiligt)   to disadvantage

benutzen (benutzt)   to use

bequem   comfortable

der *Berg (-e)*   mountain

der *Beruf (-e)*   job, profession

beruflich   career-wise, in terms of a job

berühmt   famous

beschäftigt   busy

beschließen   to decide

beschreiben (berchrieben)   to describe

beschweren (sich) (beschwert)   to complain

besetzt   occupied

besichtigen (besichtigt) to see (while sightseeing)

besonders   particularly

besprechen (besprochen) to discuss

die *Besprechung (-en)*   discussion, meeting

besser   better

bestehen aus (bestanden)   to be made of, to consist of

bestellen (bestellt)   to order

bestimmt   definitely

besuchen (besucht)   to visit

beten (gebetet)   to pray

das *Bett (-en)*   bed

betrunken   drunk

bevor   before (time)

bevorzugen (bevorzugt) to prefer, to favour

die *Bewegung (-en)*   movement

sich um etwas bewerben (beworben)   to apply for sth.

der *Bewerber / die Bewerberin*   applicant

die *Bewerbung (-en)*   application

das *Bewusstsein verlieren*   to lose consciousness

die *Bibliothek (-en)*   library

das *Bier (-e)*   beer

bieten (geboten)   to offer

billig   cheap

die *Biokost*   organic food

Biologie   biology

der *Biomüll*   organic waste

bis   until, as far as

Bis bald!   See you later!

ein bisschen   a little

Bitte!   please

blau   blue

„blau" machen   to skip work

bleiben (geblieben)   to remain, to stay

der *Bleistift (-e)*   pencil

der *Blitz (-e)*   lightning

Es *blitzt.*   There's lightning.

blöd   stupid

der *Blumenkohl*   cauliflower

der *Blutdruck*   blood pressure

das *Blutgefäß (-e)*   blood vessel

die *Bohne (-n)*   bean

das *Boot (-e)*   boat

böse   angry

die *Bratwurst (¨e)*   (fried) sausage

brauchen (gebraucht)   to need, to use

braun   brown

die *Braut (¨e)*   bride

der *Bräutigam (-me)*   bridegroom

breit   wide, broad

brennen (gebrannt)   to burn

der *Brief (-e)*   letter

die *Briefmarke (-n)*   stamp

der/die *Briefträger/-in*   postman/postwoman

der *Briefumschlag (¨e)*   envelope

die *Broschüre (-n)*   brochure

der *Bruder (¨)*   brother

der *Brunnen (-)*   fountain, well

das *Buch (¨er)*   book

das *Bücherregal (-e)*   bookcase

der *Buchstabe (-n)*   letter (character)

buchstabieren (buchstabiert) to spell

bügeln (gebügelt)   to iron

bunt   colourful

das *Büro (-s)*   office

der *Bus (-se)*   bus

das *Butterbrot (-e)*   sandwich

C

der *Cent*   cent (100th of a Euro)

der *Chat-Server*   chat server

chatten (gechattet)   to chat (on the internet)

der *Chef / die Chefin*   boss

(die) *Chemie*   chemistry

die *Chips (pl)*   crisps

der *Chor (¨e)*   choir

der *Computer (-)*   computer

das *Computerspiel (-e)* computer game

der *Cousin / die Cousine*   cousin

D

d.h. (das heißt)   i.e.

da   as, since, there

der *Dachboden (¨)*   attic

dafür   in favour of something

dagegen   opposed to it, against it

damals   then, in those days

damit   so that, in order that, with that

danach   afterwards

Danke (schön)!   Thank you!

dann   then

dass   that

das *Datum*   date

dauern (gedauert)   to last (time)

DB   Deutsche Bahn (German rail system)

denken (gedacht)   to think

denn   as, since

dennoch   nevertheless

deprimiert   depressed

deshalb   therefore

deswegen   because of this/that

Deutsch   German

Dezember   December

dick   fat

Dienstag (-e)   Tuesday

das *Ding (-e)*   thing

die *Disko(thek)*   disco, club

die *Diskriminierung (-en)* discrimination

doch   but, after all, on the contrary

der *Dolmetscher / die Dolmetscherin* interpreter

der *Dom (-e)*   cathedral

der *Donner*   thunder

Donnerstag   Thursday

Es *donnert.*   There's thunder.

doof   stupid

das *Doppelhaus (¨er)*   semi-detached house

das *Dorf (¨er)*   village

dort   there (fixed position)

dorthin   there (movement towards)

die *Dose (-n)*   can

draußen   outside

dreckig   dirty

das *Dreieck (-e)*   triangle

dreieckig   triangular

drinnen   inside (it)

drittens   thirdly

die *Droge (-n)*   drug

die *Drogenberatungsstelle (-n)* drugs advice centre

der *Drogenhändler (-)*   drug dealer

der/die *Drogensüchtige*   drug addict

drüben   over there

der *Drucker (-)*   printer

drücken (gedrückt)   to push, to press

dumm   stupid

das *Düngemittel (-)*   fertiliser

dunkel   dark

dünn   thin

durch   through

im *Durchschnitt*   on average

dürfen (gedurft)   may, to be allowed to

die *Dusche (-n)*   shower

E

eben   just (time), even (surface)

die *Ecke (-n)*   corner

egoistisch   selfish

ehemalig   former

ehrenamtlich   voluntary, voluntarily

ehrlich   honest

das *Ei (-er)*   egg

eifersüchtig   jealous

eigener/e/s   own

eigentlich   actually, really

eindrucksvoll   impressive

einfach   simple, simply

das *Einfamilienhaus (¨er)* detached house

der *Einfluss (¨e)*   influence

einführen (eingeführt) to introduce

eingebildet   conceited

die *Eingliederung (-en)* integration

einige   some, a few

einkaufen (eingekauft) to shop, to buy

einkaufen gehen   to go shopping

das *Einkaufszentrum (-zentren)* shopping centre

einmal   once

der *Eintritt*   admission (ticket)

der *Einwanderer (-)*   immigrant

die *Einwegflasche (-n)*   single-use bottle

der *Einwohner (-)* inhabitant

einzeln single

das *Einzelkind (-er)* only child

einziehen (in + acc.)
(eingezogen) to move into

das *Eis* ice cream

das *Eisen* iron (substance)

der *Elektriker / die Elektrikerin*
electrician

das *Elektrogeschäft (-e)*
electrical shop

die *Eltern (pl)* parents

die *E-Mail (-s)* e-mail

empfehlen (empfohlen)
to recommend

das *Ende* end

enden (geendet) to end, to
finish

endlich finally

die *Energie* energy, power

die *Energiesparlampe (-n)*
energy-saving bulb

Englisch English

enorm enormous

entdecken (entdeckt)
discover

entfernt distant

die *Enthüllung (-en)* unveiling

entlang along

entscheiden (sich) (entschieden)
to decide

die *Entscheidung (-en)* decision

Entschuldigung! Excuse me!

entsetzlich terrible

entspannen (sich)
(entspannt) to relax

enttäuschend disappointing

entweder ... oder ... either ...
or ...

die *Entziehungskur (-en)*
withdrawal treatment

(die) *Erdkunde* geography

die *Erfahrung (-en)* experience

der *Erfolg (-e)* success

erfolgreich successful(ly)

das *Ergebnis (-se)* result

die *Erholung (-en)* relaxation,
recovery

erlauben (erlaubt) to allow

das *Erlebnis (-se)* experience

die *Ernährung (-en)* diet

erst first

erstens firstly

es it

essen (gegessen) to eat

das *Esszimmer (-)* dining room

das *Etui (-s)* pencil case

etwa about, roughly

der *Euro (-s)* Euro

F

die *Fabrik (-en)* factory

das *Fach (¨er)* school subject

die *Fachhochschule (-n)*
university of applied sciences

fahren (gefahren) to travel

das *Fahrrad (¨er)* bicycle

die *Fahrt (-en)* trip, journey

fallen lassen (gelassen)
to drop

falsch false, wrong

die *Familie (-n)* family

fantastisch fantastic

die *Farbe (-n)* colour

der *Fasching* see *Karneval*

fast almost

fasten (gefastet) to fast

faszinierend fascinating

faul lazy

faulenzen (gefaulenzt)
to laze around

FCKWs CFCs

Februar February

der *Fehler (-)* mistake

feiern (gefeiert) to celebrate

der *Feiertag (-e)* holiday (one
day)

das *Fenster (-)* window

die *Ferien (pl)* holidays (time)

fernsehen (ferngesehen)
to watch TV

der *Fernseher (-)* TV set

mit etw. *fertig sein* to be finished with
sth.

das *Fest (-e)* festival, celebration

fetthaltig fatty

feucht damp

der *Feuerwehrmann / die*
Feuerwehrfrau fireman/
firewoman

das *Feuerwerk (-e)* fireworks

der *Film (-e)* film

der *Finger (-)* finger

die *Firma (-men)* company

der *Fisch (-e)* fish

fit bleiben (geblieben)
to keep fit

das *Fitnesszentrum (-tren)* fitness
centre

die *Flasche (-n)* bottle

das *Fleisch* meat

der *Fleischer /die Fleischerin*
butcher

fleißig hard-working

fliegen (geflogen) to fly

das *Fließband (¨er)* conveyor belt,
production line

das *Flugzeug (-e)* aeroplane

der *Flur (-e)* hall

der *Fluss (¨e)* river

die *Forelle (-n)* trout

Frankreich France

Französisch French

die *Frau (-en)* woman, wife

frech cheeky, impudent

frei free

das *Freibad (¨er)* open-air
swimming pool

im *Freien* out in the open

Freitag Friday

die *Freizeit* free time

die *Fremdsprachen (pl)* foreign
languages

(sich auf etw.) *freuen (gefreut)*
to look forward to sth.

der *Freund / die Freundin* (boy)
friend/(girl)friend

freundlich friendly, kind, nice

die *Freundschaft (-en)*
friendship

frieren (gefroren) to freeze

Es *friert.* It's freezing.

frisch fresh

der *Friseur / die Friseurin*
hairdresser

froh glad

Frohe Weihnachten! Happy
Christmas!

der *Fruchtsaft (¨e)* fruit juice

früh early

der *Frühling (-e)* spring

das *Frühstück (-e)* breakfast

frühstücken (gefrühstückt)
to have breakfast

(sich) *fühlen (gefühlt)* to feel

führen (geführt) to lead, to
guide

der *Führerschein (-e)* driver's
licence

für for

für jdn sorgen (gesorgt)
to look after sb.

furchtbar terrible

der *Fuß (¨e)* foot

der *Fußball* football

Fußball spielen (gespielt) to play football

der *Fußballplatz (¨e)* football pitch

die *Fußgängerzone (-n)* pedestrian zone

G

die *Gallerie (-n)* gallery

der *Gang (¨e)* corridor

die *Gans (¨e)* goose

ganz completely

die *Ganztagsschule (-n)* school that lasts all day

gar/überhaupt nicht not at all

der *Garten (¨)* garden

die *Gartenbenutzung (-en)* use of a garden

der *Gärtner / die Gärtnerin* gardener

das *Gasthaus (¨er)* guesthouse

das *Gebäude (-)* building

geben (gegeben) to give

geboren born

der *Geburtstag (-e)* birthday

geduldig patient

gefährlich dangerous

gefallen (+ dat) (gefallen) to please

gegen against

die *Gegend (-en)* area

das *Gegenteil (-e)* opposite (noun)

gegenüber opposite (prep.)

die *Gegenwart* present (time)

gehen (gegangen) to go

das *Gehirn (-e)* brain

die *Geige (-n)* violin

gelb yellow

das *Geld* money

die *Gelegenheitsarbeit (-en)* casual work

gemein mean

das *Gemüse* vegetables

genauso just as, equally

genießen (genossen) to enjoy

genug enough

die *Gepäckaufbewahrung* left luggage

gerade just (now)

geradeaus straight ahead

geräumig roomy

gern with pleasure

ich spiele gern ... I like playing ...

Gern geschehen! With pleasure! Done!

gerne willingly

die *Gesamtschule (-n)* comprehensive school

das *Geschäft (-e)* shop, business

das *Geschenk (-e)* present

(die) *Geschichte* history

geschieden divorced

das *Geschlecht (-er)* sex (male or female)

geschlossen closed

die *Geschwister (pl)* siblings, brothers and sisters

die *Gesellschaft (-en)* society

gestern yesterday

gestorben dead

gesund healthy, healthily

die *Gesundheit* health

getrennt separated

die *Gewalt* violence

gewaltig powerful, violent

die *Gewalttätigkeit (-en)* violence, acts of violence

gewinnen (gewonnen) to win

das *Gewitter* thunderstorm

gewöhnlich usually

das *Glas (¨er)* glass

glauben (geglaubt) to believe

gleich the same

die *Gleichheit* equality

gleichzeitig at the same time

das *Gleitschirmfliegen* hanggliding

der *Gletscher (-)* glacier

Viel Glück! Good luck!

GmbH (-s) Ltd.

der *Goldfisch (-e)* goldfish

grau grey

grillen (gegrillt) to grill, to have a barbeque

groß big, large

die *Größe (-n)* size

die *Großeltern (pl)* grandparents

im Großen und Ganzen by and large

die *Großmutter (¨)* grandmother

die *Großstadt (¨e)* big city, metropolis

der *Großvater (¨)* grandfather

großzügig generous

grün green

die *Grünanlage (-n)* green space/area

gründen (gegründet) to found, to set up

die *Gruppe (-n)* group

Grüß Gott! Hello! (Austria and S. Germany)

mit freundlichen Grüßen yours sincerely, best wishes

günstig reasonable, at a good price

die *Gurke (-n)* cucumber

gut good

gut bezahlt well paid

gut/schlecht gelaunt good-/bad-tempered

das *Gymnasium (-ien)* grammar school

H

die *Haare (pl)* hair

haben (gehabt) to have

die *Haferflocken (pl)* rolled oats

der *Hagel* hail

Es hagelt. It's hailing.

das *Hähnchen (-)* chicken

halb half (to)

halb neun half past eight

das *Hallenbad (¨er)* indoor swimming pool

Hallo! Hello!

die *Halsschmerzen* sore throat

die *Haltestelle (-n)* bus stop

die *Hand (¨e)* hand

Handball handball

die *Handschuhe (pl)* gloves

das *Handy (-s)* mobile phone

hart hard

hassen (gehasst) to hate

Haupt- main, central

das *Haus (¨er)* house

die *Hausaufgaben (pl)* homework

die *Hausfrau / der Hausmann* housewife/-husband

der *Hausmeister (-)* caretaker

die *Hautfarbe (-n)* colour of skin

der *Hautkrebs* skin cancer

das *Heft (-e)* exercise book

heftig violent(ly)

der *Heiligabend (-e)* Christmas Eve

das *Heim (-e)* hostel

das *Heimweh* homesickness

heiraten (geheiratet) to marry, to get married

heiß hot

heiter   cheerful

die *Heizung (-en)*   heating

helfen (geholfen)   to help

hell   light, bright

herausfinden (herausgefunden)   to find out

der *Herbst*   autumn

der *Herd (-e)*   cooker

herrlich   marvellous, magnificent

herrschend   ruling, reigning, current

herum   around

herumlaufen (herumgelaufen)   to run or go around

herumreisen (herumgereist)   to travel around

herunterdrehen (heruntergedreht)   to turn down

herunterladen (heruntergeladen)   to download

hervorragend   excellent, outstanding

das *Herz (-en)*   heart

Herzlichen Glückwunsch zum Geburtstag!   Happy birthday!

heute   today

heutzutage   these days

die *Hilfe (-n)*   help, assistance

die *Himbeere (-n)*   raspberry

der *Himmel*   sky, heaven

hinter   behind

hoch   high

hochladen (hochgeladen)   to upload

die *Hochzeit (-en)*   wedding

hoffen (gehofft)   to hope

das *Holz (¨er)*   wood

die *Hose (-n)*   trousers

das *Hotel (-s)*   hotel

der *Hund (-e)*   dog

der *Hut (¨e)*   hat

I

ich   I

ideal   ideal

die *Idee (-n)*   idea

illegal   illegal

der *Imbiss (-e)*   snack

die *Imbissstube (-n)*   snack bar

immer   always

in   in, into

die *Industrie (-n)*   industry

die *Informatik*   IT

der *Ingenieur / die Ingenieurin*   engineer

inkl. (inclusiv)   including

das *Insektizid (-e)*   insecticide

die *Insel (-n)*   island

das *Instrument (-e)*   instrument

intelligent   intelligent

das *Interesse (-n)*   interest

(sich für etwas) interessieren (interessiert)   to be interested in

das *Internat (-e)*   boarding school

das *Internet*   internet

die *Internetseite (-n)*   internet site

inzwischen   in the meantime

irgendwo   somewhere

J

Ja!   yes!

die *Jacke (-n)*   jacket

die *Jahreszeit (-en)*   season

das *Jahrhundert (-e)*   century

jahrhundertealt   centuries-old

Januar   January

die *Jeans (pl)*   jeans

jedoch   yet

jemand   someone

jetzt   now

der *Job (-s)*   job

der *Jogurt (-e)*   yoghurt

die *Jugendherberge (-n)*   youth hostel

Juli   July

jung   young

Juni   June

Jura   law

das *Juweliergeschäft (-e)*   jeweller's

K

der *Kaffee*   coffee

kalt   cold

die *Kamera (-s)*   camera

der *Kanal (¨e)*   canal

der *Kandidat/ die Kandidatin*   candidate

das *Kaninchen (-)*   rabbit

die *Kantine (-n)*   canteen

die *Kappe (-n)*   baseball cap

kaputt machen (gemacht)   to ruin, to wear out

der *Karneval*   carnival (traditional German celebration between Epiphany and Ash Wednesday)

die *Karriere (-n)*   career

die *Karte (-n)*   ticket

die *Kartoffel (-n)*   potato

der *Karton (-s)*   card, cardboard

der *Käse*   cheese

der *Kassierer /die Kassiererin*   cashier

die *Katze (-n)*   cat

kaufen   to buy

das *Kaufhaus (häuser)*   department store

der *Kaufmann / die Kauffrau*   businessman/woman

der *Kaugummi (-s)*   chewing gum

kaum   hardly

kaum vorstellbar   barely imaginable

kegeln (gekegelt)   to bowl

der *Keller (-)*   cellar

der *Kellner / die Kellnerin*   waiter/waitress

das *Kind (-er)*   child

das *Kinn (-e)*   chin

das *Kino (-s)*   cinema

die *Kirche (-n)*   church

die *Klamotten (pl)*   clothes

die *Klarinette (-n)*   clarinet

die *Klasse (-n)*   class

Klasse!   Great!

die *Klassenarbeit (-en)*   class test

die *Klassenfahrt (-en)*   school trip

das *Klassenzimmer (-)*   classroom

das *Klavier (-e)*   piano

kleben (geklebt)   to stick, to glue

das *Kleid (-er)*   dress

die *Kleidung*   clothes

klein   small

der *Klempner / die Klempnerin*   plumber

klettern (geklettert)   to climb

das *Klima (-ten)*   climate

der *Klingelton (¨e)*   ringtone

die *Klinik (-en)*   clinic

der *Klub (-s)*   club

klug   clever

die *Kneipe (-n)*   pub

der *Koch / die Köchin*   cook

kochen (gekocht)   to cook, to make (e.g. tea and coffee)

die *Kohle (-n)* coal, money
(slang)

das *Kohlendioxid (-e)* carbon
dioxide

die *Kohlenhydrate (pl)*
carbohydrates

das *Kohlenmonoxid* carbon
monoxide

der *Kollege/ die Kollegin*
colleague

kompliziert complicated

die *Konditorei (-en)* cake shop

können (gekonnt) can, to be
able to

der *Kontakt (-e)* contact

das *Konzert (-e)* concert

das *Kopfkissen (-)* pillow

die *Kopfschmerzen (pl)* headache

kopieren (kopiert) to copy, to
photocopy

der *Körper (-)* body

körperlich physical

kosten (gekostet) to cost

kostenlos free

köstlich delicious

das *Kostüm (-e)* costume

das *Krankenhaus (¨er)* hospital

der *Krankenpfleger / die
Krankenschwester* nurse

die *Krankheit (-en)* illness

der *Krebs (-e)* cancer

die *Kreditkarte (-n)* credit card

der *Kreis (-e)* circle

die *Kriminalität* crime

kritisieren (kritisiert) to
criticise

die *Küche (-n)* kitchen

der *Kuchen (-)* cake

der *Kugelschreiber/der Kuli*
ballpoint pen

kühl cool

kulturell cultural

der *Kunde/die Kundin* customer

kündigen (gekündigt) to hand
notice in

die *Kunst (¨e)*

kurz short, brief

kürzlich shortly

die *Küste (-n)* coast

an der *Küste* on the coast

das *Labor (-s)* laboratory, lab

lachen (gelacht) to laugh

der *Lachs (-e)* salmon

der *Laden (¨)* shop

das *Land (¨er)* country

die *Landschaft (-en)* landscape

der *Landwirt / die Landwirtin*
farmer

lang long

langsam slow(ly)

(sich) *langweilen (gelangweilt)* to be
bored

langweilig boring

der *Lärm* noise

leben (gelebt) to live

der *Lebenslauf (¨e)* CV

die *Leber* liver

lecker delicious

das *Leder* leather

ledig single

leer empty

die *Lehre (-n)*
apprenticeship

der *Lehrer / die Lehrerin* teacher

das *Lehrerzimmer (-)* staff room

lehrreich educational

leicht easy, light

die *Leichtathletik* athletics

Es tut mir Leid! I'm sorry!

leider unfortunately

der *Leihwagen (-)* hire car

leisten (geleistet) afford

der *Leistungsdruck* pressure to
achieve

lesen (gelesen) to read

letzter/e/es last

die *Leute (pl)* people

lieb kind, nice, lovely

lieben (geliebt) to love

lieber rather

Lieblings- favourite

am *liebsten* best of all

das *Lied (-er)* song

liegen (gelegen) to be situated
in

lila purple

das *Lineal (-e)* ruler

die *Linie (-n)* route, line

links to the left

die *Lippen (pl)* lips

der *LKW (Lastkraftwagen)* lorry

der *LKW Fahrer / die LKW Fahrerin*
lorry driver

der *Lohn (¨e)* wage(s)

losgehen (losgegangen)
to get going, to get started

die *Luft* air

die *Luftverschmutzung* air
pollution

die *Lunge (-n)* lung

der *Lungenkrebs* lung cancer

die *Lust (¨e)* desire, pleasure

lustig fun

magersüchtig anorexic

die *Mahlzeit (-en)* meal

Mai May

mailen (gemailt) to send (by
e-mail)

malen (gemalt) to paint

manchmal sometimes

der *Mann (¨er)* man, husband

die *Mannschaft (-en)* team

der *Mantel (¨)* coat

die *Marke (-n)* brand

der *Markt (¨e)* market

der *Marktplatz (¨e)* market place,
market square

März March

(die) *Mathe(matik)* maths

die *Maus (¨e)* mouse

der *Mechaniker / die Mechanikerin*
mechanic

das *Medikament (-e)* medicine,
medication

die *Medizin* medicine

das *Meer (-)* sea

das *Meerschweinchen (-)*
guinea-pig

der *Meeresspiegel* sea level

mehr more

mehrere several

das *Mehrfamilienhaus (¨er)*
house for several families

mein my

meinen (gemeint) to think

die *Meinung (-en)* opinion

am *meisten* most (of all)

eine *Menge* a lot of

messen (gemessen) to measure

das *Metal (-le)* metal

der *Metzger / die Metzgerin*
butcher

die *Metzgerei (-en)* butcher's shop

mies rotten, lousy

mieten (gemietet) to rent

die *Mikrowelle (-n)* microwave
oven

die *Milch* milk

die *Milchprodukte (pl)* dairy
produce

mindestens at least

das *Mindesthaltbark-eitsdatum (-ten)* best-before date
das *Mineralwasser* mineral water
mit with, by (transport)
miteinander with one another
mitgehen (mitgegangen) to go with sb.
das *Mitglied (-er)* member
mitkommen (mitgekommen) to come with sb.
mitmachen (mitgemacht) to join in
Mittag (-e) midday
das *Mittagessen (-)* lunch
die *Mitte* middle
mittelgroß medium-sized, of average height
mitten in in the middle of
Mitternacht midnight
die *mittlere Reife* intermediate school certificate
Mittwoch Wednesday
mobben (gemobbt) to bully
die *Mode (-n)* fashion
modisch fashionable
mögen (gemocht) to like
möglich possible
die *Möglichkeit (-en)* possibility
der *Moment (-e)* moment
der *Mond (-e)* moon
Montag Monday
montags on Mondays
morgen tomorrow
der *Morgen* morning
morgen früh tomorrow morning
morgens every morning
der *MP3-Spieler (-)* MP3 player
mühsam laboriously
der *Müll* waste, rubbish
die *Mülltonne (-n)* dustbin
multikulturell multicultural
München Munich
der *Mund (¨er)* mouth
das *Museum (-een)* museum
die *Musik* music
Musik hören (gehört) to listen to music
das *Müsli (-s)* muesli
müssen (gemusst) must, to have to
die *Mutter (¨)* mother
die *Mütze (-n)* hat
MwSt (Mehrwertsteuer) VAT

N

nach after
nachdem after, afterwards
nachforschen (nachgeforscht) to research
nachher afterwards
der *Nachmittag (-e)* afternoon
die *Nachricht (-en)* message, piece of news
nachsitzen (nachgesessen) to have detention
nächster/e/es nearest, next
die *Nacht (¨e)* night
der *Nachteil (-e)* disadvantage
nachts at night
der *Nachttisch (-e)* bedside table
nagelneu brand new
nah near
die *Nähe* vicinity, neighbourhood
in der *Nähe* nearby
die *Nahrung* food
die *Nase (-n)* nose
die *Nase voll haben* to have had enough, to be fed up
nass wet
natürlich naturally, of course
das *Naturschutzgebiet (-e)* conservation area
die *Naturwissenschaften (pl)* science
der *Nebel* fog
nebelig foggy
neben next to
der *Nebenjob (-s)* second or extra job, job outside school
Es ist *neblig.* It's foggy.
Nein! No!
nervös nervous
nett nice
neu new
neulich recently
nicht not
nicht fit unfit
nicht nur ... sondern auch ... not only ... but also ...
nichts nothing
nie never
die *Niederlande (pl)* the Netherlands
niemals never
niemand no one
nirgendwo nowhere
noch still

noch einmal once more
noch nicht not yet
der *Norden* north
im *Norden* in the north
nördlich to the north
die *Nordsee* the North Sea
normalerweise usually
die *Not (¨e)* need
die *Note (-n)* mark
der *Notendruck* exam pressure
November November
nun now
nur only
die *Nudeln (pl)* pasta, noodles
nützlich useful
nutzlos useless

O

ob whether
obdachlos homeless
oben above
das *Obst* fruit
der *Obst- und Gemüseladen (¨en)* greengrocer's
obwohl although
oder or
offen open
die *Öffentlichkeit* public
in der *Öffentlichkeit* in public
die *öffentlichen Verkehrsmittel (pl)* public transport
öffnen (geöffnet) to open
oft often
ohne without
die *Ohrenschmerzen (pl)* earache
Oktober October
das *Oktoberfest (-e)* Munich beer festival in October
das *Öl (-e)* oil
die *Oma (-s)* granny, gran
der *Onkel (-)* uncle
der *Opa (-s)* granddad, grandpa
die *Oper (-n)* opera (house)
das *Orchester (-)* orchestra
in *Ordnung* fine, okay
organisch organic
organisieren (organisiert) to organise
der *Ort (-e)* place
der *Osten* east
im *Osten* in the east
Ostern Easter
Österreich Austria

Osteuropa   Eastern Europe
östlich   to the East
die Ostsee   the Baltic Sea
das Ozonloch (¨er)   hole in the ozone layer
die Ozonschicht (-en)   ozone layer

P

ein paar   a couple
das Papier (-e)   paper
die Pappe (-n)   cardboard
der Parkplatz (¨e)   car park
passen (gepasst)   to fit
Es passt dir.   It fits you.
die Pause (-n)   break, breaktime
peinlich   painful, embarrassing
die Pension (-en)   guesthouse
die Person (-en)   person
pessimistisch   pessimistic
das Pestizid (-e)   pesticide
das Pferd (-e)   horse
der Pfirsich (-e)   peach
pflanzen (gepflanzt)   to plant
das Pflichtfach (¨er)   compulsory subject
das Pfund (-e)   pound
(die) Physik   physics
die Pizzeria (-s)   pizzeria
das Plakat (-e)   poster
der Plan (¨e)   plan
das Plastik   plastic
der Platz (¨e)   space, room
plaudern (geplaudert)   to chat
pleite   skint
plötzlich   suddenly
PLZ (Postleitzahl)   postcode
Polen   Poland
der Polizist / die Polizistin   policeman/woman
die Pommes (frites) (pl)   chips
die Portion (-en)   portion
das Postamt (¨er)   post office
praktisch   practical, practically
der Preis (-e)   price
prima   great
pro   per
probieren (probiert)   to try
der Profi (-s)   professional
die Prüfung (-en)   exam
der Pulli (-s)   pullover
die Pute (-n)   turkey
putzen (geputzt)   to clean

Q

die Qualifikation (-en)   qualification
qualifiziert   qualified
die Qualität (-en)   quality
die Quantität (-en)   quantity
quatschen (gequatscht)   to chat
die Quelle (-n)   source
die Quittung (-en)   bill, receipt

R

der Rabatt (-e)   reduction
das Rad (¨er)   wheel, bicycle
Rad fahren (gefahren)   to go cycling
der Radweg (-e)   cycle path
Rasen mähen (gemäht)   to mow the lawn
der Rassismus   racism
der Rassist (-en)   racist person
rassistisch   racist
das Rathaus (¨er)   town hall
rauchen (geraucht)   to smoke
die Raucherecke (-n)   smokers' corner
der Raucherhusten   smoker's cough
das Rauschgift (-e)   drug, narcotic
die Realschule (-n)   secondary modern school
Recht haben (gehabt)   to be right
das Rechteck (-e)   rectangle
rechts   on/to the right
die Rechtsanwaltspraxis (-xen)   lawyer's practice
recyceln (recycelt)   recycle
der Regen   rain
regnen (geregnet)   to rain
Es regnet.   It's raining.
reich   rich
reichen (gereicht)   to be enough
das Reihenhaus (¨er)   terraced house
reinigen (gereinigt)   to clean
der Reis   rice
die Reise (-n)   journey
der Reisebus (-se)   coach
reisen (gereist)   to travel
reiten gehen (gegangen)   to go riding
der Rektor / die Rektorin   headmaster/-mistress

die Religion (-en)   religion, RS
reservieren (reserviert)   to reserve
die Reservierung (-en)   reservation
das Restaurant (-s)   restaurant
retten (gerettet)   to save
die Rezeption (-en)   reception
der Rhein   Rhine
richtig   right
die Richtung (-en)   direction
riechen (gerochen)   to smell
das Riesenrad (¨er)   big wheel
das Risiko (-ken)   risk
das Risiko eingehen, etw. zu tun   to run the risk of doing sth.
rosa   pink
der Rock (¨e)   skirt
der Rosenmontag (-e)   Monday before Ash Wednesday
rot   red
die Rückenschmerzen   backache
ruhig   calm, peaceful
rund   round
der Rundflug (¨e)   a sightseeing tour by plane
Russland   Russia

S

sagen (gesagt)   to say
die Sahne   cream
der Salat (-e)   salad
sammeln (gesammelt)   to collect
Samstag   Saturday
das Satellitenfernsehen   satellite TV
satt   full
es satt haben   to have had enough of sth.
sauber   clean
sauer   cross
saurer Regen   acid rain
die Schachtel (-n)   box
schade   it's a shame
schaden (geschadet)   to damage
schädlich   damaging
schaffen (geschafft)   to manage, to pass
der Schal (-s)   scarf
der Schatten (-)   shadow
schauen (geschaut)   to look
der Schauer (-)   shower (of rain)
die Scheibe (-n)   slice

(sich) *scheiden (lassen) (scheiden gelassen)* to get divorced

scheinen (geschienen) to seem, to shine

die *Schichtarbeit* shift work

schick stylish, chic

schicken (geschickt) to send

das *Schiff (-e)* ship

der *Schinken (-)* ham

schlafen (geschlafen) to sleep

das *Schlafzimmer (-)* bedroom

schlank slim

schlecht bad, badly

schließen (geschlossen) to shut, to close

schließlich in the end, finally, eventually

schlimm terrible, awful

Schlittschuh laufen (gelaufen) to go ice skating

das *Schloss (¨er)* castle

schmecken (geschmeckt) to taste

Es *schmeckt.* It tastes good.

... *schmeckt mir (nicht)* I (don't) like the taste of ...

der *Schmuck* jewellery

schmutzig dirty

ein *Schnäppchen machen* to pick up a bargain

der *Schnee* snow

schneien (geschneit) to snow

Es *schneit.* It's snowing.

schnell quick, quickly

die *Schokolade (-n)* chocolate

der *Schokoriegel (-)* chocolate bar

schon already

schön beautiful

Schöne Ferien! Have a great holiday!

Schottland Scotland

der *Schrank (¨e)* cupboard

schrecklich terrible

schreiben (geschrieben) to write

das *Schreibwarengeschäft (-e)* stationer's

der *Schriftsteller / die Schriftstellerin* writer

der *Schuh (-e)* shoe

Schuld an etw. sein to be to blame for sth.

die *Schule (-n)* school

der *Schulhof (¨e)* playground

die *Schulordnung (-en)* school rules

die *Schulter (-n)* shoulder

die *Schuluniform (-en)* school uniform

schützen (geschützt) to protect

der *Schützenzug (¨e)* parade of riflemen

schwarz black

schwatzen (geschwatzt) to gossip, to chatter

das *Schwefeldioxid (-e)* sulphur dioxide

die *Schweiz* Switzerland

die *Schwester (-n)* sister

Schwieger- -in-law

schwierig difficult

schwimmen (geschwommen) to swim

das *Schwimmbad (¨er)* swimming pool

der *See (-n)* lake

die *See (-n)* sea

segeln (gesegelt) to go sailing

sehenswert worth seeing

die *Sehenswürdigkeit (-en)* sight (thing worth seeing)

Sehr geehrte Dame Dear Madam

Sehr geehrter Herr Dear Sir

sehr very

sein (gewesen) to be

seit since, for (a length of time)

seitdem since

die *Seite (-n)* page, side

der *Sekretär / die Sekretärin* secretary

der *Sekt* sparkling wine, champagne

selbstständig independent

selten rarely

die *Sendung (-en)* TV programme

sensibel sensitive

September September

der *Sessel (-)* armchair

sicher sure, safe

das *Silber* silver

Silvester New Year's Eve

simsen (gesimst) to send text messages

sitzen bleiben (geblieben) to repeat a school year

die *Sitzung (-en)* meeting, session

Skateboard fahren (gefahren) to go skateboarding

Ski fahren (gefahren) to go skiing

das *SMS (-)* text message

so ... wie as ... as

so viel ... wie as many ... as

das *Sofa (-s)* sofa

sofort straight away

sogar even

der *Sohn (¨e)* son

die *Solarenergie* solar power

sollen (gesollt) should, ought to

der *Sommer* summer

der *Sommerschlussverkauf* end of summer sales

das *Sonderangebot (-e)* special offer

der *Sonnabend* Saturday

die *Sonne* sun

sonnen (sich) (gesonnt) to sunbathe

der *Sonnenbrand (¨e)* sunburn

die *Sonnenterrasse (-n)* sun terrace/deck

sonnig sunny

Es ist *sonnig.* It's sunny.

Sonntag (-e) Sunday

sonst else, otherwise

die *Sorge (-n)* worry

sorgen für (gesorgt) to ensure

das *Souvenir (-s)* souvenir

das *soziale Netzwerk* social networking site

der *soziale Wohnungsbau* social housing

Spanien Spain

Spanisch Spanish

sparen (gespart) to save

der *Spaß* fun

Spaß haben (gehabt) to have fun

spät late

spazieren gehen (gegangen) to go for walks

speichern (gespeichert) to save (files on a computer)

die *Speise (-n)* dish, food

die *Spende (-n)* donation

spenden (gespendet) to donate

das *Spiegelei (-er)* fried egg

das *Spiel (-e)* game

spielen (gespielt)   to play

der Spielplatz (-e)
    playground

der Spinat   spinach

Spitze!   Great!

Sport   PE

Sport treiben (getrieben)
    to take part in sports

die Sportart (-en)   type of sports

die Sporthalle (-n)   sports hall

der Sportplatz (-e)   playing fields

die Sportsachen (pl)   things for
    sport (PE kit)

die Sportschuhe (pl)   trainers

das Sportzentrum (-zentren)
    sports centre

das Sprachlabor (-s)   language
    laboratory

die Spraydose (-n)   aerosol

die Spritze (-n)   syringe

die Spülmaschine (-n)   dishwasher

die Staatsangehörigkeit (-en)
    nationality

das Stadion (-ien)   stadium

die Stadt (-e)   town

die Stadtmitte/das Stadtzentrum
    town centre

der Stadtrand (-er)   outskirts of
    town

am Stadtrand   on the outskirts of
    town

der Stadtteil/das Stadtviertel
    area of a town, quarter

stattfinden (stattgefunden)   to
    take place

der Stau (-s)   congestion, traffic
    jam

staubsaugen (staubgesaugt)   to
    vacuum

stecken (gesteckt)   to put

stehlen (gestohlen)   to steal

Es steht dir.   It suits you.

die Stelle (-n)   job, position

sterben (gestorben)   to die

Stief-   step-

die Stiefel (pl)   boots

Stimmt!   That's right!

stinken (gestunken)   to stink

stolz   proud

stören (gestört)   to bother, to
    disturb

der Strahl (-en)   ray

der Strand (-e)   beach

die Straße (-n)   street

die Straßenbahn (-en)   tram

(sich) streiten (gestritten)   to argue

streng   strict

der Stress   stress

stressig   stressful

das Stück (-e)   piece

studieren (studiert)   to study
    (at university level)

die Stunde (-n)   hour, lesson

der Stundenplan (-e)   timetable

der Sturm (-e)   storm

stürmisch   stormy

suchen (gesucht)   to look for

die Sucht   addiction

süchtig   addicted

der Süden   south

im Süden   in the south

südlich   to the south

surfen (gesurft)   to surf

süß   sweet

sympathisch   nice, kind

T

der Tabak (-e)   tobacco

diese Tabletten   these tablets

der Tag (-e)   day

täglich   daily

das Tal (-er)   the valley

die Tante (-n)   aunt

der Tante-Emma-Laden   corner
    shop

tanzen (getanzt)   to dance

die Tasche (-n) (Schultasche)   bag
    (schoolbag)

das Taschengeld   pocket money

die Technologie (-n)   technology

der Tee   tea

teilen (geteilt)   to share

Teilzeit-   part-time

das Telefon (-e)   telephone

telefonieren (telefoniert)
    to telephone

die Telefonnummer (-n)
    telephone number

der Tellerwäscher / die
    Tellerwäscherin   dish washer
    (person)

die Temperatur (-en)
    temperature

Tennis spielen (gespielt)
    to play tennis

der Tennisplatz (-e)   tennis court

der Teppich (-e)   carpet

teuer   expensive

das Theater (-)   theatre

das Thema (-men)   topic

der Tiefkühlschrank (-e)   freezer

das Tier (-e)   animal

der Tierarzt / die Tierärztin   vet

tippen (getippt)   to type

die Tochter (")   daughter

die Toilette (-n)   toilet

toll   great

die Tomate (-n)   tomato

tot   dead

total   totally

töten (getötet)   to kill

der Tourismus   tourism

der Tourist (-en)   tourist

die Touristeninformation   tourist
    information

die Tradition (-en)   tradition

trainieren (trainiert)   to train

der Traum (-e)   dream

traurig   sad

der Trauring   wedding ring

die Trauung   wedding

(sich mit) treffen (getroffen)   to meet
    (with)

treiben (getrieben)   to drive, to
    do

der Treibhauseffekt (-e)
    greenhouse effect

(sich) trennen (getrennt)   to separate

treu   faithful

trinken (getrunken)   to drink

trocken   dry

der Trommler (-)   drummer

diese Tropfen (pl)   these drops

trotzdem   nevertheless

Tschüss!   Bye!

das T-Shirt (-s)   T-shirt

die Türkei   Turkey

türkis   turquoise

der Turm (-e)   tower

turnen (geturnt)   to do
    gymnastics

die Turnhalle (-n)   gymnasium

die Tüte (-n)   bag

typisch   typical

U

die U-Bahn (-en)   the
    underground

über   over, above

überall   everywhere

die Überdosis   overdose

überhaupt nicht   not at all

übermorgen   the day after
    tomorrow

übernachten (übernachtet) to stay the night

überrascht surprised

die Überstunden (pl) overtime

übrig bleiben (geblieben) to be left

sieben Uhr hour, 7 o'clock

um at, around

die Umfrage (-n) survey

die Umgebung (-en) surrounding area

der Umkleideraum (¨e) changing room

umschauen (umgeschaut) to look around

umsteigen (umgestiegen) to change (trains, buses etc.)

umtauschen (umgetauscht) to exchange

die Umwelt environment

umweltbewusst environmentally aware

umweltfeindlich environmentally unfriendly

umweltfreundlich environmentally friendly

umziehen (umgezogen) to move house

der Umzug (¨e) parade, (house) move

unabhängig independent

unbedingt without fail, definitely

und and

unfair unfair

ungefähr about

ungerecht unjust

ungesund unhealthy, unhealthily

unglaublich unbelievable

die Uni(versität) (-en) university

unmöglich impossible

unordentlich untidy

Unrecht haben (gehabt) to be wrong

unsicher unsure

unten underneath, below

unter below, under

unterbringen (untergebracht) to accommodate

(sich) unterhalten (unterhalten) to talk

die Unterkunft (¨e) accommodation

das Unternehmen (-) business

unternehmen (unterommen) to undertake, to do

unternehmungslustig likes doing lots of things (adj)

der Unterricht lessons, classes

der Unterschied (-e) difference

unterschiedlich different

unterschreiben (untergeschrieben) to sign

unterwegs on the move

der Urlaub (-e) holiday (trip)

die Urlaubspläne (pl) holiday plans

usw. (und so weiter) etc.

V

der Vandalismus vandalism

der Vater (¨) father

der Vegetarier / die Vegetarierin vegetarian

vegetarisch vegetarian

Venedig Venice

(sich) verabschieden (verabschiedet) to say goodbye

die Verantwortung (-en) responsibility

verbessern (verbessert) to improve

die Verbesserung (-en) improvement

verbieten (verboten) to forbid, to ban

die Verbindung (-en) connection

das Verbrechen (-) crime

verbringen (verbracht) to spend (time)

verdienen (verdient) to earn

der Verein (-e) club, society

die Vergangenheit past

vergessen (vergessen) to forget

der Vergleich (-e) comparison

vergleichen (verglichen) to compare

Mit Vergnügen! with pleasure!

das Verhältnis (-se) relationship

verheiratet married

der Verkäufer / die Verkäuferin shop assistant, salesperson

der Verkehr traffic

das Verkehrsamt (¨er) tourist information

verkleidet dressed-up, disguised

verlassen (verlassen) to leave

(sich auf etw.) verlassen (verlassen) to rely on sth.

verlobt engaged

der/die Verlobte (-n) fiancé(e)

vermeiden (vermieden) to avoid

die Verpackung (-en) packaging

verpesten (verpestet) to pollute

verrückt crazy

die Versammlung (-en) assembly

verschieden different

die Verschmutzung pollution

verschwenden (verschwendet) to waste

verstecken (sich) (versteckt) to hide

verstehen (verstanden) to understand

(sich mit) verstehen (verstanden) to get on with

verursachen (verursacht) to cause

verwenden (verwendet) to use

Verzeihung! Sorry!

viel a lot, much, many-

viele lots of

vielleicht perhaps

viereckig quadrangular

Viertel nach quarter past

Viertel vor quarter to

die Vitamine (pl) vitamins

der Vogel (¨) bird

voll full

völlig completely

die Vollpension (-en) full board

Vollzeit- full-time

von from, by, of

vor in front of, before, ago

vor kurzem until recently

im Voraus in advance

vorausgesetzt dass provided that

vorbei past, by

vorgestern the day before yesterday

der Vorhang (¨e) curtain

vorher before

der Vormittag (-e) morning

vorschlagen (vorgeschlagen) to suggest

vorsichtig careful

vorstellen (vorgestellt) to introduce

das *Vorstellungsgespräch (-e)* job interview

der *Vorteil (-e)* advantage

das *Vorurteil (-e)* prejudice

vorwärts forwards

vorziehen (vorgezogen) to prefer

W

wählen (gewählt) to choose

das *Wahlfach (¨er)* optional subject

während while

wahrscheinlich probable, probably

der *Wald (¨er)* forest, wood

das *Waldsterben* dying of the forests

die *Wand (¨e)* wall

wandern (gewandert) to hike, to go on walks

wann? when?

warm warm

warum? why?

was? what?

(sich) *waschen (gewaschen)* to wash

die *Waschküche (-n)* laundry room

das *Wasser* water

die *Webseite (-n)* webpage

weder ... noch ... neither ... nor ...

wegen due to, because of

wegwerfen (weggeworfen) to throw away

... *tut weh* ... is hurting

Weihnachten Christmas

der *Weihnachtsmarkt (¨e)* Christmas market

weil because

weinen (geweint) to cry

weiß white

weit far

weiterstudieren (weiterstudiert) to do further study

welcher/e/es? which?

die *Weltreise (-n)* tour of the world

wenigstens at least

wenn if, when

wer? who?

werden (geworden) to become

das *Werken (pl)* D&T

der *Westen* West

im *Westen* in the West

westlich to the West

der *Wettbewerb* competition

das *Wetter* weather

der *Wetterbericht (-e)* weather report

die *Wettervorhersage (-n)* weather forecast

wichtig important

Das *Wichtigste ist, ...* The most important thing is, ...

wie? how?

wie lange? how long?

wie viel(e)? how many?

wieder again

wiegen (gewogen) to weigh

Herzlich willkommen! Welcome!

der *Wind (-e)* wind

windig windy

Es ist *windig.* It's windy.

der *Winter* winter

wirklich really

wo? where?

woanders somewhere else

die *Woche (-n)* week

das *Wochenende (-n)* weekend

woher? where from?

wohin? where to?

die *Wohltätigkeit* charity

der *Wohnblock (-s)* block of flats

wohnen (gewohnt) to live (in a particular place)

die *Wohnung (-en)* flat

der *Wohnwagen (-)* caravan

das *Wohnzimmer (-)* living room

die *Wolke (-n)* cloud

wolkig cloudy

Es ist *wolkig.* It's cloudy.

die *Wolle* wool

wollen (gewollt) to want to

womit? what with?

wunderbar wonderful

wunderschön gorgeous, very beautiful

wünschen (sich) (gewünscht) to wish, to want

die *Wurst (¨e)* sausage

Z

z.B. (zum Beispiel) for example

der *Zahnarzt /die Zahnärztin* dentist

die *Zahnschmerzen* toothache

zeichnen (gezeichnet) to draw

der *Zeitpunkt (¨e)* point in time

die *Zeitschrift (-en)* magazine

die *Zeitung (-en)* newspaper

Zeitungen austragen (ausgetragen) to deliver newspapers

das *Zelt (-e)* tent

zelten (gezeltet) to camp

das *Zentrum (-tren)* centre

das *Zeug* thing

das *Zeugnis (-se)* school report

ziemlich quite

die *Zigarette (-n)* cigarette

das *Zimmer (-)* room

der *Zoll (¨e)* customs

der *Zoo (-s)* zoo

zu to, too, by

zuerst first

zufällig by chance

zufrieden content, happy

das *Zuhause* home

die *Zukunft* future

zumachen (zugemacht) to close

zunehmend growing, increasing

zurück back

zusammen together

zusammenleben (zusammengelebt) to cohabit

der *Zuschlag (¨e)* supplement (to pay)

zustimmen to agree

der *Zweck (-e)* cause, goal

ohne *Zweifel* without a doubt, doubtless

zweitens second(ly)

die *Zwillinge (pl)* twins (noun)

Zwillings- twin (adj.)

zwischen between

zwitschern (gezwitschert) to twitter

der *Zug (¨e)* train

Acknowledgements

The authors and the publisher would like to thank the following for permission to reproduce material:

pp24-25, Schweizerische Fachstelle für Alkohol- und andere Drogenprobleme (SFA), & Bundesamt für Gesundheit (BAG) (Eds.). (2008) Alkohol-, Tabak- und Cannabiskonsum bei Jugendlichen – Zahlen und Hintergründe. Lausanne/Bern: SFA/BAG; pp38-39, Perpherie, Institut für praxisorientierte Genderforschung, from http://www.peripherie.ac.at/; pp40-41, from www.schule-ohne-rassismus.org; p54, IASO, from www.iaso.org; p54, from www.bpd.de/sozialesituation; p92, Tatsachen über Deutschland, from www.tatsachen-ueber-deutschland.de; pp114-115, from www.greenpeace.at.

Illustrations:
Kathy Baxendale pp11, 12, 21, 27, 45, 61, 75, 131, 146; Mark Draisey pp37, 64, 70, 139, 153; Robin Edmonds pp70, 103, 158; Tony Forbes pp10, 16, 57, 66, 158; Dylan Gibson pp142, 143; Celia Hart pp29, 39; Abel Ippolito pp47, 57, 77, 119, 147; Martin Sanders p10

Photographs courtesy of:
p13 © iStockphoto.com / trait2lumiere; p15 Nelson Thornes; p18 © iStockphoto.com / Chelnok; p19 © iStockphoto.com / shorrocks; p20 © iStockphoto.com / Stockphoto4u, © iStockphoto.com / attator; p22 © iStockphoto.com / luoman, © iStockphoto.com / track5, © iStockphoto.com / track5, © iStockphoto.com / Fly_Fast, © photoconcepts1 – Fotolia.com; p24 © Stephen Coburn – Fotolia.com; p26 © micut. Image from BigStockPhoto.com, © WoodyStock / Alamy.com, © AdisX. Image from BigStockPhoto.com, © STAB. Image from BigStockPhoto.com, © Jiri Miklo/123rf.com, © stocksnapp. Image from BigStockPhoto.com; p32 © Steve Pepple. Image from BigStockPhoto.com, © Sandymaya. Image from BigStockPhoto.com; p33 © Luminis – Fotolia.com; p34 © ZanyZeus – Fotolia.com, © cenorman . Image from BigStockPhoto.com, © Cathy Yeulet / 123rf.com; p36 © Phil Date / 123rf.com; p38 © Patrick Hermans / 123rf.com, © Moodboard / 123rf.com, © merrilld. Image from BigStockPhoto.com, © iStockphoto.com / Ayakovlev; p40 © selanik. Image from BigStockPhoto.com; p41 © Bundeskoordination SOR-SMC; p42 © Simone Van Den Berg / 123rf.com, © Peteralbrektsen. Image from BigStockPhoto.com; p44 © Sabphoto – Fotolia.com; p54 © anweber – Fotolia.com, © Fotolia XII – Fotolia.com; p55 © Andres Rodriguez – Fotolia.com; p57 © Alta.C – Fotolia.com; p58 Nelson Thornes, Nelson Thornes; p59 Nelson Thornes, Nelson Thornes; p60 © deanm1974. Image from BigStockPhoto.com, © SCGstudio. Image from BigStockPhoto.com, © imagerymajestic / 123rf.com, © Willee Cole. Image from BigStockPhoto.com, © Ramona Smiers / 123rf.com; p62 © iStockphoto.com / blackred, © iStockphoto.com / Mac99, © iStockphoto.com / ALEAIMAGE, © Mikael Damkier – Fotolia.com, © Paul Cowan – Fotolia.com, © iStockphoto.com / fotolinchen, © Philip Date – Fotolia.com, © iStockphoto.com / aabejon, © iStockphoto.com / barsik; p68 © Action Press/Rex Features; p74 © Maxim Petrichuk – Fotolia.com, © VISUM Foto GmbH / Alamy; p76 © luminis / 123rf.com, © iStockphoto.com / pkline, © iStockphoto.com / cobalt, © Anatoly Tiplyashin – Fotolia.com, © iStockphoto.com / sjlocke, © iStockphoto.com / JoanVicent; p78 © Bernd Kröger – Fotolia.com, © ReSeandra – Fotolia.com, © Thomas Röske – Fotolia.com; p79 © Neelrad – Fotolia.com, © SamK2. Image from BigStockPhoto.com, © iStockphoto.com / webphotographe, © iStockphoto.com / agentry, © iStockphoto.com / anouchka, © Alice – Fotolia.com, © Mikael Damkier – Fotolia.com; p80 © Monkey Business – Fotolia.com, © iStockphoto.com / kevinruss, © iStockphoto.com / track5, © iStockphoto.com / Paul Gibbings, © iStockphoto.com / stray_cat; p82 © iStockphoto.com / antebante, © iStockphoto.com / PeterJobst; p84 © Henry – Fotolia.com, © Nicola Gavin – Fotolia.com, © dinostock – Fotolia.com, © jeff gynane – Fotolia.com, © Klaus Eppele – Fotolia.com;

p92 © Julia – Fotolia.com; p93 © iStockphoto.com / JLGutierrez; p94 © Andrey Andreev – Fotolia.com; p95 © Somatuscani. Image from BigStockPhoto.com; p97 © madaboutart. Image from BigStockPhoto.com, © Victoria Alexandrova/123rf.com, © Moodboard/123rf.com, © kropka! – Fotolia.com, © dragon_fang. Image from BigStockPhoto.com, © MKL. Image from BigStockPhoto.com; p98 © collindale. Image from BigStockPhoto.com, © ZDM – Fotolia.com, © Sylvain Bouquet – Fotolia.com; p100 © Joe Gough – Fotolia.com; p104 © iStockphoto.com / thelinke; p106 © Ewe Degiampietro – Fotolia.com, © R.R.Hundt – Fotolia.com; p108 © martini – Fotolia.com, © Sandy Stupart. Image from BigStockPhoto.com, © gaja_tz. Image from BigStockPhoto.com, © alamar. Image from BigStockPhoto.com, © Valeria73. Image from BigStockPhoto.com, © Buckland. Image from BigStockPhoto.com; p109 © cenorman. Image from BigStockPhoto.com; p112 © INSADCO Photography / Alamy; p113 © Rob Toone/123rf.com, © Birds Eye. Image from BigStockPhoto.com, © MLFoto – Fotolia.com, © joegough. Image from BigStockPhoto.com, © philippe simier – Fotolia.com, © wrangler – Fotolia.com; p114 © iemily – Fotolia.com, © Anthony Jay Villalon – Fotolia.com, © iStockphoto.com / mphotoi, © iStockphoto.com / Ralph125, © TMAX – Fotolia.com; p115 © Superstars_for_You – Fotolia.com, © Greenpeace; p116 © kolesn – Fotolia.com, © Glaflamme. Image from BigStockPhoto.com; p118 © GVision – Fotolia.com, © Alexander Potapov – Fotolia.com, © vekha – Fotolia.com, © Springfield Gallery – Fotolia.com; p120 © Monkey Business – Fotolia.com, © David Davis – Fotolia.com; p128 © iStockphoto.com / ncn18, © Falk – Fotolia.com; p129 © iStockphoto.com / RichVintage; p130 © Nikolay Titov / 123rf.com; p132 © Wolfgang Cibura – Fotolia.com, © Cathy Yeulet / 123rf.com; p133 © Alexander Oshvintsev – Fotolia.com, © Lev Olkha – Fotolia.com; p134 © iStockphoto.com / SteveStone, © Cathy Yeulet / 123rf.com, © flippo. Image from BigStockPhoto.com; p136 © ajn. Image from BigStockPhoto.com, © iStockphoto.com / Stockphoto4u, © Anyka – Fotolia.com; p138 © iStockphoto.com / attator, © digitalskillet / iStockphoto.com, © iStockphoto.com / eurobanks; p140 © Barbara Schniebel – Fotolia.com, © iStockphoto.com / AndreasWeber; © Leah-Anne Thompson – Fotolia.com, © iStockphoto.com / tarajane; p146 © sparklingmoments. Image from BigStockPhoto.com, © rgbspace. Image from BigStockPhoto.com, © iStockphoto.com / quavondo; p149 © RazvanPhotography. Image from BigStockPhoto.com; p151 © Jaimie Duplass – Fotolia.com; p152 © Pavel Losevsky – Fotolia.com; p153 © Cathy Yeulet / 123rf.com, © Cathy Yeulet / 123rf.com, © iStockphoto.com / TriggerPhoto, © iStockphoto.com / quavondo; p154 © philw. Image from BigStockPhoto.com, © Stanislav Popov. Image from BigStockPhoto.com, © visual28. Image from BigStockPhoto.com; p156 © csabafikker. Image from BigStockPhoto.com, © andres. Image from BigStockPhoto.com, © pudding. Image from BigStockPhoto.com, © EastWest Imaging – Fotolia.com; p166 © Pictorial Press Ltd / Alamy, © Monkey Business – Fotolia.com

Every effort has been made to contact the copyright holders and we apologise if any have been overlooked and would be happy to rectify any errors or omissions at the first opportunity.